Discovering a New Freedom

"Much distress, fatigue, loneliness and inner emptiness could be eliminated if people had a deeper understanding of how to live fruitfully with their 'inner child of the past.' Such understanding could help married couples meet one another's needs more fully. It should help parents create a childhood for their own children that will be free of the attitudes that pile up future trouble. This book is an effort to provide, in understandable language, a working knowledge of the root causes of emotional disturbance, and a method of dealing with them."

—W. HUGH MISSILDINE, M.D.

Your Inner Child of the Past

W. Hugh Missildine, M.D.

PUBLISHED BY POCKET BOOKS NEW YORK

POCKET BOOKS, a Simon & Schuster division of
GULF & WESTERN CORPORATION
1230 Avenue of the Americas, New York, N.Y. 10020

ISBN: 0-671-43261-3

First Pocket Books printing April, 1982

10 9 8 7 6 5 4 3 2 1

POCKET and colophon are trademarks of Simon & Schuster.

Printed in the U.S.A.

Contents

PART III

Changing Yourself and Your Life

Preface

This book attempts to explain you to yourself so that you can live with yourself and others more fully, more freely and more comfortably. Explaining you to yourself is quite a task because nobody really understands you very well. Truth, especially about human feelings and behavior, is a very elusive thing; as St. Paul says, "For now we see through a glass darkly."

In order to write the complete truth about you and your life I would have to wait many years for hundreds of scientists to obtain results from thousands of experiments. Even then we will probably still "see through a glass darkly." Therefore, this book is the closest to truth about you that I can achieve today. Even though we know so little, we know enough to help you understand and deal with some troubled feelings more satisfyingly. At the present time all of us suffer in our feelings too much. We cannot wait for further knowledge; we must actively apply what we do know without delay.

Many of my patients are described in this book. I have changed their histories slightly to keep them anonymous. I hope that I have presented their stories with the dignity that their actual lives deserve. I am grateful that they have allowed us to learn from them.

I also want to thank Harry Henderson, who has helped me transform my skeletal prose into a more complete work.

It is my hope that you will find yourself in this book, and that as a result of finding yourself you will begin to regard yourself a little more respectfully.

W. HUGH MISSILDINE

recognize any connection between this and the results of
264

PART I

*Recognizing and Accepting
Your Inner Child
of the Past*

CHAPTER 1

WHO IS YOUR INNER CHILD OF THE PAST?

The Persisting Child of the Past

Somewhere, sometime, you were a child. This is one of the great obvious, seemingly meaningless and forgotten common denominators of adult life. Yet the fact that you were once a child has an important bearing on your life today. In trying to be adults we mistakenly try to ignore our lives as children, discount our childhood and omit it in our considerations of ourselves and others. This is a basic cause of much adult distress and unhappiness. It is a way of mistreating ourselves.

Whether you are now rich or poor, pleasantly satisfied with your lot or bitterly discontented, a housewife or a career girl, married or divorced, in jail or in your own home, your childhood and the child you once were are not something wholly behind you, long ago and far away. Your childhood, in an actual, literal sense, exists within you now. It affects everything you do, everything you feel.

These childhood feelings and attitudes influence, often actually determine and dominate, your relations with friends, colleagues, your mate, even your own children. They can interfere with your ability to work or to love. Such feelings may be a significant part of your fatigue, your inability to relax, your irritating headaches, your upset stomach.

What happened to the child you once were? Did he or she die? Was he outgrown and cast aside, along with old toys, overshoes and sleds? Was he somehow abandoned? Was he lost somewhere in Time, eventually forgotten?

3

Troublemaking Attitudes

As a child psychiatrist who has had the opportunity to observe the inner feelings of both children and adults as they struggle with their problems, I have been in a unique position to see *in the adult* what has happened to the child he once was. I often observe, *in their very origins,* the development of troublemaking attitudes in the child. They are the child's way of dealing with the often unreasonable or excessive attitudes and demands of his parents, the all-important people in his life. I see the end result of these childhood reactions in the adult—loneliness, anxiety, sexual difficulties, depression, fears, marital discord and compulsive striving for success.

The child you once were continues to survive inside your adult shell. "Thrive" would perhaps be a better word than "survive," for often this "inner child of the past" is a sprawling, bawling, brawling character—racing pell-mell into activities he likes, dawdling, cheating, lying to get out of things he doesn't like, upsetting and wrecking others' lives—or perhaps this child is the fearful, timid, shrinking part of your personality.

Whether we like it or not, we are simultaneously the child we once were, who lives in the emotional atmosphere of the past and often interferes in the present, and an adult who tries to forget the past and live wholly in the present. The child you once were can balk or frustrate your adult satisfactions, embarrass and harass you, make you sick—or enrich your life.

How Do You Deal With Your "Inner Child of the Past"?

You are already dealing with your "inner child of the past" in one way or another. This is what lies behind many of your problems. Actually, from adolescence on, we are each dealing with our respective "child of the past." But not understanding how childhood influences continue in the adult, we ineffectively exhaust ourselves and continue our frustrations.

Most of us try to root out these childhood feelings. We

disown, ignore or dismiss them, "overcome" them, scolding and belittling ourselves as "childish" and for not being "grown up." Yet the very nature of emotional development makes it impossible for us to do this.

If you were not already trying to deal with your "inner child of the past," you would have no conflicts, feel no pain or distress. Some people, in fact, do just that. They let the "child of the past" take over their adult lives—inevitably bringing them into serious conflict with others and often with society. A young child, for example, has no concept of private property. He takes whatever interests him. If he continues to act this way as an adult, he will land in jail.

Recognizing and accepting the needs of your "child of the past" does not mean indulging in childish behavior, impulsiveness or temper tantrums. Limits must be established for him—very much in the same way that a parent sets firm street-crossing limits to protect his child.

The Seriousness of the Problem

Today the conflict between the "inner child of the past" and the adult of the present has caused such serious emotional distortions that nearly one in ten of us is under treatment in mental hospitals, clinics and by physicians in private practice. Much of this conflict in others is concealed in symptoms of physical illness. Approximately 30 to 50 percent of the practicing physician's time is spent on complaints that originate in emotional difficulties. Though millions of dollars are spent each year in treating such sickness, the ailments continue because their emotional character is not recognized and treated.

Years ago, the answer seemed to be that more psychiatrists and more research would someday solve the problem. But this hope has not been realized. We are on the edge of disaster in the field of mental health. We have only 10,000 psychiatrists—about one to every 18,000 persons. At the rate our population is growing, we cannot even maintain this inadequate proportion, let alone make progress in the field.

But the problems we are going to talk about in this book are, for the most part, not those troubling deeply disturbed persons in need of specialized psychiatric treatment. They are the problems of ordinary people in everyday life—problems that we can do much to solve on our own, if we understand what caused them and how to deal with them.

Much distress, fatigue, loneliness and inner emptiness could be eliminated if people had a deeper understanding of how to live fruitfully with their "inner child of the past." Such understanding could help married couples meet one another's needs more fully. It should help parents create a childhood for their own children that will be free of the attitudes that pile up future trouble. This book is an effort to provide, in understandable language, a working knowledge of the root causes of emotional disturbance and a method of dealing with them.

Three Major Ideas

You will find three major ideas in this book. These ideas grew out of my experiences, first as a physician, then as a child psychiatrist concerned with children and their parents, and finally as a teacher of psychiatry at Ohio State University College of Medicine working with medical students and young physicians.

These concepts are:

1. *Your "inner child of the past"*—literally the child you once were, who continues to exist in your life as an adult.

2. *Being a parent to oneself*—you are already acting as a parent to your "child of the past," whose reactions to your parental attitudes often cause you trouble.

3. *Mutual respect*—the basis of getting along with your "inner child of the past" and with others.

These ideas were developed when, after opening the Children's Mental Health Center in Columbus, Ohio, in the postwar years, I was faced with the problem of trying to help the hundreds of troubled children and parents who poured into the clinic. My patients needed help and needed it quickly—a situation duplicated everywhere.

Ideas that People Can Use

Most of my patients in Columbus were earnest, hard-working, often well-educated but disturbed American parents. I found that psychoanalytically oriented psychother-

6

apy often did not help them much. It did not fit their problems. And it did not work because they did not understand either the terminology or the basic concepts—and often rejected these ideas when they did understand. Above all, it was too slow, too time-consuming. Lastly, the great number of persons seeking help forced me to realize that some way other than the lengthy techniques of psychoanalysis must be found.

None of this means that psychoanalysis or psychoanalytically-oriented therapy cannot or does not work. But often it is inappropriate and wasteful of the time of the trained psychiatrist—not to mention the time and cost to the patient. In view of the exceedingly long period required to train psychoanalysts, their skills should be reserved, so to speak, for the most severely disturbed.

If we try to adhere rigidly to the concepts of Freudian psychotherapy, we cannot reduce our shocking incidence of emotional illness. I believe the general practitioner offers us the greatest hope in this respect. By virtue of his training and his intimate relationships with families, he is in a strategic position to recognize and alleviate emotional disturbance early. As of now he has to rely primarily on the theoretical framework of Freudian psychiatry, which is too cumbersome and too removed from daily experience for him to use effectively. However, if equipped with more practical diagnostic and therapeutic tools, the practicing physician can treat the bulk of emotional disturbances.

We obviously need more psychiatrists, psychologists and other skilled professional workers. We desperately need more research. But it also seems obvious to me that we need to give each man and woman some sound understanding, in familiar language and concepts, of how and why their disturbing tensions and anxieties arise.

In Columbus I gradually began to discontinue using the concepts of orthodox Freudian psychiatry. I sought to develop ideas which my patients could use more effectively in understanding and dealing with their emotional difficulties. Because I was working with both children and adults, I could often observe the child wrestling with the parental attitudes surrounding him—*and I could see the adult patient still wrestling with the attitudes of his parents with which he had grown up and which be continued to apply to himself.* These attitudes, no longer enforced by his parents' presence, were nevertheless still powerful—

7

and he continued to react to them as he had as a child. Thus, the idea of the "inner child of the past" persisting in the adult was developed.

These concepts—*inner child of the past, being a parent to oneself, mutual respect*—helped my patients as soon as I applied them. They have been in use some years now. I have taught them to others and seen them applied successfully. Many people have found in them a way to begin to understand their own troubled feelings and how to cope with them. If your problems seem severe and you wish to talk to a physician or psychiatrist after you have read this book, you may find the book helpful in indicating where your difficulties lie.

Reading this book will not, of course, automatically solve your problems. But it may illuminate them in such a way as to make it possible for you to apply yourself to the real cause of your loneliness, anxiety and exhausting conflicts.

You can learn to look at yourself and your childhood in a new way.

CHAPTER 2

WHY YOUR FEELINGS
ARE DISTURBING

Our Unreasonable Feelings

Feelings that seem undesirable and unreasonable keep recurring throughout our adult lives. We may blush if someone admires our clothes or compliments us. We may feel
embittered toward those who love us. We may suspect
without one iota of evidence that a storekeeper has short-
changed us or that a neighbor gossips about us. We may
feel deeply annoyed by a child's casual acceptance of a
gift into which we have put much thought.

We may often be embarrassed and feel guilty about
these unreasonable feelings. We may laugh on hearing
bad news—and then scold ourselves. A child's grimace
may rub us raw. We may, in our eagerness to develop
friendships with people we admire, "put our foot in it" by
saying the very thing we know will alienate them—and
thus deprive ourselves of friendship. We may feel quite
sad and blue at events we planned and hoped for. And
who does not know the seemingly inexplicable private
sigh of regret when one is consciously happy and con-
tented?

Frequently our feelings are so intense and so uncalled
for, so unrealistic and inappropriate, that we try to hide
them and the intense inner discomfort they cause. Ashamed
of our troubled feelings, we call them "silly" and scold
ourselves for having them.

Such attempts to suppress or disavow our feelings actually make our discontent with ourselves greater. Moreover, scolding ourselves leads to feeling alone and isolated.

Such efforts to deal scornfully with your feelings are doomed to failure. You can't turn against yourself and have inner security.

Our inability to control these unacceptable feelings may arouse the fear that we are really incapable, different, deeply inadequate, perhaps hopelessly neurotic. To mention these feelings and fears seriously to anyone seems even more threatening. Thus, many of us blame our feelings on fatigue, the weather, our work, the inconsiderateness of our friends, employers, or family. Yet as the cycle repeats itself, we develop in our misery an ever-deepening sense of being alone, alienated and separated from people we love, and unable to participate effectively in life. The feeling of being alone is one of the most devastating and most common experiences in our society.

Actually much of our loneliness is simply the result of the way in which we treat ourselves. Our attitudes toward ourselves are largely formed by the family attitudes and emotional atmosphere of our early childhood. I do not mean by this that each of us has suffered from some severely traumatic experience as a child which has resulted in a deep-seated neurosis. Instead I mean that our attitudes toward ourselves were created more by the general atmosphere and attitudes of our families than by any single "traumatic" experience.

Not Unreasonable in a Child

Each of us carries within him his "inner child of the past"—a set of feelings and attitudes brought from childhood. These feelings may be hard to recall and identify, for our memories of being a child are both sharp and vague, fleeting and recurring, seemingly disconnected. You may remember anything—from your mother's dismay over spilled coffee at a church social, to a party dress or a specific punishment, the way a room looked, another child's toy, or longings to be a cowboy or a nurse. You may say, "Oh, that was long ago when I was a kid," and thus dismiss it.

Yet none of us can remember the day when we were no longer children, when we were grown up. The "child of the past" actually continues, with all his feelings and his attitudes, to the very end of our lives. *While these feelings may seem undesirable and unreasonable to you as an adult, they are not at all unreasonable in a child—specifically, your "child of the past" and the emotional atmosphere in which he lived.*

An Essential Difference

Our child-guidance clinic gave me many opportunities to observe how the feelings of children at every age are affected by the attitudes of their parents. The child's emotional distress may register itself in such forms of behavior as bed-wetting, refusal to eat, shyness, tantrums or unprovoked attacks on other children. Because parental attitudes are significant elements in creating the child's reactions, the child's behavioral problem usually disappears if the parents can alter the troublemaking attitude.

In such a clinic one can observe the child's efforts to establish his own evaluation of himself—for a child literally discovers what kind of a person he is and how he feels about himself by the reactions of his parents to him. We can follow in this way the creation of problems in childhood—and their continuation in adult life when the individual recreates within himself the emotional atmosphere of his early home.

In the clinic, dealing with hundreds of disturbed children and their parents, one can isolate and identify certain parental attitudes which are pathogenic—by which I mean excessive or troublemaking. These attitudes will almost certainly cause trouble for the child both in childhood and later when he is an adult contending with the feelings of his "child of the past." In later chapters these excessive attitudes will be examined, one by one, so that you can identify those causing your difficulties.

If we look at adult problems from the viewpoint of a child psychiatrist dealing with harmful parent-child relationships, we can immediately make two revealing, simple and important observations:

1. *One essential difference between adults and children in an emotional sense is that children have parents who provide in many different ways an inner sense of direction and guidance, reassurance, esteem and worthiness—while adults act as parents to themselves, giving themselves the guidance and direction, the reassurance or the scolding that parents give to children.*

11

2. *Adults (as parents to themselves) continue the parental attitudes that were imposed on them in childhood, perpetuating these attitudes toward themselves in adult life.*

This is fundamental in understanding how your personal problems as an adult arise. Childhood is customarily considered a period of growth and training, terminating when you no longer need the guidance and protection of your parents and can live as an independent human being. As you assume the posture of an adult, you become, in effect, your own parent. In doing this, you utilize the feelings and attitudes of your parents toward yourself.

What Kind of a Parent Are You to Yourself?

In unraveling a personal difficulty, ask yourself, "What kind of a parent am I being to myself? Am I treating myself with belittling scorn and disrespect? Am I punishing myself? Am I indulging myself? Am I expecting and demanding too much of myself? Am I treating myself the same way my parents treated me in such situations?"

As you grow up, you gradually adopt or "borrow" the attitudes of your parents toward yourself. I use the term "borrow"—prefer it, in fact—because *these attitudes are those of your parents and are not yours.* Many adults are often unaware of the fact that many of their attitudes, both toward the world in general and toward themselves in particular, are simply repetitions of their parents' attitudes and not independently formed. *When you realize these attitudes are not yours, you can really begin to form attitudes toward yourself that are your own.*

The sum of your early childhood feelings adds up to an alive, active portion of your adult self—your persisting "child of the past." When you treat yourself with the attitudes of your parents, you awaken certain responses of your "child of the past" to that treatment.

You may call some of these reactions "childishness." Generally we try to hide our "childishness" from others in order to appear more "mature" or "adult." We may flail ourselves for being so "childish" as to let our feelings show when we are hurt.

12

The Vitality of Childhood Feelings

Probably the most conspicuous example of the vitality of the "child of the past" in men is the emotional intensity and enthusiasm with which they follow the favorite athletic teams of their childhood. As a boy learns to play ball, he develops deep feelings of loyalty to his school and its team. He attaches this same loyalty to a major league team. As an adult he often continues to follow the team's ups and downs, hooting derisively at opponents, suffering shame and embarrassment if the team plays badly, rejoicing with deep satisfaction over victories. Going to a ball game permits the child who once was to give vent to his feelings exactly as he did years ago.

Many people mistakenly believe that all childhood feelings are bound to be troublemaking. Actually, the "child of the past" participates in everything we do as adults—in our pleasures as well as our difficulties. When we can recognize these feelings as stemming from childhood, we have made a big step forward.

Our Past-Colored Glasses

Our "inner child of the past" causes us to see life, in a sense, with double vision. The adult-of-the-present gives us one view—which may be quite intelligent, level-headed and mature. At the same time the "child of the past" sees the same situation through the emotionally colored glasses of past family relationships. The two views may be so different that we are pulled in two directions at once.

Sometimes we say, "The way I think and the way I feel are not the same at all," or "Why do I act this way when I don't really want to?" These are familiar questions when the "child of the past" and the adult-of-the-present are contending.

I have found, from teaching medical students in my psychiatry classes, that even when this concept of the "child of the past" existing actively within the adult is understood and accepted intellectually, there is a strong tendency to minimize the significance of feelings that stem from childhood. *You will have to struggle within yourself to accept their existence as an influential part of your adult make-up.*

In our adult lives the "child of the past" is constantly trying to make us live as we lived "at home" in childhood. Due to this influence, we keep twisting our present circumstances and relationships to resemble those we knew in the past. It is not much different in some respects from twisting, curling and rearranging the bedclothes in a certain way as we try to fall asleep in that individual way which each of us has. In this manner we get the "security of the familiar" that we knew as children. While the circumstances and relationships of our early years may not have been entirely comfortable, we learned about life and the world at large in this special childhood setting. We learned to adjust ourselves to this special emotional atmosphere and to call it "reality." As adults we tend to continue to see things in terms of the "reality" of this early family setting.

CHAPTER 3

HOW THE CHILD OF THE PAST
INFLUENCES ADULT LIFE

Let me give, in quick succession, some incidents which show that the "inner child of the past" continues in adult life. These incidents may help clarify the role of the "child of the past."

No One Outgrows His Feelings of Childhood

No one outgrows or becomes too old to have an "inner child of the past." A few years ago when President Dwight D. Eisenhower announced a new record-breaking budget, newsmen promptly interviewed his older brother, Edgar, for his views. Edgar severely criticized the budget as inflationary. Next morning the President was asked what he thought of his brother's comments. According to *The New York Times*, the President, smiling broadly, said, "Edgar has been criticizing me since I was five years old." His remark, frank in its human quality and its implication that he had learned in childhood not to heed Edgar, drew laughter from the correspondents. It revealed one facet of the President's "child of the past"—the attitude of Edgar toward his younger brother and the attitude which young Dwight had developed to cope with Edgar's criticism. More than half a century later these attitudes were still functioning vigorously.*

---

* Bela Kornitzer's book, *The Great American Heritage: The Story of the Five Eisenhower Brothers,* reveals Edgar and Dwight often quarreled and fought as boys, as brothers often do. In 1953, when both were in their sixties, Edgar boasted to Kornitzer: "I can still

A Man Who Couldn't Love His Wife

Your "inner child of the past" may at times so dominate your adult self that your opportunities for self-expression and satisfaction are frustrated or destroyed. Most of us have at some time seen an irascible and discontented child dominate an embarrassed and harassed parent. This is exactly the kind of a struggle that goes on inside many people without their realizing it.

For example, Fred, a young businessman, has successfully launched his own firm. Outwardly bright and chipper, clean-cut and competitive, he suffers from impotency with his wife Helen. He looks at her pretty face, her glossy abundance of dark brown hair, her fulsome figure, and wonders why he has no feeling for her. This worries and depresses him. "Any man would be attracted to her," he says, adding with self-contempt, "any man but me, that is."

He knows that Helen loves him and would welcome his embraces. Yet they are not lovers. A ritual of empty small talk is virtually all their marriage consists of at the moment. Wondering and worrying about what is wrong, Helen waits as patiently as she can for him to put his arms around her. He tells himself he ought to, but for some reason he cannot bring himself to do it. Yet other girls in the building where Fred works attract him.

At home, when small talk fails, Fred picks irritably at Helen over trifles—and has even slapped her. He then criticizes himself for abusing her. Yet his irritability with her seems to be increasing.

In my office he asked, "Why is this happening to me? I wasn't this way when we married. But now it seems that just because I have love in abundance at home, I must refuse it. In the midst of Helen's willingness to love me, I am lonely, miserable, unable to help myself or her. Why?"

Of course, his behavior did not make sense. Were there

lick him anytime." President Eisenhower discounted their early wrangling, but when Kornitzer told him of Edgar's boast, "the President drew back in his chair and threw up his hands as if in shocked amazement. He had just heard something utterly incredible. Oh no, Edgar couldn't whip him! The grin returned. And then he repeated that his brother couldn't lick him."

16

other problems? No, none. He got along fine in his work. Everybody liked him. He just couldn't bring himself to make love to his wife. That was all there was to his problem. Nonsense, you may say; he can *if he just forces himself a little* because people don't react this way. However —and unfortunately—this *is* the way many people react to their marriage partners. This is one way in which the "inner child of the past" often interferes in the present.

A search for Fred's "child of the past" helped clarify his behavior. He grew up in a home where his father frequently exploded in scorn and mean temper outbursts, and often struck his wife and Fred.

When Fred finally married, everything was fine at first. However, as he settled down in his own home he began to treat himself with the past attitudes of his father. That meant he had to be stern with himself. Being stern with himself, he then began to react in the same way he had when his father was stern with him in his childhood. He began to be resentful toward the only other adult in his present home—his wife Helen. And so he could not react to Helen as his attractive, loving wife. The more he scolded himself for his treatment of his wife, the more he reacted with resentment—as if his father were scolding him—and the more irritable he became with his wife. Thus, the "child of the past" took over Fred's life and made it impossible for him to make love to his wife, or even show her affection.

His feeling that he "ought to" love his wife was only the first phase of his crippling self-criticism. It triggered the stern, scolding disapproving attitude with which he was treated as a boy. This, in turn, activated the great burden of resentment which he had built up as a child. In this fashion Fred's "inner child of the past" dominated his adult life. It didn't matter how attractive Helen was and had nothing to do with sex.

Such problems are almost never completely one-sided. Helen's father was a "do-it-yourself" man, always helping her mother around the house. Since Fred wasn't helpful in this sense, her "inner child of the past" interpreted this as a lack of love for her—and she subtly sniped at him, opening the old wounds of childhood resentments and making him irritable.

When Fred realized he was continuing the stern, critical attitudes which his father had had toward him, his impotency slowly disappeared. Interestingly, when he was finally able to stop saying to himself, "I ought to love Helen," he was able to—and freed himself of the deprecating tyranny of past parental attitudes. Helen was helped to see that lack of "fixit" know-how did not mean lack of love for her and she stopped sniping and nagging at him.

The "Inner Child of the Past" Interferes With Penicillin

A lifetime of bacteriological research had prepared Alexander Fleming to recognize the significance of a bit of fluff which had blown into a culture dish and stopped the growth of bacteria there. Something in the fluff, he reasoned, prevented this growth, and in publishing his observations he noted it could have usefulness in treating infections. When he tried it on persons with infections, it sometimes cleared the infection miraculously and at other times did nothing. If the mysterious germ-inhibiting factor could be extracted and purified, it was clearly going to be a powerful, life-saving drug. But, to quote Fleming, "I . . . failed to advance further for want of adequate chemical help."

Though he continued to maintain cultures of the peculiar penicillium substance for the next twelve years, nothing happened. Fleming could not convince his superiors at the research institute that it was worth the attention it needed. Finally, in 1940, the biochemist Chain came across Fleming's original paper by chance. Impressed, and believing Fleming dead, he enlisted two other chemists. Within a matter of months they had purified and synthesized the germ-killing substance in "penicillium"—penicillin.

Fleming's "inner child of the past," continuing to assert itself despite his knowledge of what penicillium could do, had made it impossible for him to convince the brilliant but talkative and dogmatic scientist Sir Almroth Wright, his superior at St. Mary's Institute of Pathology and Research, of the need for expert chemical help. Fleming was particularly handicapped by an almost complete inability to express himself and to confide his feelings to anyone.

Fleming's Childhood

Fleming grew up on a remote Scottish farm with three sisters and five brothers. He was the next to last son of his father's second wife. Some brothers were considerably older; Tom, for instance, was already at the University of Glasgow when Alexander was born. His father, who had remarried at sixty, had a stroke after the birth of the youngest son. He survived two years. Fleming's only memory of him, according to André Maurois' biography of this great scientist, was that his stricken father, kindly but gray and disabled, sat by the fire worrying about what would become of his children after he died.

It is not hard to imagine how silence was imposed on this entire anxious household while the father's illness ran its fatal course. No doubt there were infractions, for children are inevitably noisy, but this must have brought swift disapproval from their busy mother. Undoubtedly this long illness, ending in his father's death when young Alexander was four years old, contributed to Fleming's unusual inability to express himself. Moreover, his position in the family would tend to make him feel that what he thought, felt and said was not as important as what his older brothers and sisters said.

His sports and games were the solitary ones of a farm boy—hunting and fishing. He walked long, lonely distances to school, four miles each way. He grew up accustomed to having no one to talk to, to silence, and the satisfaction of observing bright older brothers and listening to them. When he was thirteen years old, he went to London to live with his older brothers and a sister who kept house for them, an arrangement that persisted even after he had become an Institute researcher. In forty-odd years of daily association, meals and scientific bull sessions at the Institute, Fleming rarely said anything. He sat smiling, likable and affectionate in his manner, but always silent, unable to talk. Thus, Fleming's silent "child of the past" continued—in fact, thrived unchallenged—and even though he knew he had a life-saving drug in his laboratory he could not effectively alter the situation by convincing anyone of its importance. Fleming's patience in maintaining the cultures during these twelve years of silence was heroic. It was all he could do with his limitations—and he went right on doing it.

Later, when fame was heaped on him, this same "child of the past" inability to speak made it nearly impossible for him to propose marriage to a young woman physician who worked with him. Both went through a long period of unnecessary anxiety and loneliness because of this. Even when he finally proposed, it was an unintelligible mumble which might have been missed if the young woman had not insisted that he repeat it. Thus, Fleming belatedly gained some well-deserved love and warmth amidst his honors. Yet this dedicated man suffered all his life from the attitudes and feelings of his "child of the past," which severely limited his own great work and personal happiness.

The Story of Linda

Linda's story demonstrates how her "inner child of the past" kept her from doing what she wanted to do—marry and become a mother. An attractive but quiet girl with a self-contained air, Linda told me she was single and worked in a nursery school. She enjoyed working with children and they loved her. She wanted very much to get married and have children of her own. She had twice been engaged. But each time when the wedding date approached, she broke off the engagement in panic.

After her first visit, she could scarcely talk to me. She sat silent. Why could she not talk? Why did she have such a struggle to say anything? Bit by bit, the outline of a life pattern emerged.

Her mother had died when Linda was two. Then she lived with her grandmother, who took care of her during the week. Her father kept her with him on weekends. When she was four, her grandmother died and her father hired a housekeeper. At six her father died. She then went to live with an elderly, rather formal aunt and uncle who were childless. During her first two years in their house she had frequent nightmares, but she was afraid to tell her aunt and uncle about them. She acquired a surface conformity, tried not to be a burden to her uncle and aunt. She became a good student and a "good girl," as she put it.

By the time she was grown, she had a vague but compelling feeling from her early experiences that to have a deep attachment to anyone was dangerous, the "kiss of death" for the person she liked. She kept all her relationships friendly but distant. Anyone coming too close, she felt, would be abruptly snatched away. Even talking to me was a threat because we talked about beneath-the-surface things. Something inside told her, "Don't talk to the doctor about how you really feel because he too will be snatched away."

This was the voice of her "child of the past." It had also spoken when, in spite of her wish to marry, the close relationship of marriage was near. If she allowed herself to feel deeply enough about someone to accept him as her husband, he certainly would have been "taken away," as her mother, grandmother and father had been.

Illogical? No, this was not illogical in the light of her childhood experiences. We actually feel things inside with the logic of this kind of experience. By working to respect yet limit the fearful feelings of her "inner child of the past," Linda was eventually able to marry and have her own children.

Present and Past and Future

We can acquire a three-dimensional appreciation of our attitudes instead of seeing only the surface of today. Some people seem to have moved lightly through childhood. They have not been deeply hurt or scarred because no harmful parental attitudes were focused on them in those early years. As adults they can, with relative ease, modify their own attitudes toward themselves. Others, who experienced deeply wounding attitudes, have greater difficulty in treating themselves with the approach of a kindly parent.

It has been my experience that often with very little help, many people caught up in the grip of seemingly hopeless anxieties and fears can sort out for themselves the true causes of their emotional difficulties and reduce them to the point where these past attitudes no longer dominate their lives.

The *first* step is to recognize these disturbing feelings and their childhood origin. The *second* is to accept and respect these feelings as part of oneself—as unavoidable as childhood itself. The *third* step is to establish limits so

21

that these old childhood feelings do not control or dominate one's actions and ability to function. All this takes hard, patient, repetitious work.

Grieving, complaining or blaming gets us nowhere. But we can, by following the steps outlined above, begin to alter the way we feel about ourselves—and to deal through our "child of the past" with both the present and future *today*.

CHAPTER 4

OUR ATTITUDES ABOUT CHILDHOOD MISLEAD US

Few of us escape the belittling of children and their feelings, which is part of our general culture. Parents are inevitably the "carriers" or transmitters of cultural attitudes —and when you understand this you will not be inclined to blame them for some of their attitudes reflecting broad cultural views. You can help yourself by realizing such attitudes frequently lay a basis for—and continue to support—self-contempt both in childhood and in later life.

One of the most repeated themes of a generation ago was that "children should be seen and not heard." Our culture requires constant moral judgment of children as "good" or "bad" while other cultures do not, *accepting their behavior as that of children.* If you want to free yourself from the tyranny you knew in childhood, you must objectively examine the role played by these dominant cultural attitudes in your past home life and the extent to which your parents followed them. Such an examination will help you to understand why your parents behaved as they did.

Millions of us grew up in a kind of moralizing atmosphere that is burdensome to children—but the burden is seldom recognized by adults. Because children do not have adult responsibilities, our culture holds that they live a carefree, problemless, happy life. Part of the adult exasperation with children is that they complain of small responsibilities after the parents have worked hard to provide comforts and pleasures. Have you not heard a parent say to a child: "Can't you even pick up your clothes? After I've worked hard all day to provide a nice home for you, you complain!" These attitudes, expressing continual disappointment and complaint, create feelings of guilt and inadequacy in the child, which eventually echo in the adult.

Our traditional cultural view belittles childhood and everything about it. We tend to continue and to repeat, parrot-like, attitudes toward children—even our own— which are derogatory, belittling and the basis for later self-contempt.

Adult Expectations

This is not a plea to let children dominate parents, be rude or disobedient. We live in a world which adults necessarily dominate and control. As Dr. B. I. Beverly, a psychiatrist who took a special interest in the emotional development of children, has pointed out in his well-known book *In Defense of Children,* "Society, from the parents in the home to the broadest social concepts, is made by and for adults. The child, as a child, in this scheme of living is entirely disregarded. He is expected to understand, appraise, and adjust himself to those adult standards as an adult would. By great effort and well-meaning he may act rightly hundreds of times; yet any such desired behavior is usually ignored, while one wrong act on his part brings down upon him the wrath of the gods—of his parents, older relatives, teachers, and other adults. The child, who necessarily lives in a mental world of his own, is expected to think and conduct himself according to adult standards."

Only in relatively recent times has the child been recognized for what he is—a child. Our heritage includes subtle pressures to make children into "little men" and "little women," but historically the main reliance has been upon a heavy-handed discipline, absolute obedience and learning by rote.

"Childish Things" Are Never Put Away

One of the most powerful and pervasive attitudes regarding childhood in our culture is the idea that at some point you cease to be a child and are an adult forever after. This is completely contrary to the facts of emotional

24

growth and development, resulting in much confusion and often severe, unnecessary self-contempt in adults. The demand is that you must be "grown up" at all times because of varying conditions or responsibilities: you have graduated, reached twenty-one years of age, gotten married, obtained a job, become a parent. Therefore, any feelings or actions, or even wishes, that might be regarded as "childlike" are considered as signs of unworthiness, contemptibility, a demonstration of inadequacy. Often people who thus belabor themselves have been raised in an unnecessarily strict environment with a constant parental demand for "grown-up" behavior. As adults, such persons continue to place such demands on themselves—which the "inner child of the past" defies, arousing their self-contempt.

Sometimes moralizing parents with this mistaken idea quote St. Paul: "When I was a child, I spake as a child, I understood as a child, I thought as a child, but when I became a man, I put away childish things."* However, St. Paul is not castigating childhood or childlike behavior. He is, it is generally agreed, referring to his conversion and assumption, as a man, of the responsibility of leading a spiritual life in accordance with Christ's teachings. But this has often been misinterpreted to belittle the feelings of the "child of the past" and is coupled with the idea that at a specific time you leave childhood feelings behind. While you can make a serious and sincere effort to be responsible and mature, you cannot manage the feelings and actions of your "child of the past" by putting them away. They are part of you and must be accepted before you can give your attention to your mature goals.

Yet scores of adults turn on themselves in this coercive fashion if they find themselves doing anything they consider "childish." The child we once were continues to exist in our adult selves and it is totally impossible to banish such feelings. Yet we will ignore, as Dr. Beverly has noted, hundreds of instances of adult behavior and let one act, feeling or thought of the "child of the past" bring "down the wrath of the gods," taking on the role of our parents, older relatives, teachers and other adults in our self-punishment. Whatever critical, hurtful, punitive comments our parents applied to us, we now apply to ourselves.

* I Corinthians, 13:11.

As long as we do not realize that adults act as parents to themselves, we can only pursue the fruitless and hopeless task of trying to put away childish things.

Perspectives and Persistence

You can relieve yourself of much anxiety, tension and chafing irritation if you can learn to be a kindly but firm parent to yourself by looking upon the feelings of your own "inner child of the past" tolerantly. You can also more truly be yourself than you have ever allowed yourself to be. Much of your tension and anxiety may simply be due to your own fears of your childhood feelings revealing themselves—and your efforts to suppress and hide these feelings, to disown and deny them.

To learn to recognize the feelings of your "inner child of the past," to respect and accept these feelings as a kind parent might accept them in a child, is not easy. Habits are not easily changed and your habitual way of treating yourself, "borrowed" from your parents, will not yield quickly.

Yet with persistent effort you can accept the feelings of the child you once were in your daily activities. These feelings are a part of you and always have been. They are nothing to be ashamed of. Such acceptance will ease your anxious efforts to suppress them and help you find satisfaction in their uniqueness and depth.

These are the basic perspectives in taking a new look at the child you once were. How your "inner child of the past" affects your job, your marriage and capacity for sexual pleasure, your money worries, your health and relations with others are important aspects of your life which can be seen in a new and different light.

How You Feel About Yourself

How you feel about yourself—and how you judge or evaluate your own feelings, thoughts and actions—is central to living your own life. What you do, and often what you *feel* you cannot do, is for the most part determined by how you feel about yourself.

These feelings about oneself are subject to enormous distortions which are rooted in childhood and cause much unnecessary pain. The man who feels stupid and weak and the girl who feels awkward and ugly are rarely as stupid and weak, awkward and ugly as they feel. In most instances these feelings are continuations of childhood feelings which were created by parental attitudes of long ago.

A child develops his sense of being a worthwhile, capable, important and unique individual from the attention given him by his parents. He "sees" or feels himself reflected in their love, approval and attention to his needs; he also learns in early childhood how to seek and win their approval as well as what will bring disapproval.

Psychiatry and Emotional Growth

In psychiatry it has long been recognized that how one feels about himself is a basic and decisive aspect of the personality. Strenuous efforts have been made to discover what influences and experiences affect the feelings of a child about himself. Such research, having fully established the primary importance of parental attitudes toward the child, has made the primary goal of child psychiatry the task of helping children develop sound feelings of self-esteem.

Freud's clinical studies of adults resulted in his theories of oral and anal libido fixation, which so shocked and disturbed people a generation ago. Today these theories have been modified by recognition of the importance of emotional attitudes and their constant interplay between parents and children. At the time when Freud did his work, such a specialized body of knowledge as child psychiatry did not exist and he was forced to make enormous guesses, based on relatively few observations almost exclusively of adults, and chiefly guided by his own insight.*

During my first years of psychiatric practice, it gradually became apparent to me that some of Freud's most widely known concepts of infantile sexuality were not necessarily the common denominators of my patient's problems. For instance, according to psychoanalytic theory, character is "fixated" at the "anal stage" by undue attention to this region in the two-to-three-year-old period, resulting in a character who later takes pleasure in compulsive, mean,

---

* Freud did not see his first child patient until three years after he had written his work on infantile sexuality. See L. Kanner, *Child Psychiatry*, 3rd ed., Springfield, Ill.: C. C. Thomas, 1957, p. 7.

sado-masochistic withholding activities. But I had a patient with "Hirschsprung's disease," which meant that every few months he had to have his bowels cleaned out surgically. Since birth he has had enemas. His mother has poked, prodded and fussed with his little behind all his life. Is he an "anal character"? He is not. He is a generous, loving, laughing and happy little boy because his relationship with his mother is sound. So-called fixations are really reflections of unhappy, crippling parent-child relationships.

"There Was a Child Went Forth"

During childhood, parental attitudes, whatever they might be, are gradually absorbed and used in self-guidance. Thus, the feelings of your "inner child of the past" are not related to a specific aspect of the personality, but encompass and include virtually everything a child encounters. Walt Whitman, in his memorable poem "There Was a Child Went Forth," describes the process of a child's growth in his environment with precision and beauty:

There was a child went forth every day,
And the first object he look'd upon, that object he
    became,
And that object became part of him for the day or a
    certain part of the day,
Or for many years or stretching cycles of years.

The early lilacs became part of this child,
And grass and white and red morning-glories,
    and white and red clover, and the song of the
    phoebe bird . . .
His own parents, he that had father'd him and she
    that had conceiv'd him in her womb and birth'd
    him,
They gave this child more of themselves than that,
They gave him afterward every day, they became part
    of him.

The mother at home quietly placing the dishes on the
    suppertable,
The mother with mild words, clean her cap and
    gown, a wholesome odor falling off her person and
    clothes as she walks by,

The father, strong, self-sufficient, manly, mean,
    anger'd, unjust,
The blow, the quick loud word, the tight bargain, the
    crafty lure,
The family usages, the language, the company, the
    furniture, the yearning and swelling heart,
Affection that will not be gainsay'd, the sense of what
    is real, the thought if after all it should prove unreal,
The doubts of day-time and the doubts of night-time,
    the curious whether and how,
Whether that which appears so is so, or is it all
    flashes and specks? . . .

This excerpt describes how the experiences, images,
scenes and wonder of childhood are retained forever, literally becoming part of us.

In childhood, in order to win the warmth, affection and
attention of his parents, the child absorbs and imitates
even the gestures and grimaces of his parents as well as
their way of looking at himself and the world in general.
The most important of these attitudes, is, of course, how
the parents feel about the child. This determines how the
child feels about himself. He has no other guide, no other
mirror that reflects what kind of a person he is and
whether he is worth loving.

As the child grows older, as year is piled on year, the
illusion develops that these attitudes of his parents are
indeed his own attitudes—when the truth is that they are
not his attitudes, formed independently by him. Instead
they are his parents'. Yet the child perpetuates these attitudes toward himself and calls them the "truth" long after
he has reached physical maturity.

Thus, the "inner child of the past" in the adult continues not only the general cultural attitudes of his parents
toward food, home life, religion, education, sex and money,
but *particularly the attitudes which his parents had toward
him.* We have a persistent inclination to recreate within
ourselves this past family atmosphere and the attitudes of
our parents toward us even if they are hurtful. As many
a patient has told me even after he has recognized the
falseness of a deprecating parental attitude, "it feels right."
The security of the "child of the past" lies in these old,
harmful parental attitudes. When you attempt to change
such attitudes, the "child of the past" protests, often so

strenuously that the adult portion of yourself permits him to interfere with adult goals and satisfactions.

Each of us grew up in a family and became accustomed to its many facets, its "feeling tones" as well as what Whitman calls "the family usages, the language," which were peculiar to our particular family. We absorbed what would make our father laugh and what would make him angry, what would shock our mother and how they really felt about other people and everything from money to love and food, how they set themselves apart from all others. In this way we learned to like or dislike fried potatoes, gravy, chocolate pudding and other foods. As adults we continue these patterns of likes and dislikes because these foods are familiar, "old friends." This too is part of our "child of the past" continuing in the present.

Life, as you understand it and live it, was learned in this past setting. Whatever its peculiarities, you gained from your family the feeling of being "at home." It is this feeling that your "inner child of the past" constantly seeks.

Not to Blame Your Parents

Even if our childhood home was unhappy at times, it nevertheless provided the "at home" feeling. We can all recall painful childhood experiences. Many of us were forced to eat foods we did not like—and as adults we shun them. We may, as adults, stay up too late because as children we were sent to bed too early—and resented it. There were attitudes taken by our parents, brothers and sisters that hurt us, but we coped with them to the best of our ability at that time. Scoldings, spankings, refusals and deprivations may have made us feel unacceptable, inadequate and isolated.

However, now that we are grown, we can begin to see our parents as they really were—and not as the all-powerful, all-wise persons we saw as children. We now see them as just plain human beings with problems of their own, not very different from other people's. While they undoubtedly made some mistakes in rearing us, they did the best they could with the understanding they had. As Whitman points out, parents "give this child more of themselves" than birth: "They gave him afterward every day, they became part of him."

In learning to recognize your "inner child of the past,"

30

you should examine carefully the hurtful attitudes you encountered as a child. They are easily identified: they still hurt. The purpose of identifying them is not to blame your parents, but *so that you will not continue to inflict these hurtful attitudes on yourself in acting as a parent to yourself.*

CHAPTER 5

WHEN THE CHILD OF THE PAST TAKES OVER

Annette's Story

It may seem incredible that an adult continues to apply to himself the harsh criticisms and derogatory or belittling attitudes of a parent. Yet this is precisely the case. To provide some firsthand evidence of how this affects adult life, I should like to describe the case of "Annette." For many months I sat listening to a bitter repetitious monologue which this hurt, angry young woman hurled at me at every session:

"You hate me, don't you?" she would cry. "You wish I would die. I don't mean anything to you. Don't pretend I do. You don't even know me!

"You're sitting there thinking how ugly I am! I'm not asking you to lie to me. You're just sitting there wishing this session was over. Why don't you go home? Don't you have anything better to do? Do you want me to leave? You poor thing! The great doctor who is such a martyr! Well, you're not a martyr to me! You're a fake—a big fake, that's all. You have no feeling for anybody. You're just a phony and I can't stand phonies!

"Oh God, I don't know what makes me talk like this . . ."

What was I doing? Just sitting there. Did I threaten or insult her? I didn't. I merely asked her how she had been feeling since the day before. This tirade was her answer. She couldn't possibly know whether or not I was a fake —she didn't really know me. Besides, if I am so obnoxious, why did she keep coming to me? Why did she have to be so concerned about whether she was making me angry?

32

This is unreasonable behavior. Yet Annette knows very well where the reality boundaries are. She manages a house and three children. Her friends find her sympathetically understanding but more silent than most people. Her husband finds her irritating and he frequently tells her about her shortcomings. But he finds his employers and his children irritating too. Annette tolerates his tirades in silent submission. She has anxiety attacks when she walks along the street and in stores. She feels, despite evidence to the contrary, that she is ugly and stupid. When she is not overcome with anxiety, she lives in a bleak, utterly lonely world which has no niche in it for her.

But none of this, not even the irritability of her husband, tells us why she has to be so self-critical or why she must misinterpret the people around her, including her physician, when they are often really quite friendly and sympathetic to her.

Her past life provides a basis for understanding why she behaves in this fashion. Her father was neglected in his early life. He grew up with a number of brothers and sisters in a poverty-stricken home. He went to work at an age when he should have been playing and worked hard from then on. He grew up with little loving interchange and found it difficult to be close to anyone in his family. He could only be close to his work. He took his wife's nagging without rebuttal—except to spend more time at his job. As a result his children saw little of him.

Annette's Mother

Annette's mother was a domineering woman subject to violent temper outbursts. She grew up quarreling with, demanding from and ordering about her own mother, my patient's grandmother. When she married, she continued the quarrel with her husband but most of her fury was spent on her child—my patient. She would say to Annette: "You are awkward and ugly. You will never be pretty, not worth looking at. What a stupid, ugly child! What a pity I couldn't have had a decent-looking child!" This was her day-in, day-out comment.

If angry or annoyed with Annette, she would scream: "You ugly fat little pig! Get out of my sight!" Once, when she took the child to the seashore, she told her, "Look, the ocean is right there. Why don't you walk out into the ocean—and just keep walking. Then I'll be rid of you!"

You may think that people never say such things to their children. You are mistaken. If you have any doubts, stand in a busy supermarket for an afternoon and listen to the comments of mothers to their children.

When a child is spoken to in this fashion repeatedly, he begins to speak to himself in the same way. "You are ugly" becomes "I am ugly." And "You are stupid and no good, bad" becomes "I am stupid and no good, bad." Such verbal comments are often reinforced with facial expressions of disgust or gestures that convey the parent's attitude silently when used alone.

As the child reaches adolescence he gradually becomes his own parent—and treats himself with his parents' attitudes, even though they are harsh, painful and continually downgrading and damaging.

I asked Annette, whose tirade I described earlier, to write out how her "inner child of the past" functions within her and how it affects her life today. This is what she wrote:

"My particular 'child of the past' has forced me to tear up the last fifteen things I have tried to write because I am ashamed of what I said and the way that I have said it, and also consider them unworthy. This is by way of apology in advance, so as to protect myself. Why am I like this?

"The criticism that has paralyzed my every thought and action is within myself. I am sitting here and judging my every word, judging them to be bad. This reaction to my performance is ever within me whether it be in regard to writing or cooking or driving or walking down the street (an act that is almost impossible for me).

"I believe I can give a description of the 'child of the past' in action. Today is Sunday and on Sundays I revert almost completely to my past life. There is no respite from it anywhere. I am, or feel myself to be, completely alone in a frightening world that I cannot cope with. Everyone is angry and I am bad and not capable of an action that will please. I have taken my temperature eight times today, watching the red line with great anxiety and feeling relief from the anxiety for only a moment or two when the thermometer says normal, and then a few moments later repeating the procedure again. I am also fat today, although the scale said that I weigh 102 and I am five feet three. I had tried on my tightest clothes and felt no relief from the fear of being fat when they fit as they always have.

"I had company for dinner. My hands shook and my heart pounded because in my opinion the meal was terrible and the people were thinking how inadequate I am, and most terrible of all, how ugly and repellent I am. I actually have no way of telling how I look. To me, every woman in the world is pretty and only I am hideous. I have been told that I am attractive and some men seem to find me so but their words make no impression at all on me or on my opinion of myself.

"As I sit here now, I can remember the words most frequently said to me when I was a child, words I now use on myself when I fail to live up to my expectations. The words? 'Ugly, fat cow,' and even as I write this, I cringe as I cringed when they were used about me all of my childhood years. However, the fact that I cringe does not alter the fact that I said them to myself this very day when I cooked the roast too long and when I tried to walk into the drugstore and had to retreat in abject humiliation because of anxiety that threatened to become panic. Shame, anxiety, and self-criticism are almost all of the emotions that I have on Sunday.

"What were Sundays like in the past? What is different about Sunday? On Sundays my mother was angry. When I would wake in the morning and go down to the library I would see her sitting in the tall wing chair and I could tell by one look at her face that she was not going to speak to me today. Her face was a mask of hatred, and I could feel the familiar tightening in my chest and the stomach ache and horrible anxiety about it all and the dull fear of cancer or bleeding to death and the resolve never to tell anyone of this shameful thing. I would try to talk to her, but she hated me today and so I couldn't speak. I would go into the kitchen and prepare breakfast for my brothers, and my dad. I would listen with fear for a sound of her coming into the kitchen—and soon she would. She would set the table, all the time giving me looks of hatred from under her thick and beautiful eyebrows. I would think, from the few looks I would glimpse of her from under my lowered and ashamed eyes, how beautiful she was and how beautiful she had always seemed to me.

"I would think of how ugly I was and of her hatred when she would tell me how wonderful it would have been to have a tall, thin, dark-haired little girl with blue eyes. A little girl who looked like my cousin and not 'like his family.' I could feel her eyes on my fat arms and stomach and I would have liked to hide but there was no escape. I could feel her hatred of me permeate the room, and I could feel the lump in my throat when my older brother came down. She fussed over him, giving him food and attention. When she would do the same for my little brother and, dutifully and resentfully, feed my father, I could hardly control my tears. She would never make any attempt to see that I had anything to eat. Of course, I was dreadfully overweight, a shame and a humiliation to her, and I didn't and don't blame her. As I would walk across the room or try, very inadequately, to do the dishes, she would mutter her favorite words about me: 'Ugly, fat cow!' The lump in my throat would grow almost balloon-size and then she would mutter, with unconcealed hatred in her voice and face, 'She's crying again!'

"Then I would spend the rest of the day in the bathroom, overcome with fear and shame. The same thing would be repeated at dinner and at night.

"Yes, there was my father but I knew from past experience what he would say: 'Pay it no mind,' or 'Here's a dollar. Go to the movies and forget it.' There was no one I could turn to. I was alone. I was alone as I am today. At nine or ten o'clock I would go to bed. I would lie there and cry with the pillow over my head, so that no one would hear me. The silent tears are what I remember of the nights—that and not being able to sleep. The anxiety would grow greater and greater as sleep would fail me.

"Yet in a way I didn't want to sleep, because if I did, it would be morning too soon. 'Please God,' I would murmur, 'let me be a grownup.' But I was only ten and the years until I would be grown were interminable. Still no sleep. At one o'clock, if I could hear the sound of their voices, I would sit outside their door and listen . . . I heard a great many things about me that way. All of the things I heard hurt me. I was a humiliation to her, just as I am to me today. I had no enthusiasm or verve. I was unhappy and a trial to them both, as I am to me today.

"Listening was no help to my self-esteem. At two or three o'clock I would finally sleep, but the awakening was all that I expected. I would hardly open my eyes before the tears would come, and the dread of day would overwhelm me, as every morning it does now. As an adult, sleep is a constantly elusive treasure. As I write now, I thank God for the sleeping pills that I took an hour ago that will enable me to lay this Sunday down and hurry it with a long list of Sundays that I thank the fates have passed. I also am grateful to the pills because they have put the censor of my every act and deed to sleep so that I am able to write of my feelings with more ease and with a 'what the hell' feeling. I do not know if I have made the similarities of the past and present clear. I have tried to point out the way the past is still operating. I am no longer a child, but the hurts, the self-devaluation, the terrible phobias remain. 'In the darkness of Age a child lies weeping.'

"I hope some day to begin anew. The slate will be wiped absolutely clean and there will be no reflection in the mirror at all. I will no longer see me through my mother's and my own eyes, but will gradually be able to see me as perhaps I really am. If my mother's interpretation of me is wrong, then in reality I have no existence and will have to be reborn. Certainly that is my hope. A chance to start again. A chance to live for the first time in my life."

The "At Home" Feeling

Annette's story is, of course, an extremely severe example of how a person continues parental attitudes toward himself, but this does not make it less valid. Treating herself in this scornful, lacerating way, my patient is forced to see the people around her as if they had the same harsh, belittling and hateful attitudes she knew in childhood. Her "child of the past" feels more secure in this harsh abuse. Any lack of harshness from the adults she meets arouses suspicion and anxiety in her because it is strange and unfamiliar. If she can provoke hostility, she feels more "at home."

If we cannot find, recreate or simulate the emotional atmosphere we knew as children, we feel "strange," "foreign," "lost" or "not at home." If we succeed in simulating it, we have the old familiar "at home" feeling. It provides a certain kind of security, *but it contains all the restrictions and hurts we knew as children.*

When Another Type of "Child of the Past" Takes Over

Rex, a brilliant college senior, came to see me about his temper outbursts and difficulties with girls. He was handsome, but with a rather wild, unruly look. His hair was always tousled and his necktie askew. He would pace up and down, then collapse in a chair and put his feet on my desk (I would firmly tell him to remove them) and call me "Doc, old buddy."

He had a girl friend but said she didn't love him. Why? Because she didn't "listen" to him. "Listening" meant obeying, because he knew what was best.

He wanted to pry into every aspect of his girl friend's life. He wanted to dictate what she should do in everything: what kind of stores to shop in, what color hose to wear, what kind of toothpaste she should use—and how often. When the girl rebelled, Rex was both enraged and hurt. "She doesn't love me or she would do what I say," he complained.

Jealous of the time she spent in charity work, he ordered her to quit. After taking his dictates—and his rages—for a long time, the girl broke off with him. This left Rex desolate—for a while. Presently he found another girl whom he soon made miserable in the same way with his dictums and temper outbursts. This process had already been repeated with a number of girls, in whom his handsome but sloppy appearance originally aroused a maternal interest. His bossy dictates, at least initially, even appeared quite masculine. But inevitably his all-consuming demands, prying and dictating caused the girl to break off the relationship. Each time he was deeply hurt and disconsolate.

Why did this young man's endless repetitious pattern go on? Why did he have so little insight into others and their feelings?

When Rex was a child, his mother boasted that she never left him with a baby-sitter. He was her "life"—and she was literally his devoted slave. Practically from the time he could talk, he ordered his mother about. Adoring him, proud of his quick, bright mind, his mother was always ready to obey him—and to admire his developing intelligence and sense of taste. She wanted to make him feel important and obeyed his slightest whim. Just as he dictated to his girl friends, he still dictated to his mother.

His "child of the past" had never had any lessons in respecting the feelings and rights of others. Rex constantly invaded the privacy and rights of his girl friends—and then misinterpreted their protests as lack of love. Because his mother had never protested against his abrogating her rights during his childhood, he had no insight into his girl friends' feelings. He felt the girls really didn't accept him or they would "listen" to him. In fact, anyone who refused to obey him, to accept his word as law—and admire him for being so bright—obviously didn't love him. His "child of the past" said, "If you love me, you will cater to my whims as my mother always has." This is what love meant to him.

This young man's hurt feelings were genuine. He wanted and needed very much to be loved. But to win and hold a girl's love, Rex had to learn, by becoming a different kind of a parent to himself, to set limits on his impulsive "child of the past." These limits and respect for the rights of others had not been developed in childhood.

You Are a Parent to Yourself

Despite their seeming dissimilarity, in both Rex's case and that of Annette the "inner child of the past" took over and controlled their adult existence. Both were eventually able to recognize their individual "child of the past," diminish their self-administered defeats and begin to increase their satisfactions by becoming more kindly and firmer parents to the children they once were.

Let me say again: regardless of your particular childhood or present problems, you are already acting as a parent to yourself. We all necessarily do this. We tend to use the same techniques to comfort or punish ourselves that our parents used. The way you treat yourself determines how secure you are going to feel. If you treat yourself exactly as your parents treated you, you may feel a certain security, but you are continuing the old—and now unnecessary—painful attitudes that hurt you deeply as a child. These old attitudes now limit your opportunities and satisfactions as an adult.

In being a parent to yourself, you do not have to continue these hurtful attitudes. You can be a better parent to yourself than your parents' attitudes permitted. You can learn that *the process of maturing is the accepting of these childhood feelings as a respected part of ourselves. You can learn to live with them—in your way.*

Your "child of the past" can be an asset if you are a good parent to him. He can provide an enriched appreciation of your efforts and help to keep your world young, fresh and full of wonder.

CHAPTER 6

ARE YOU DIVIDED
AGAINST YOURSELF?

Emotionally, we grow like the layers of an onion. Each day, as Whitman puts it, "becomes part" of us. The struggles and longings of our childhood and adolescence will always remain deep within us. It takes time to get used to the idea that these old feelings and struggles are not "over and done with" and that the core of childhood lives on, exerting its influence.

Most of us never emotionally accept this fact. We seek to stifle or root out this part of ourselves. It is unwelcome because it doesn't confirm our adult view of ourselves. From my own experience I know that some people grow very resentful of the idea that they have within them a lively and persistent "child of the past." Often these are people who have carried out a harsh, painful battle or "put away childish things," sternly punishing and denying themselves in the effort to be mature.

No one should expect to be completely adult all the time. If we turn against ourselves in bitterness, we are divided and helpless, unable to function. This is what Annette did. This bitterness does not destroy the "inner child of the past." Instead the so-called childish feelings are driven in deeper, making their expression more urgent. Depending on how you felt about parental scoldings years ago, your "child of the past" responds to such treatment with fear, rebellion, hurt feelings and sullenness. The more we try to ostracize this part of ourselves, the more abandoned and lonely we are bound to feel.

The "Inner Child of the Past" and the Unconscious

Sometimes my medical school students ask: "Is the 'inner child of the past' the same thing that Freud calls the 'unconscious'?"

The answer is "no." There is a great difference.

Books, articles and movies have created a picture of the "unconscious" as an all-powerful reservoir of feelings within us which lies beyond our control. The persons portrayed in such books and articles are pictured as being helpless because their condition arises from the need to satisfy "unconscious" demands, demands of which they are not aware and which they cannot control. Thus the "unconscious" seems to consist of frightening, unseen, mysterious and overpowering forces which cause people to harm themselves and others.

After considerable experience as a psychiatrist and as a teacher of psychiatry, I seriously question the usefulness of the idea of the "unconscious" in explaining to anyone how and why his feelings are troubled. The "unconscious" frightens people—makes them feel they have within themselves a murky pool inhabited by hobgoblins which they cannot manage.

I tell my medical students that they know the facts of their present and past lives as well as they know the backs of their hands, that they have lived through every minute of it. We all recall the attitudes our parents had toward us when we were children. These are the essential attitudes. We are familiar with them because they are the ones we apply to ourselves now—and which we must modify in order to feel better.

We may forget our childhood reactions toward our parents because if they had been expressed then they might have jeopardized our acceptance in the family. Often we had to hide these reactions to feel safe. But we rarely forget our parents' attitudes that hurt us.

With this understanding we can immediately get rid of the hobgoblins and mysterious demons that popular usage has attributed to the "unconscious." We have put the problem of emotional distress in its proper perspective —*namely, that the conscious adult can be an accepting,*

42

firm and appreciative parent to his well-known *"inner child of the past."* This means that while respecting the feelings of his "child of the past" he recognizes that these feelings were often the reactions to his parents' attitudes years ago and he does not allow this part of him to interfere with his adult goals and satisfactions.

We are, in this way, not talking about something mysterious, unseen, vaguely felt. We are talking about the needs and feelings of a known child who once was and who now continues to exist within a known adult—*you.*

Living in Harmony with Yourself

Mutual respect is the principle which can help you live in harmony with yourself. This means that, as a good parent to yourself, you respect the feelings of your childhood, your "inner child of the past." This also means that you require your "child of the past" to accept limits which keep him from infringing on your life as an adult and on the rights of others.

All of your feelings must receive serious consideration. Hiding, denying or belittling any feeling you have is an act of disrespect toward yourself and it automatically divides you, creating conflict—renewing conflict, I should say—between your "child of the past" and you as a parent to yourself. Therefore, the way to accept your "child of the past" is to give all your feelings serious respectful consideration. If your desires do not interfere with your adult goals or the rights of others, you should try to fulfill those desires.

However, if the feelings from your childhood are permitted free expression, they may interfere with your adult life or the rights of others. To use a broad, perhaps ridiculous example, if your "child of the past" doesn't want to get up in the morning and go to work, and you indulge this feeling, you are letting these childhood feelings interfere with your adult life. You may lose your job—and be unable to do the things that you, the adult, really want to do. In a similar fashion you may have trouble limiting your anger because your temper tantrums were indulged by your parents. You may eat too much or "want what you want when you want it" regardless of others because someone indulged your whims in childhood.

Therefore, you must set firm limits in allowing these

feelings to be expressed. Controlling these feelings often hurts. All children howl at times when needed restrictions are imposed and your "child of the past" is no exception. In imposing limits, you must not criticize or belittle these feelings. Yet you must not allow them to be expressed in a way that interferes with your adult living. The pain you experience when you impose limits is not damaging and it will become less intense as you continue to set them.

To be productive, this change of attitude toward yourself requires a conscious effort on your part. You may be surprised to discover how constantly and continually you belittle your "child of the past" and his feelings. You may have trouble in learning to accept these feelings as a natural part of yourself. And you must accept some anxiety while your "child of the past" is becoming accustomed to a new emotional "home"—one that may be more respectful and more limiting, but in the long run more satisfying.

In this way you will find yourself developing more energy for your adult activities. Yet by treating these feelings differently you will feel somewhat uneasy, "not at home" with your new parental attitudes. If you are used to clobbering down with contempt and shame the feelings of your "child of the past," for example, you will find it difficult to tolerate and respect these feelings, to accept this part of yourself with kindness and appreciation.

Changing Your Attitudes Toward Yourself

Whatever parental attitudes you have been using on yourself, it takes time, patience, repetition and willingness to stand the gaff in order to change them. Some people have more ability to live outside the old "at home" atmosphere of their childhood than others. Past patterns are often clung to tenaciously—even though they hurt—because they are familiar. It takes real effort and work to live "in the present" rather than with the old, past patterns of self-evaluation. If you do not work to change some of these old patterns, you are destined to long, needless stretches of unrest and loneliness. You are never so alone as when you turn against yourself in criticism and disgust.

In later chapters specific parental attitudes which have been found to be emotionally damaging to children and which are commonly encountered in our culture, such as perfectionism and overcoercion, are discussed at length. You will be able to pick out specific parental attitudes to which you were subjected as a child and which you may still be applying to yourself, thereby limiting your capacity as an adult.

CHAPTER 7

IT TAKES FOUR TO MAKE
A MARRIAGE

Because each of us has within himself a "child of the past," marriage requires that four—*not two*—persons adjust to one another. If one of the four dominates, there is bound to be trouble. Not understanding that marriage basically involves four persons is the cause of much of the anguish of our unhappy marriages and divorce courts. Our romantic attitudes toward love and marriage, which inundate us in song and story, give us a misleading picture of marriage—"just us two." After looking forward to marriage, we are then disappointed, frustrated and eventually embittered or resigned because "just us two" are somehow "so complicated"—and not at all as compatible, appreciative, loving and sympathetic as we had imagined, hoped, dreamed.

We are simply not told that marriage involves four persons—two adults acting in the present and two children acting according to their respective and different family backgrounds.

The idea that four distinct people are involved in marriage startles and shocks some people. It amuses others. Some people immediately visualize four individuals rollicking in a marriage bed. In a way this is true, although they may be quite unhappy instead of rollicking; I shall try to explain how this happens in later chapters. There is nothing amusing about this. It is often sad and pathetic because the interference of the "child of the past" in the present is often the basic cause of marital difficulties regardless of whether sex, money, jealousy or nagging seems to be the problem.

46

Marriage Is Naturally Complicated

Because there are four people involved, *any* marriage is naturally complicated. If we were taught this as young men and women, we might be more realistic in estimating our possibilities for marital happiness—and less disturbed by the difficulties that inevitably do occur in marriage. The wife would understand that her husband still has within him "the boy who once was," who never picked up his clothes and didn't come to supper the minute he was called. And the husband would understand that his wife has within her "the girl who once was," who needed to be reassured that she was attractive and capable, who was afraid of mice and timid about speaking up.

What Happens When You Marry

In marriage the child you once were expresses his needs, wants, attitudes, ways of behaving and desires more fully than in any other situation. He may, quite literally, bawl and balk over every frustration and task, storm and rage in tantrums, or withdraw in icy silence. This is why the most common complaint made about marriage partners is: "She's so childish," or "He acts like a kid."

Why does this happen? It happens because marriage and the establishment of a home promises to restore the comfortable, familiar "at home" feelings of childhood—and the "inner child of the past" in both husband and wife rushes to the foreground. This is why there is often bitter conflict about what seem to be trivial things in marriage. For instance, a young couple once came to see me because the husband took off his shoes and went about in his stocking feet from the moment he arrived home. This offended his wife. She felt it showed complete disrespect for their home. "He doesn't take off his shoes in the office. Only at home! He has no standards!" she complained. "Why should I keep the living room looking beautiful if he's going to sit around in it in his stocking feet?" Her husband said, "My God, what's wrong with being comfortable at home?"

Of course, this conflict over stockinged feet vs. shod ones was only the visible portion of the iceberg of conflict between them. Discussion of their past homes, the homes

47

of their childhood, brought out that each was trying to duplicate that past home. The husband had been raised in a home where the father worked hard all day, came home, took off his shoes and was comforted by his wife's ministrations. The wife was brought up in a home with severe housekeeping standards, where no one went into the living room except for almost formal occasions, and where her mother's wishes were scrupulously followed by her father. The "child of the past" of each expected, in marriage, to find things exactly as they had been in their childhood homes. When each got some insight into the other's "child of the past," their iceberg of conflict and discontent gradually melted.

A Fresh Perspective

If you understand that you have within yourself a persisting "inner child of the past"—and that your spouse also has an active "child of the past," quite different from yours—you will gain a fresh perspective on your marriage. Difficulties and misunderstandings arise in marriage because there really are *four* persons whose feelings and attitudes must be adjusted in areas that are deeply emotional—sexual satisfaction, money and economy, foods and eating habits, recreation, prestige, neighbors' values, and the meaning of "home" to each.

When I reach this point in my lectures on psychiatry at Ohio State University School of Medicine, the married medical students often approach me with a request. "Would you mind if I brought my wife to the next class? I can see her 'child of the past,' but she can't see mine." As these capable young medical students demonstrate, none of us escapes this problem. Because "home" and marriage provide the opportunities for affection, intimacy, warmth and security, and involve food, sex, and money as well, the feelings of our childhood home are most intensely expressed within marriage. Inevitably, we all tend to flavor our marriage with the feelings of our childhoods—which make us feel "at home."

Generally, in order to achieve the "at home" feeling within our marriage, we treat ourselves in the same way our parents treated us. The old "at home" emotional atmosphere of childhood is copied as precisely as possible, including any painful attitudes that may have characterized our family life in the past. We frequently even invite our spouses to treat us the way our parents did—unknowingly seeking their approval and depending on their evaluation of us in the same way that we once sought the approval and love of our parents. This is, in a way, what is happening when your spouse refuses, perhaps by default or abdication, to assume responsibility or "acts like a baby."

Four Making Plans

Few people can explain very well why they happened to marry when they did. The feelings that led them to marry are often closely and intimately connected with the feelings of aloneness experienced in childhood.

In childhood such feelings arise at times when we feel left out, unaccepted, disapproved of or isolated. We can all remember some occasion when other children in our class left us out of some activity and how lonely, hurt and isolated we felt. Still more painful were occasions when our feelings of ineptness and inadequacy, or the belittling attitudes of those around us, often placed us in the uncomfortable position of being separated from others in our family.

As our world expanded, we found that we had to exert ourselves to win a place for ourselves in school, with friends and on the job to keep from being left out, isolated and alone. As children we may have endured some exploitation from other children in order to "belong to the gang" or to have the friendship of another child. On reaching adolescence we found ourselves dreaming of establishing a close, loving and rewarding relationship with a dream person whom we had never met. This dream shifted slightly as we grew, becoming a dream of establishing a home with the idealized person, where the close, loving intimacy and companionship we sometimes knew as young children would be re-established with the added joys of adult sexual satisfactions and independence. "How can I possibly feel alone again," our inner feelings told us, "with someone loving me who will share my life completely?" Marriage would be the answer!

Marriage, we believed, was to have all the advantages of dating without the anxieties and wounded feelings involved in the "trying-out" character of dating. When we at last found someone who seemed to meet our needs, we married. For a while both before and after marriage it seemed as though our hope never to feel lonely and left out would be realized. Then misunderstandings developed. We found that we could live very close to another person and yet be apart, even though we didn't want to be. We found ourselves complaining, "If she would only understand how I feel," or "He could change if he wanted to. It would mean so much to me."

Four in Love

When two persons marry, they are "in love." This usually means that two adults are reasonably companionable and physically attracted to one another, and that the two "children of the past" see in the opposite adult the promise of fulfillment of past longings. Then, either gradually or suddenly, each marital partner comes face to face with the "child of the past" of the other—the "childish" part of your spouse, the part that seems unreasonable.

Many marital difficulties and incompatibilities might be avoided—or at least foreseen—if the prospective bride and groom visited one another's homes casually and observed the relationship between the "intended" and his parents. The way he looks at his parents will be the coloration through which he will see his spouse. One must ask: "Do I want to be treated as he treats his parents?" And the way his parents treat him will be a good indication of how he will treat himself and how he will expect you to behave toward him—after the honeymoon.

The satisfactions and success of the marriage depend on how well *each* of the four—the two adults and the "inner child of the past" of each adult—can adjust on a basis of mutual respect for the other three.

Because four persons are involved, a balanced state of mutual respect is seldom achieved easily. We traditionally and habitually think of marriage as involving only two people. Often—indeed, generally—contention among the four is masked by what appear to be genuine problems and differences. Let me cite some brief, simplified illustrations of this.

In one family there is endless irritation and anxiety over entertaining others. Eleanor's "child of the past" feels most at home only if people within the family connection or very old friends are invited to dinner. In her childhood home strangers—any persons outside the family relationships—were never invited to the house. As a child she sometimes wished she could get her parents to invite the parents of other children to dinner. However, her parents always refused. "The family table" had an exclusive character in their home. The only way a stranger could get an invitation, her older sister once told her, would be to marry one of them.

When Eleanor got a job after college, she was attracted to a crowd-loving, gregarious, generous and openhearted man, Ernest, whom she met at a party. He promptly invited her to a supper he was giving. At the supper Eleanor was both astonished and pleased when he invited his housekeeper, who had prepared the meal, to sit down and eat with the guests. It seemed to Eleanor that he did all the things she used to wish her family, particularly her father, would do.

Ernest's "child of the past" had known an easygoing, happy and informal home where everyone was welcome, where a constant stream of strangers appeared for supper, where there was "always room for one more." "All people are interesting" was the creed of Ernest's father and it had become Ernest's. Eleanor's shyness was quickly overcome by Ernest's warmth and appreciative interest in her.

But when they married, much as Eleanor liked the idea of entertaining in her own home, she found the actual entertaining to be very difficult and trying. She worried for days over everything and couldn't talk to her guests when they did come. At first Ernest's gregariousness made up for it. But gradually he noticed she was a "cold clam," as he put it in a moment of irritation. Actually, she felt comfortable only when her parents or other relatives came. She had to steel herself to entertain her husband's business friends. One night he brought home a complete stranger —an unemployed man who had approached him on the street seeking money for a meal. Ernest had simply brought him home. Eleanor was shocked and upset, completely unable to feel any sympathy for the stranger, who was very ill at ease, and she was furious with Ernest. When her husband gave him bus fare and sent him on his way, they had a furious argument. The pent-up feelings of her "child of the past" against "strangers at the family table" poured out of her. Her husband, astonished, called her "narrow

51

and stupid." She says, "I'm being made into a servant for Ernest's friends. In fact, just anybody, complete strangers!"

Actually, their respective "children of the past" are completely at loggerheads. Yet this aspect of their different backgrounds is never discussed and when brought to their attention is dismissed as something that happened "long ago." Neither sees how it affects their lives today.

In another family the "child of the past" of the wife, Marion, expresses itself in worry over illness—and in illness. Listen to Marion's story:

"I've been sick for about ten months. My doctor has given me vitamin shots but they haven't helped. Ten months ago I had a touch of the flu. When I got sick, I just collapsed. I couldn't get up, I was so weak. My nerves are shot and I just can't do anything. Two doctors examined me and they say there is nothing wrong. But I'm afraid to go out because I might get so sick I couldn't get back to the house.

"Until I got sick, I worked as a stenographer. I worked hard, trying to run my home and hold a full-time job.

"I was sick a lot when I was a child. I had all the childhood diseases as well as pneumonia and a ruptured appendix. My whole family was especially kind to me when I didn't feel well. My mother worried a lot about my health. She was always doing things to protect our health. My father was sick a lot and he worried about my health."

This woman was overwhelmed by the drudgery of her life. Under the pressure of her job and her responsibilities as a wife, her "child of the past" gradually took over and sought the reward she had received in childhood when ill. She adopted her parents' solicitous attitude toward herself —which forced her into bed for months. After much inner struggle she realized that she did not need to treat herself as her parents had and that her unrealistic worries about her health were efforts to enjoy both the sympathy and the freedom from responsibility of her childhood. She decided to cease being "a poor sick child," which is what her parents always called her in anxious, solicitous tones.

This was a hard decision to make—to abandon her childhood retreat. And it took courage and persisting determination for her to refuse to coddle her whimpering, whining, protesting "child of the past," who kept crying of aches and pains and the need to rest. Yet, with the kind of quiet, patient persistence with which many women meet great problems and real pain, she overcame these parental attitudes within herself and gained a real life as a mature woman. She no longer begged off from her husband's embraces and from social engagements because she "wasn't feeling well." Instead she was able at last to enjoy them. She now says, "I am surprised at myself. I would never have thought I could do these things."

Every married person can gain considerable perspective on his marital difficulties by recognizing the part played in them by his "inner child of the past." You can recognize that there are certain areas where you and your spouse have differences. Such differences are natural to some extent, but you need to ask yourself: What role does my "child of the past" play in these differences, in the demands I make and in what I consider desirable?

CHAPTER 8

AREAS OF CONFLICT

Money, Sex, Fun

There are certain areas where the "child of the past" is more clearly in control of the adult than at other times. For example, the home itself may be such an area. Several men I know are interesting, outgoing persons when away from home. If you meet them at their work or at a party or in transit, they are warm, outgoing persons. Yet whenever any one of them steps inside the door of his home, he crawls into an army-tank attitude, bristling with machine guns. He becomes remote and caustic. His wife complains, "I just can't get to him! I can't get through his shell. He won't listen, and he says such cruel, ugly things."

These men had to build protective, combative armor in childhood to cope with a sharp-tongued, battlefield home atmosphere. They still feel too vulnerable to step out of their protective shells in the present, even though the battlefields of childhood have long since disappeared. Often their wives, out of loneliness and in a frantic attempt to "reach" these husbands, quarrel with them. This recreates the battlefield atmosphere of their past home life—and more firmly entrenches these men in their armored tanks.

Money

Much friction between husbands and wives occurs over money. Many people are unreasonable about money as adults simply because in their childhood they were surrounded by persons who were anxious about money. To

54

the "child of the past," money can mean security, a means of expressing individuality, a way of getting away from circumstances that are unpleasant, a promise of good things. Conversely, it may mean control, deprivation, withdrawal of love or status. These strong childhood reactions can easily obscure adult goals.

For example, I know a professional man whose annual income is about $65,000. Yet his wife is not free to buy soap chips for her dirty dishes without pleading for money. If she wants to buy clothing for the children, she has to prepare her arguments in advance. Maybe she will get the money; maybe she won't.

This man's wife finally took a job as a secretary so that she would have sufficient money to run the household without having to beg for every penny. She recognized that as far as money is concerned, her husband lives in the past of his childhood where money was scarce and he was taught that poverty and starvation lurked just ahead. She can see that her husband is deeply hurt in the area of money and she has adjusted to it. She now doesn't have to react as though he were just arbitrarily mean and stingy, but she can genuinely sympathize with his "child of the past" who has been hurt.

In another case a man, who had known real poverty as a child, married a woman whose early life had been affluent. They had a son who took advantage of his indulgent mother. This man spent hours lecturing his son on the virtues of hard work and thriftiness. The boy, rebelling against his father and riding roughshod over his mother, was a careless spender who indulged himself in sweets, sodas and candy—and later on pinball machines, cars and beer. When confronted with his son's excesses, this man ached with the enormous hunger of his own childhood deprivations. He deeply resented his son's easy living. This resentment produced more lectures which the son continued to rebel against—in further excesses. This man had to learn that his son was not bad, and that his own deprived life kept a wall between him and the boy. This wall of resentment kept him from accepting the boy sufficiently so that reasonable limits from both parents could gradually be imposed.

Show of Affection

A woman, the child of a college professor and a woman writer, grew up in an intellectual home atmosphere where there was little show of affection. Her family was generous with material benefits, with unusual educational trips, but they could never show her that they loved her as much as she wanted them to do. She married a man whose mother and grandmother showered him with affection—so much that he became conditioned to feeling suffocated and encumbered by the attention of women. After a brief, intense honeymoon, he began to move away from his eager and demonstrative wife. A vicious cycle began. Her "child of the past" continually wanted more affection and attention while his "child of the past" felt continually hemmed in by her attention and concern for him.

A couple I know almost divorced because of their continual "arguments." Edna came from a home where everyone in the family grumbled and griped at all the others, constantly complaining of abuse and infringement of their rights. In fact, her family was a continual hubbub of petulant chatter. Her husband, on the other hand, came from a home where there were often intense arguments between his mother and father. As a child he always felt that his entire world was about to collapse when his mother and father started at one another.

Thus, she came to marriage feeling that arguing was a natural part of the home atmosphere. He came to the marriage with a feeling of anxiety and impending catastrophe if there was an argument. Edna felt that she had to let off steam over things that irritated her or that she would burst inside. He felt that *any* blowing off of steam was too much, because his "child of the past," after many early years of conditioning, still panicked at the sound of an irritated raised voice.

In another family quarrels may not have this effect. For instance, Cathy and Bert quarrel and fight—at least verbally—a great deal for people who have been married six years. If you pass by their home when a quarrel is on, you may think someone is about to be killed. Outbursts of profanity, epithets and furious accusations are exchanged. At least once a week there is such an explosion. Sometimes they occur more often. Both of them come from homes where violent verbal outbursts were common. Each remembers clearly furious, abusive quarrels between their respective parents.

Yet both Cathy and Bert are happier than their furious quarrels and arguments would seem to indicate. In these explosions of wrath they recreate the wrangling, quarreling, verbally abusive images of their parents—with which they feel quite at home. They themselves recognize their arguments to be a form of affection. They do not hold grudges. Their neighbors are astonished to hear them quarreling bitterly one minute and a short time later see them out in their yard laughing and walking arm in arm.

Recreation

Another area in which many couples find themselves in bitter conflict is recreation. What to do on leisure time and on vacations can become a disaster area when the "child of the past" asserts himself. Millions of wives are dragged protesting on hunting and fishing trips which they hate. Millions of husbands sulk at resorts and at the seashore because they came only to please their wives.

In addition, innumerable tennis matches, bowling and golf games are played each year which have nothing to do with recreation or family fun. They are simply competitive contests in which the more skillful spouse beats the daylights out of the other, who often has little interest in playing and is virtually forced to play in the name of "togetherness." Such games allow the "child of the past" to express resentment and to triumph over his partner in a way which, as an intelligent adult, he could not condone.

The "child of the past" is particularly likely to assert himself in the question of recreation because it is an area which in certain respects resembles the carefree days of childhood. For instance, Carl came from a family in which there was much partying, bridge-playing and trips which were planned for adults. He grew up wanting a quiet, stable home without the frantic running about that characterized his early home life.

His wife, Vera, grew up in a home very unlike his. Her home was under the domination of a matriarchal grandmother who ruled the others with a fierce determination—and kept the household in misery. Occasionally Vera's immediate family could slip away from the grandmother and have a little trip in glorious freedom from her domination. Otherwise they stayed home and could not even enjoy visits from their friends because the grandmother did not like them.

When Vera and Carl married, he wanted to stay home during summer vacations, claiming one can relax and get more rest at home than anywhere else. But Vera, responding to the needs of her "child of the past" just as Carl was responding to his, felt the old hemmed-in feeling which had made her life as a child so unhappy. This led to much discontent and quarreling, with Vera projecting visits and Carl finding reasons for scuttling them. Neither understood for many years the role their early home life was playing in this conflict.

Four in Bed

The marital bed often becomes overcrowded because there are four in bed—not two. Each of the four has a distinctive and individual feeling about being there. In this way the "inner child of the past" of both man and wife plays an important part in their sexual relationship. In most instances where there is embarrassment, shame, humiliation, resentment, guilt or sexual exploitation, there is a "child of the past" dominating the sexual scene.

There has been more written and said about sexual problems, satisfactions and maladjustments since publication of the Kinsey reports on human sexual behavior than in all the previous years of man's history. But most of this literature, even when it attempts to discuss the most intimate details of sexual behavior and the techniques of love-making, often just arouses more anxiety and fails to help the man or woman who is troubled by his sexual difficulties.

What is not usually understood is that each person takes into the sexual situation both his present adult self and the child he once was. Moreover, because close, intimate feelings of loving affection are involved, strong and deep feelings of the "child of the past" are likely to emerge in one or both of the partners—to sabotage their adult sexual satisfactions. For instance, if the prevailing atmosphere in your childhood home forced you to have anxious, guilty attitudes about your sexual feelings, you may have a guilty, anxious "child of the past" in bed with you and

58

your spouse. These childhood feelings and anxieties, emerging in either husband or wife, can make adult sexual functioning difficult—even impossible.

A man was attracted to an intelligent woman who seemed to need his loving protection. When they married, she wanted to be babied in the marital bed—cuddled, tenderly fondled and caressed, but not vigorously loved in a physical sense. Sexual love, she said, continuing her mother's attitude, was disgusting, animal, "like stupid beasts." Because her husband demanded it, she complied with his wishes for intercourse, but she made it plain that she did not enjoy it.

Her "inner child of the past" so dominated this aspect of her life that sexual intercourse was barely tolerable. Not until she learned to set limits on her "child of the past" did she begin to find that she actually had the capacity for adult sexual enjoyment. When this woman recognized that her feelings and attitudes were not hers, but were simply continuations of her mother's narrow and bitter views, she was able, with much work inside, to set limits on her "child of the past"—and begin to find sexual satisfaction and pleasure for her adult self.

In the same way the "child of the past" often impairs the ability of men to function adequately in a sexual sense. Not long ago an energetic, well-built young man told me, "My wife and I have been having trouble with our sex life. I am just not able to make love to her in that way. I get aroused by thoughts of other women when I am away from home. But I don't feel the same way about my wife when I'm home. My wife is attractive and affectionate. But something just happens to me. Except for this, we're happy together. I think she's disappointed in me.

"My folks were fine, churchgoing people. My dad was a quiet man. I didn't see much of him. My mother was very anxious for me to be a good boy. Everything was either 'good' or 'bad' around our house. Nobody ever mentioned sex—it was not part of our lives. I never heard either one of my parents say anything about it. Once when a cousin said something that was a little off-color, my mother frowned and took me out of the room. She was quite upset and said he was very bad—'a bad man' was the way she described him. When I got to be an adolescent, I kept my sex feelings a secret. I even tried to deny them to myself. When other boys told about their experiences, I felt they were very 'bad.' I knew my feelings would be disapproved and that I would be a disappointment to my parents if they knew I had them.

"And here I am married—and I feel that I'm a real disappointment to my wife, even though she doesn't say so. I feel I'm just not a man. My spirits get low when I think about this and then it's a strain to be with people —any people."

This man was stopped short of adult loving by a striving, too "good" "child of the past" who felt anxious, guilty and criticized when his own sexual feelings were aroused. These childhood feelings were so strong that they formed a barrier between him and his wife that he could not penetrate. Gradually he learned to recognize his "child of the past" and that his sexual feelings were not bad in a man, but natural. Gradually the interference of his "child of the past" in his sexual relations with his wife diminished. His wife patiently helped him by showing him that, unlike his mother, she did not consider sex "bad" but something she too wanted.

I wish to stress the consideration which each marriage partner must have not only for his or her own "child of the past," but also for the "child of the past" of the partner. In the intimacy of sex, profound respect must be shown all four in the marital relationship. A man has difficulty in loving his wife if his "child of the past" feels that women are humiliating, hurtful individuals. Nor can a husband be close to his wife if he does not temper his aggressive impulses and allay her childhood fears. For example, if a woman's childhood idea of men interprets them as powerful, rough, whiskery creatures who grab little girls out of the dark and hurt them, her husband must respect these fears and be more gentle. Lack of gentleness will reinforce her fearful feelings of the past.

Adults can, in general, easily adjust their glandular responses to one another. If the past conditioning of the partners is known, understood and respected as separate entities, the physiological side of sex will tend to function smoothly. No one of the four persons in a marriage should dominate the sexual relationship; each must receive respectful consideration.

This is, as my patients have often told me, easier said than done. For example, your opinion of yourself in a sexual situation is extremely important. It can mean the difference between pleasure and pain, between functioning and not functioning. If your "child of the past," continuing the general belittling attitude of your parents, belittles your sexual adequacy and attractiveness, your capacity for sexual pleasure will be limited in the same degree. Sexual intercourse will be something you bumble anxiously through. You particularly tend to bring to a sexual situation not only your own childhood desires and attitudes toward sex, but also your parents' reactions toward those feelings when you expressed them in your childhood. As children we naturally became interested in our bodies and those of others. Our parents, aware of these interests and experimentations, may have swiftly reacted with fear, worry, condemnation or disgust.

If our parents did not accept our childhood interest in sex, we tend to regard ourselves now as unacceptable in sexual situations. We may feel guilty, as though we are stealing pleasure. Obviously a satisfactory sex experience is difficult if you have to choose that time to scold yourself.

There are men who look upon the sexual act as a contest in which they have to "achieve" something. Their parents have stressed "performance," and at the same time given these men the lifelong feelings that their achievements never quite measure up. Such men have difficulties in marriage because they have adopted toward themselves the same parental attitude of failure-in-performance, even about sex. They are so driven that they cannot deeply enjoy sexual intercourse and they worry later about whether they couldn't have done better, achieved "more."

In the same way parental attitudes may continue to plague women. Even in this day of the bikini, there are women who feel embarrassed, shameless and immodest in the nude because their mothers hissed, "Never let a man see you naked." There are women who, like their male counterparts, are "achievers," who try so hard to achieve an orgasm that they cannot—and then they denounce themselves as "frigid." There are women so frightened of sex or pregnancy that, even though they are married, they try to ignore the whole thing. There are women who exploited their parents as children and who now use sex as a bargaining weapon to get their way with their husbands. This belittles the husband and is bound to be resented by him, but more than that it denies sexual pleasure to the woman. Her exploiting "child of the past" comes between her and her opportunity for loving interchange on the adult level.

Although the puritanical characteristics of our culture have lessened, many people have had the term "badness" pinned to their sexual feelings. The idea that only "bad" women enjoy sexual intercourse and that "good" women do not is a characteristic of many "children of the past." Many men are plagued with impotence with their "good" wives and feel that they cannot express their so-called "bad" impulses with them. Yet they often can express these impulses in daydreaming or with persons whom they do not respect, whom they consider "bad" or do not know. In this way the "child of the past" often contributes to the casual character of the sexual relations of many people.

Much of the interest in burlesque shows, "girlie" magazines and risqué literature comes primarily from our curious, peeking "child of the past." He is not interested in integrating his sexual feelings into a fully developed, personalized emotional relationship with another complex human being, which is the goal of the adult. If these impersonal fantasies of the "child of the past" preoccupy the mind, sexual relations with the marital partner may become more and more meaningless, if not disappointing, and one can find oneself quite alone in reality, even though preoccupied with a copious fantasy life.

One of the interesting aspects of the "child of the past" is that if his parents, for some reason, did not create strict, harsh prohibitions against sex, an adult can freely enjoy sexual activities—even though he is dominated by a belittled, humiliated "child of the past" in areas of living other than the sexual one. Parental attitudes often continue selectively in the adult as they were in childhood.

In general, however, the sexual relationship reflects the solid mutual respect—or lack of it—in other aspects of the marriage. If the four persons involved in the marriage are in conflict in the less intimate aspects of marriage, they tend to be in even more conflict when crowded closely together in bed.

Because sex involves such powerful and intimate feelings, any deviation from mutual respect in this intimacy is sharply outlined and accentuated. Any hurts are deeply felt because they contrast so sharply with the affection, trust and fulfillment expected and sought in the sexual experience.

It takes four to make a marriage. If you work toward understanding and respecting all four, you will lessen the differences and misunderstandings that wreck many marriages. This can help you find greater harmony within yourself and within your marriage.

CHAPTER 9

WHAT KIND OF A CHILD
WERE YOU?

Because your ability to "live" with an increasing inner harmony and enjoyment depends on respecting the feelings of your particular "inner child of the past," you must make an active search to discover what kind of a child you were. What were your prevailing moods as a child? Do you remember, for example, times when you demanded, when you whined and felt sorry for yourself, when you felt lonely, when and how you were punished, when you had a tantrum and how you set about getting the approval and praise of your parents? Were you happy? Do you recall times when you were raging—inwardly or outwardly? What do you remember about being afraid? Are you still afraid? Of what?

Your answers to such questions are important in helping you to recognize yourself as a child. However, they are secondary to your major problem—that of recalling what were the prevailing attitudes of your parents toward you. All of us can remember times when we were lonely, happy, angry or felt abused. But such memories may be confusing and lead you into blind alleys unless you realize the primary importance of your parents' attitudes toward you. These attitudes created your own basic attitude toward yourself—which is why they are important. The main purpose of this chapter is to provide some time-saving directions on what to look for—and how to do it. Using these guides, you need to recall, as specifically as you can, the emotional attitudes and feelings of your parents—about their ways of doing things, about specific activities and areas of life, such as work, play, cleanliness, sex, love, what they liked and disliked.

This takes hard, patient, repetitive work. You will not be able to remember immediately all of these things, all the twists and turns, the ins and outs of your parents' attitudes, the subtle shadings of feeling that made you know exactly what your parents wanted. What you need to find are those distinct attitudes which made you a member of a particular family—and a complete stranger in the home next door, where other attitudes prevailed.

Take Notes

Take a notebook and keep notes on what you recall. Try to set a regular time when you can relax and jot down whatever you remember about your parents' attitudes, likes and dislikes.

But do not expect these notes to do anything except clarify your own attitudes about yourself—and where you got them. These notes will not solve your problems. What will become gradually clear is that you grew up in a certain emotional atmosphere and were naturally shaped by it. Just as trees are shaped by the soil in which they grow, by the sun, the winds and the rain, so did the climate created by your parents' attitudes influence your emotional development and outlook.

Sometimes, in seeking to understand themselves, people wander aimlessly through memories. Some mainly dwell on painful memories, returning to them again and again, proving they were innocent and were wronged, suffering all over again. This sort of recollection, like woolgathering, is usually fruitless. When you know what you are looking for you can save yourself much time and make the effort genuinely rewarding.

In this search we are seeking the main trends of your parents' attitudes in their handling of everyday problems with you. Were they generally easygoing? Were they stern? Was one parent sterner than the other? About what? What made them annoyed with you? What made them laugh? What did they tell you about the way you looked? What did they warn you against? Were they always fussing about your health? Did your parents quarrel? What about? What was their attitude toward your brother or sister— and how did it differ from the way you were treated?

What you need to recall is the day-to-day flavor of your parents' attitudes and your reactions. What did you do to win their approval? What was their attitude if you did something well? How did they express disapproval? Of what did they disapprove? What children did they want you to play with—and why? What was your father's attitude toward you? How did it differ from your mother's? When did you first get any money to spend? When did you feel most dressed up? What was your mother's main worry? What was considered "bad"? What was considered fun? What did your mother and father tell you about their childhoods? Did you ever "play hooky"—and then what happened? Was your family religious? What was its attitude about sex? What were the forbidden things—things everyone knew should not be discussed? What was your parents' attitude about your growing up and marrying? About the attitude of children toward their parents? Do you remember defying them?

Such questions should provide you with a start toward recalling the parental atmosphere that dominated your early life. As a child you absorbed these moods, feelings and values automatically. They were almost literally a part of the air you breathed and the food you ate.

Pathogenic: Excessive: Troublemaking

Certain parental attitudes are the prime factors in creating emotional disturbance—first in the child, later in the adult. The following pathogenic or "troublemaking" parental attitudes, briefly defined, provide a quick checklist to help you discover which of them affected your "child of the past." In later chapters each of these parental attitudes will be discussed in detail. Your identification of the attitudes which were important in creating your "child of the past" can help you understand why certain aspects of living as an adult trouble you today—and help to free you from this enslavement to the past.

A word of caution may also be useful. The parental attitudes listed below are the common attitudes of parenthood. Their pathogenic or troublemaking quality comes from the excessive degree with which they were applied. When trouble has been caused by a particular parental attitude, it is because the attitude has been used excessively, or, to quote a former patient of mine, "overdone."

66

Can you find among these attitudes those which were important in your early home life and which contributed to the creation of your particular "inner child of the past"?

PERFECTIONISM: This is a common pathogenic attitude among "successful" people who strive endlessly and fruitlessly for still more "success," for perfection. Perfectionism is created in the child by the parent's withholding acceptance of the child until his behavior is more mature than he can comfortably achieve at the time. The child responds to this demanding attitude with a striving, over-serious preoccupation with physical, intellectual or social accomplishment and the persistent belittling of whatever he does accomplish. See page 75.

OVERCOERCION: The most common pathogenic parental attitude in America, this viewpoint is typically expressed by the parent who constantly directs, supervises, redirects the child with an endless stream of anxious reminders and directions. Because the child's need to initiate and pursue his own interests as part of his own development is ignored by this coerciveness, the child may learn to rely excessively on outside direction. Often, because he must assert his independence as an individual some way, he reacts to this constant coercion by dawdling, daydreaming, forgetting, procrastination and other forms of resistance. See page 91.

OVERSUBMISSION: Almost as common as the overly coercive parent, the overly submissive type capitulates to the child's immature whims and demands, ignoring and sacrificing his own needs and rights. Such a parental attitude makes the child the "boss," the parent a slave. The child responds to this parental attitude by demanding more, becoming impulsive, flying into temper outbursts if his demands are not met. He has difficulty in considering the rights of others. See page 113.

OVERINDULGENCE: A parent with this attitude constantly showers the child with presents, clothes, "treats" and services—often without the child's desiring them and without any consideration of the child's needs to develop his own ways of affecting his environment. While the overly submissive parent waits for the child's demand—

and obeys it—the overly indulgent parent showers gifts and presents without the child's asking. The child eventually responds to this inexhaustible cornucopia with bored, blasé behavior. Both as a child and later as an adult, he has difficulty in initiating any effort and has little persistence. See page 131.

HYPOCHONDRIASIS: This common and disabling parental attitude morbidly focuses attention on body functions or organs—even when they are healthy. Minor aches and pains are exaggerated. The child, growing up in this atmosphere of anxiety about health, absorbs his parents' excessive concern, discovering that this may gain sympathy and provide a reason for inactivity and nonparticipation. See page 156.

PUNITIVENESS: A common parental attitude, often combined with perfectionism and overcoercion, punitiveness is widely accepted in our culture as something necessary for the "disciplining" and "training" of children. Actually, the punitive parent vents his personal hostility and aggressions on the child, his subjective feelings—not the child's error—determining the punishment. Usually the parent has been similarly treated in his own childhood and often believes sincerely that this is only "discipline." Actually, punitiveness creates a need for punishment— virtually a reliance on it in some persons—and a fierce desire for revenge which may dominate adult life. See page 178.

NEGLECT: Hard to define because it often results from the absence or busy preoccupation of the parent, neglect is widespread, often afflicting children of prominent and economically successful people; it also frequently afflicts the children of mothers overwhelmed with overwork, alcoholism, poverty and other problems. Such a parent has little time for the child—regardless of the cause of this situation. Death and divorce may be factors. The neglected child often lacks capacity to form close, meaningful relationships. See page 214.

REJECTION: This parental attitude grants the child no niche of acceptance in the family group. The child responds with bitter, anxious feelings about his isolation and helplessness and with severe self-devaluation. However, popularization of the concept of the "rejected" child has caused much confusion. The realistic need to set limits on unacceptable behavior is not rejection. True rejection is relatively rare. See page 247.

SEXUAL STIMULATION: A pathogenic parental attitude which causes the parent, either with or without awareness of what he is doing, to stimulate the child's sexual feelings excessively. This causes the child to be prematurely preoccupied with sex, creating guilt and hostility. However, not all or even most adult sexual problems result from this; sexual activities often serve as an outlet for many other pathogenic attitudes, such as perfectionism and punitiveness. The prudish "hush-hush" atmosphere of a generation ago created many sexual problems, including the current mass sex stimulation via advertising and other mass media. As a people, we treat our sexual feelings with disrespect. See page 260.

Are Your Parents to Blame?

Young children see their parents as all-powerful, almost godlike beings whose approval they need. As they grow older and begin to assume more responsibility for themselves, this godlike stature of the parent diminishes. In time father and mother are gradually recognized as ordinary human beings, with all the needs, difficulties, weaknesses and quirks of other human beings. Accepting the human frailties and qualities of your parent is an indication of maturity. With rare exceptions and often despite severe limitations, most of them have done "the best they could."

However, on becoming aware of how the old pathogenic parental attitudes of their childhoods have limited their capacities as adults, people sometimes feel resentful and angry toward their parents. Initially this is a normal, healthy and human reaction in some respects, especially if it is recognized that you no longer have to treat yourself with these old hurtful attitudes.

But some people continue to keep their resentment boiling day after day. They make their parents into a kind of scapegoat to be blamed for every dissatisfaction in their adult lives. And, indeed, these parental attitudes do explain why life has often been so unrewarding and why, for example, an attractive and gifted person punishes himself with self-devaluation.

Are parents to blame?

When you first look at it, this might seem to be an open-and-shut case. Did not the parents create the emotional atmosphere of one's childhood? Did they not hold the hurtful parental attitudes in which you grew up? Thus, a certain kind of logic holds that they are indeed responsible.

But logic cannot be applied to human life in this fashion—and even this kind of logic requires recognition that some of your positive and useful attitudes came from your parents even if other attitudes were hurtful.

The real difficulty with this kind of thinking is that it avoids the question of whether something can be done about the root of your present difficulties—your continuation of old parental attitudes which hurt you. Blaming your parents is often simply a way of continuing feelings of hostility and aggression which were too dangerous to express in childhood. And you can, in this fashion, continue your childhood, still looking upon your parents as godlike, all-powerful beings who should prevent our wounds instead of hurting us.

Sometimes people are frightened by *any* question about their parents' attitudes, the way they lived, their attitudes and their own experience with their parents. They are particularly frightened by questions on what effect this has had on their lives. It sometimes seems disloyal and disturbing because in many cases their resentment over hurts had to be concealed in childhood and has never been recognized and expressed. Such persons are often still frightened by the violence of resentments pent up since childhood. They can only gradually recognize and express these hurt feelings.

Others are frightened because the overemphasis of sex in popularizations of early psychiatric theory always left the implication that incest marked every family. Today it is obvious that psychiatry is concerned with all aspects of human life, not just sex. Yet this idea continues to frighten people who loved their parents.

Because of all these factors, it is important to be clear as to why we are identifying and examining past parental attitudes. Our purpose is not to create a case against our parents. Our purpose is to free ourselves from whatever damaging effects such attitudes may have had.

Parents Are Human Beings

In my own experience with thousands of parents, ranging from the domineering to the absent and alcoholic, I have rarely found a parent who was not concerned about his children, who did not love them and attempt to provide for them to the best of his ability. What often prevented this was the parent's own "inner child of the past," who had in many cases achieved a complete mastery of the adult. In these instances one could see how a troublemaking attitude had been passed from the grandparent to the parent, who was in turn passing it to the child—overcoercion, for example. This becomes a difficult pattern to change because it is reinforced by our cultural background. Within a family such an attitude may be considered the "right way" to deal with a child. Yet, what often impressed me was the fact that a mother or a father who had suffered from this pathogenic attitude and who was now inflicting it on his child recognized that there was something wrong with it and had come to the clinic for help. "I'm hitting her and yelling at her the same way my mother did," a mother told me recently of how she handled her daughter.

As you become a considerate parent to your own specific "child of the past," accepting these feelings from childhood and establishing new parental attitudes and values, you will begin to be able to see your parents as human beings. You will see how they had to struggle with their own "child of the past" without ever being aware of what the problem was. You will see more clearly that often excessive parental attitudes, such as punitiveness ("spare the rod, spoil the child"), are deeply rooted in our cultural heritage. Our parents are often merely the carriers of these attitudes from one generation to the next. You will see that if your father was a demanding, perfectionistic person, he learned this in his own childhood. You will find that if your mother was oversubmissive, she developed this characteristic in her childhood home. You may also recognize how undue anxiety about health and the exaggeration of minor aches and pains is also transmitted from generation to generation. You will see, in your parents' choices of recreation, in their weaknesses, in their quarrels and in their ambitions and whatever they

71

considered "nice," something of the individual "inner child of the past" within each of them.

How each of the various excessive parental attitudes can be identified, how it operates and what its effects are on both the child and the adult he becomes will be described in the next chapters. For the sake of clarity we must describe each attitude in a "pure" form which does not exist in life. Perfectionism, for example, rarely occurs by itself; usually it is reinforced with overcoercion and punitiveness, perhaps compensated for with overindulgence. However, descriptions of these mixtures would not clarify their characteristic distinctions at this time. Once the excessive character and mechanisms of these attitudes are understood, their mixtures and common combinations can be readily recognized as they exist in life.

PART II

Excessive Parental Attitudes—
How They May Be
Influencing You Today

CHAPTER 10

PERFECTIONISM—
If you must strive to "do better"

YOUR INDEX OF SUSPICION: *The adult who suffers from the results of perfectionism in his childhood is apt to be intelligent, well educated and economically better off than most people. Belittling his own accomplishments, he drives himself with ever stiffer demands to "do better." If these words describe you, you should carefully consider the possibility that your difficulties arise from an "inner child of the past" who strives to gain parental acceptance—which was withheld in the past, because of the ever present parental pressures to "do better."*

Recognizing Your Perfectionism

If you are perfectionistic, you probably already know it. You demand perfection of yourself, perhaps of others too, and exert arduous efforts to achieve it. You must have things "just perfect"—everything in its place, the right color with the right color, the window blinds adjusted at the "perfect angle," the silver on the table perfectly positioned, the perfect word at the perfect place and time, arriving and departing on time and the punctilious observance of manners and polite forms. If you are a perfectionist, you pursue your work methodically, systematically and strenuously, with meticulous attention to detail, often to the point of exhaustion. Often far more effort is expended in accomplishing tasks than is warranted; and far exceeding what the average person would do is frequently a source of pride to the perfectionist. Yet these strenuous efforts and often genuine accomplishments bring him no lasting satisfaction. He is miserable in spite of his success and must strive to do "still better," underrating whatever he has accomplished.

The perfectionistic housewife who wears herself out in an exhaustive daily routine of housecleaning even when she recognizes it to be unnecessary is a common example of this type of striving. Such persons cannot accept any irregularities—or even the thought of them—in anything which they consider to be theirs, whether it is a child's behavior, a speck of dust, or their work. Often such persons learn of their superhuman efforts to achieve perfection through the amused teasing or annoyance of friends when they complain their efforts were not good enough.

"Be human, relax!" friends tell them. However, this is just what the perfectionistic person cannot do. He must strive and strive and strive—and still will gain no satisfaction.

Often perfectionistic people, who are generally very intelligent, realize they are pushing themselves far beyond what is necessary—or human. As an explanation to themselves, they say that they feel ordinary standards do not apply to them.

The perfectionistic individual may feel superior to others and look down on less-driven people as his inferiors. Yet he yearns for the human satisfaction which he sees ordinary people enjoying, their genuine pleasure in life and the enhancement of their self-esteem through their accomplishments.

The Successful Failure

Objectively, the relentless driving to achieve which the perfectionist subjects himself to generally results, by most social and material standards, in his being considered very "successful." But his striving, while it has brought him status, leaves him feeling empty and dissatisfied. He may call himself a "successful failure."

Sometimes the perfectionistic person tries to explain— to himself, perhaps to others—that only by such strenuous and relentless striving are great things accomplished. Citing the efforts of artists and scientists, he may thus convince himself his striving is necessary.

However, not all striving for excellence is perfectionistic in a psychologically troublemaking sense. Any field of endeavor, whether it is music, science, art, plumbing, cooking or shoe repairing, has its masters. Their mastery was attained through patient, diligent, persistent work and the excellence of their product is useful and beneficial to others, which is often not true of the perfectionistic person's striving. Indeed, perfectionistic striving may be detrimental to sound family relationships, as witness the mate who drives his spouse to help meet his perfectionistic demands.

One of the most important distinctions between the efforts of the true masters of their craft and those of the perfectionistic person is that the striving of the first group brings them solid satisfaction. They are happy with the results. Their efforts enhance their self-esteem. They rejoice in their mastery. This is not true of the perfectionistic person. His striving is accompanied by the corrosive feeling that "I am not good enough. I must do better." This robs him of the satisfaction which his superior performance should bring.

Areas of Perfectionism

Many people do not realize how much their perfectionism troubles them because it is limited to certain areas or activities. Such persons are generally able to enjoy and take satisfaction in other areas of life. But in specific areas they are perfectionistic, eternally dissatisfied with themselves even though their achievements surpass others and their shortcomings are not noticed by others.

As George, one such person, put it recently: "Ordinarily I get along fine. If I make an error in grammar or English when I'm speaking to someone, if I use the wrong word, I am ready to die. I can't stand it. I turn red as a beet, my heart pounds, I get so flustered and mad at myself that I can't sleep. I wonder how I, of all people, could have made such a boner. Later I realize nobody cared, but I still can't stand it. I expect more of myself in that respect than other people do. My mother taught English and she drilled me constantly in perfect speech and grammar. The way I see it, there is no reason why I shouldn't use perfect English. God knows, I know the stuff. It's been drilled into me since I could talk. When I make an error, especially if I'm talking to a stranger, I feel I've made a hopeless, irremediable error because first impressions are everything. Consequently I am especially afraid of making an error. Therefore, I train myself, prepare myself for such a meeting if I have the chance. The result is that I generally make a good impression and whatever I say comes out perfectly.

"In fact, because of this, my boss, who often speaks poor and even ungrammatical English, sometimes takes me along to an important client to help sell a contract. I just can't sleep the night before and sometimes, if I know the people we are going to be meeting are really well educated, I am hardly able to talk when we get there. Everything I might say—and it is important in selling and negotiation to be able to talk freely—becomes dangerous. I just dry up. I have to go over everything two or three times in my mind to make sure I'm going to say it in perfect English, and that's aside from the appropriateness of the thought content of what I am saying. It's a terrible strain.

"Sometimes I have made errors. Once I grew so flustered I just barely stammered out the rest of the sentence. But neither my boss nor the other people noticed anything until I started to stammer. They thought something had stuck in my throat. We got the contract anyhow, but I couldn't sleep for nights afterward."

This is the kind of "area perfectionism" that afflicts nearly all of us to some extent. In this case George recognizes the perfectionism which he demands of himself in English grammar but he does not also realize the "perfectionism" which he also demands of himself on "first meeting." His requirements far exceed those of his employer, who feels his own poor English to be a handicap even though he has been quite successful. These self-imposed demands, increasingly severe—and bound to become more severe in time—not only cause anxious striving but actually may cause his occasional lapses from perfect grammar and syntax.

Such "areas" are those in which the child you once were had to meet the perfectionistic demands of your parents. For example, some parents stressed perfectionism in cleanliness, developing elaborate scrubbing rituals; others stressed perfection in scholastic standing, social grace, table manners. Still others, not at all concerned about these activities or about dress, may have been perfectionistic about athletic skills and demanded Big League performance from Little Leaguers.

Work is one general area where perfectionism often operates in a flagrant fashion. The perfectionistic person drives himself and those about him. He is exhausted by his efforts. He pays meticulous attention to every minute detail. His accomplishments, even when substantial, do not let him feel satisfied with himself—and he must always turn to still greater efforts to find relief from his own self-belittlement.

In some respects the perfectionistically driven person may seem to be a great competitor. Yet actually his strenuous striving is only a measure of his own self-belittlement rather than any desire to accomplish things for their own sake. He has little interest in competition itself because he is forever driven to outdo himself in an attempt to gain his own reluctant approval. Because his striving demands tend to alienate others, many perfectionist persons tend to move into intellectual or creative fields where the individual works alone, rather than in a group or team. Thus, he creates a situation in which he truly competes with himself, drives himself and is constantly dissatisfied, and in this fashion conceals even from himself his excessive demands on himself.

Perfectionism in Marriage and Sex

The perfectionistic person generally has his greatest difficulties in his intimate contacts with others. His polished manners carry him through business or social relationships in a fashion that is quite attractive to others. If love and affection could be casual, the perfectionist would sail through them. But the close, intimate and affectionate acceptance on which human love is based makes this difficult—and unhappiness often results.

Because the perfectionist is forever striving to achieve, ordinary social intercourse, the amiable enjoyment of companionship, the human need for closeness, the free-flowing interchange of feelings are difficult for him to respond to. These relationships are based on acceptance of one's self and others. But his constant self-belittling corrodes this base.

Because he did not get full acceptance in his childhood, the perfectionist seeks areas in which his performance is measurable, such as work, athletic contests and social status. He continues the striving which was his "at home" feeling in the past, pursuing the will-o'-the-wisp promise of eventual full acceptance. He tends to view life as participation in a race and to feel the intimate and mutual interchange of a close relationship binding and distracting, something which keeps him from running at full speed. The loving acceptance of his wife or sweetheart is, he feels, nothing compared to what he will have if he succeeds in winning the race—"does better." Any "stopping" of his striving in order to enjoy companionship or affection makes him fearful that he will lose the race.

The prize he seeks is his childhood one—the promise of full acceptance held out by his parents. This past goal blocks his ability to feel comfortable in enjoying human interchange and his self-belittlement forbids any cessation of his striving. He fears the time and energy spent in companionship will cost him the race and its main prize —the promise of full acceptance.

Life with a perfectionistic person puts a heavy burden on the partner, who must also strive to meet his unattainable demands. Much of what most people find satisfying, pleasurable, comfortable—and comforting—is likely to appear to the perfectionist as a blank waste of time, baffling to the point of being hard to understand because he can see and feel nothing achieved.

The perfectionist often carries his striving to achieve into his sexual activity. Unable to find satisfaction in ordinary social intimacy, driven by his continual self-devaluation and fear of failure, he tries to make performance, rather than human feeling, the important aspect of sexual relations. Inevitably it becomes performance without any satisfying emotional content and loving interchange—and the perfectionist, forever dissatisfied and blaming himself, seeks a still better performance.

Thus any lack of sexual potency, in such a man, is a severe blow; if the woman does not respond "perfectly," he counts it as his failure. He strives to do better. Similarly the woman perfectionist seeks performance, to achieve, and any failure results in self-devaluation. The result is anxiety and depressed feelings of worthlessness. And so great is the fear of failure that often sexual activity is curtailed.

All of this makes for a severe problem in marriage. In the first place, the perfectionist person has great trouble

80

in finding an acceptable marriage partner, for he wants a "perfect" mate, not a human one. Thus he tends to reject potential mates, often until he has delayed marriage for years. He has difficulty forming a relationship that would be close enough to lead to marriage. Some such persons give up the attempt to form close human ties and devote themselves to work, not realizing that it lies within their power to alter their attitude toward themselves. This is the situation of some of our successful bachelors and striving career girls.

The perfectionistic person often looks upon marriage as another achievement. Once married, he does not know how to enjoy it. He generally continues his old perfectionistic attitudes, demanding perfect order. He becomes anxious if the house is not in order at all times, with eggs done to a split-second three minutes, toast to a certain shade of tan, shirts starched a certain way, and perfect children from his perfect wife. His anxiety leads him to demand these things because anything less than what he considers "perfect" arouses his childhood patterns of self-belittlement. Many a husband silently accepts his perfectionistic wife's demands that he not wear shoes in the living room because she fears marks on her perfect rugs, endures her corrections of his speech, and indeed never feels comfortable himself.

The Case of Willard and Kay

But most of all the "perfect" bride or "perfect" groom is hard to live with if you like warmth and closeness. For example, Willard is a personally attractive and brilliant young chemist, but he and his wife may yet separate because of his perfectionism. His research in polyester molecules has already won him a place of distinction. Along with his intelligence and willingness to work hard he is friendly and courteous to those about him. But at home his wife, Kay, cannot get close to him.

On coming from his lab, Willard buries himself after dinner in his scientific journals and advance planning for new experiments. He is distantly polite but obviously annoyed if Kay tries to talk to him, his facial expression saying, "Can't you see I'm busy?" while verbally he says, "Yes, dear?"

Feeling pushed out and as though she is not really very

important to him, Kay often becomes irritated. At first she was just hurt. Then she tried, by punning about "polyester" being the same as another woman, to cajole him into conversation and doing things with her. Initially this amused him somewhat, but her continued need for attention, her natural expectation of his participation in "plain living" as she called it, and her increasing tone of bitterness gradually drove him further into his work. He thinks she is very unreasonable not to applaud his hard, constant work. "After all, I'm doing it for you, for us if you will," he said rather primly once when Kay was demanding that he stop his night work.

Willard's father was a successful businessman whose interests required him to be away from home considerably. And when he was talking or "thinking about business" at home, he was not to be disturbed. Willard's mother was a busy writer of local history and chairman of many projects for the betterment of the community. As a young boy, Willard fitted into this achievement-studded family only by striving at school. In this way he got some acceptance and recognition from his preoccupied parents. He led his class academically and was president of his class. He even excelled in athletics, although physically he was not a "born athlete." All the members of his family were so busy with their individual projects by the time he was a high school senior that they had very little time for any family interchange that was not tied into someone's accomplishment of something.

In adult life Willard continued the same accomplishment-driven attitudes he had known all his life. It was literally the only kind of life he knew how to lead with other people. But it left out his wife, whose own "inner child of the past" had strong needs to form close, somewhat time-consuming family attachments which were enriched with trivial, warm chitchat. These were the characteristics of her childhood background—and for a long time she could not understand Willard's preoccupation. But even after she understood it, she resented it. Eventually Willard had to recognize that the excessive striving that had always seemed necessary wasn't really a good idea—if he wanted to stay married.

What Drives the Perfectionistic Person

Impressed by the perfectionist's need to achieve, some psychiatric theories attribute his relentless striving to an effort to win mastery over his environment and to feel superior to others. In this view the perfectionist, completely identifying himself with his standards, looks upon his prosperity and general success as being a reward for being a good person. He sees his success as proof of his virtue. Only if misfortune or failure occurs, according to one psychiatric theorist, does he realize his human fallibility, and "self-effacing trends and undiluted self-hate, kept in check successfully hitherto, then may come to the fore."

While this describes some secondary characteristics of perfectionism, such as the confusing of striving with virtue, which does happen, it fails to emphasize sufficiently that the so-called standards are excessive. More important, it does not recognize that the perfectionist constantly feels that he has not succeeded—despite his obvious success. The perfectionist must go on striving to escape his own awful feeling that he "could have done better."

Our clinical work with children clearly indicates that this continual self-belittlement—rather than a desire to master the environment—is the real driving force behind the perfectionist's unending efforts. Self-effacement and self-hate do not rise to the fore only when misfortune or failure occur, but are constantly destroying self-satisfaction. While actual failure or misfortune may precipitate a severe emotional crisis because these are the opposite of accomplishment, it is the continual self-belittlement and downgrading that drive the perfectionist day in and day out to "do better." As long as the pressure of self-belittlement is being generated, the perfectionistic person cannot find satisfaction in his efforts.

Origins of Perfectionism

The perfectionistic person continues the downgrading-striving cycle which the child he once was *had* to accept from his parents as the way of life. Perfectionism was created in the child by persistent parental demand, expressed in terms of what was expected from the child. His behavior and development had to be more advanced and more mature than the child could comfortably achieve at the moment.

Children need—and seek—the affectionate acceptance of themselves through their efforts to please their parents. However, perfectionistic parents tend to withhold acceptance of the child until he is striving at an upper level of performance. Even when the child does accomplish something, which may be anything from moving his bowels to using correct manners and making good grades, the parent subtly defers full approval and acceptance and urges the child to "do better." In this fashion whatever the child has achieved is belittled. What the child gets is the promise of eventual acceptance if only he will "do better." If the parent gave the child full acceptance and approval, the child would feel satisfied with himself and more confident about his abilities. But the perfectionistic parent keeps the child straining on tiptoe, anxious about himself and his abilities. One of the striking things about the perfectionist is that, despite all he has accomplished, he has little or no confidence whatever in himself.

This results from the fact that as consequence of the partial withholding of parental acceptance and subtle demands for more effort, the child learns to belittle his own effort. He comes to believe that no matter how hard he strives, he will not succeed fully. He comes to believe that he has not done enough to merit full approval because he did not try hard enough. His only guiding authority—and his most important source of acceptance—is his parent. Thus, there is in fact no way for him to know anything different. Striving and self-belittlement become his way of feeling "at home." And never having known full satisfaction with himself as a child, he cannot give full approval to his efforts as an adult. As a parent to himself, he belittles his achievements and insists he do "still better."

The Subtlety of Parental Disapproval

The perfectionistic demands of some parents may at times be reinforced with overcoercion and even punitiveness. Others use a subtle, vague expectancy of peak performance and a sweet expression of sad disappointment in actual performance, with an implicit promise of eventual full approval pending better effort. In doing this the parental smile turns into a sad face, a frown, a sigh of disappointment or exasperation, a gentle suggestion for more effort, more care, more attention, more thoughtfulness, more consideration and so on.

This disapproval—and the promise of eventual acceptance—keeps the child striving relentlessly, dissatisfied and doubting himself and his abilities.

The subtlety of these belittling expressions, their constant application, their accumulating pressure and hinted promise of eventual full approval create a difficult background pattern for the adult suffering from perfectionism to recognize immediately. Such a person may turn to a search for the cause of his misery after some incident in which he felt he "fell short," or upon recognition of his difficulties in establishing a close relationship.

It is sometimes difficult to recognize your own self-belittlement. Your treatment at the hands of your parents may have seemed "perfect"; you may find no seriously traumatic incidents in your childhood which would explain either why you must drive yourself or why you are so unhappy. Individual incidents of parental disapproval always seem too mild and trivial in retrospect to constitute the basic problem.

Yet only when he recognizes the subtlety and daily repetition of these belittling parental expressions, and the fact that they often extended into every aspect of living from study to play, can the perfectionistic adult begin to understand how he acquired his basic dissatisfaction with himself. If you have continued to apply these same belittling expressions to whatever you do, you are undermining yourself.

The Case of Leslie

The generally outstanding success of the perfectionist obscures the inner devastation of continuous self-belittlement. This is what lies behind the pathetically empty lives of many otherwise successful people. It accounts for many suicides that may seem to be complete enigmas. Dr. Leo Kanner,* the "dean" of American child psychiatry, has

* Leo Kanner, *Feelings and Their Medical Significance*, Vol. I, No. 4, March, 1959.

reported the case of Leslie, a highly intelligent and attractive daughter of an economically well-to-do family. This young girl attempted suicide. Although her parents constantly assured her that her happiness was uppermost in their minds, Leslie could find no satisfaction in living because, under belittling pressures, she felt that she had not "measured up."

Why did this happen? Leslie's mother was always flawlessly attired, polished in her manners, intelligent and poised. "Had you been a guest in her home, you would have gone away with the feeling that no child could have asked for a better environment," says Dr. Kanner. Yet Leslie, in spite of scholastic brilliance and beauty, had virtually no confidence in herself. She was convinced she had let her mother down, saying, "If I were a mother and had a daughter like me, I'd be horrified." Unable to accept herself, she wished only "that my mother wouldn't have to worry about me."

In raising her, Leslie's parents had left nothing to chance, for they hoped and expected to raise a perfect child. She was not born until their housing and income were more than adequate. When Leslie was born, her mother was determined, as a good and dutiful mother, to see to it that Leslie was a perfect baby. She set up rigid rules and regulations for herself and Leslie. All routines, such as bathing and feeding, were meticulous and on schedule. Bowel training was begun when she was only three months old.

As the child grew older, much attention was given every aspect of her life: diction, posture, cleanliness, demeanor, obedience, choice of playmates, studies—and her reading, television programs, school homework and social manners. Her dress, physical status and appearance were sources of endless concern.

Her mother, says Dr. Kanner, "never spanked or scolded. She expressed her disapproval ever so subtly: 'You are getting a bit fat, honey. Don't you think we might go to the doctor and have him prescribe a diet for you?' Or: 'Your friend Dorothy is a nice girl all right, but did you notice how sloppy she is and the bad grammar she uses? How about inviting Alice, sweetheart? She comes of such a fine family.' Or: 'Of course, dear, I want you to select your own clothes. But don't you think that the dress you put on is just a bit too loud for this occasion? Be a good girl and change into the blue one.'"

Although Leslie tried hard to win her mother's full approval she could not always achieve 100s in her grades, she could not hold her weight on the line set forth on the "ideal weight chart" for her age, she guiltily liked Dorothy better than Alice. Leslie felt her own taste in color and clothes was horrible because her mother, who had once dabbled in art, implied it was not really very good.

"The child, endeavoring to please, set up the highest imaginable standards for herself and was full of guilt and contrition when she found that she could not live up to them. She herself became a perfectionist, forever displeased with her inability to excel in everything," says Dr. Kanner. The subtlety of this kind of disapproval is difficult to recognize and deal with, Dr. Kanner points out in summing up, saying, "You can resent beatings and harsh censure but you are hopelessly disarmed and crushed by the 'sweetness-and-sunshine' kind of disapproval." In Leslie's case she was eventually driven by her own self-belittlement to believe, in a desperate moment, that she preferred death. But learning that she did not have to continue her parents' attitudes and that she could really take satisfaction in what she accomplished altered this perspective for her.

The Transmission of Perfectionism

Perfectionism is often transmitted from generation to generation. It literally "runs in families." The perfectionistic parent is also entrapped in his own belittling-striving cycle—and so was his parent. Even though the modern perfectionistic parent may recognize the mistakes of her own parents' perfectionism, it remains difficult for such a parent to accept her own efforts and her children if they are less than perfect. If she tries to depart from the old perfectionistic standards, anxiety rising from self-belittlement hampers the effort to establish more realistic and human standards.

Not long ago a trim, pert woman, who seemed both efficient and forceful in the very way in which she stepped into my office, told me: "I want to feel less dissatisfied with my life and myself. Before I married I worked for several years as a dietitian. I have a master's degree in home economics and most of the work completed for my doctor's degree. After I married, I had two girls, one right after the other. I try to live up to the standards of house-keeping and child-rearing that I have learned at the university—but I can't meet them and I feel very guilty. What's the good of learning superior standards if you can't live up to them? My oldest is now five. She is so demanding, and I'm always wondering if I'm doing the right thing in the way I handle her.

"What really upsets me is my girls' untidiness. It really irritates me to see them dirty. That's not the way my little girls should look, I say to myself, and I start cleaning them up. I can't stand to see them in soiled clothing. Yet I feel guilty because I'm always fussing at them. Do this, do that. I know that's not right. I'm sure I'm not being as good a mother to my children as I should be."

When I asked her about her own upbringing, she said, "My mother expected us to live up to high standards—and I've certainly tried to achieve nothing but the best. That's one reason why I've continued my education. My father was a professor, and I was always told I was on display as a professor's child. My father was especially concerned about my grades, and my mother about how I looked and how I behaved. I pushed hard and my grades always were good. When I fuss at my little girls about being dirty, I frown and scowl like my mother did. I know from my own reading that this is wrong. I hated all this trying to be better and do better when I was a child, all the reminders I got from my parents. You've got to allow kids to get dirty once in a while. If I read that in a book, I nod and say, 'Of course.' But now when I see my kids in dirty dresses, I can't rest until they are clean, just as my mother did."

This woman, despite her education, simply continued the attitudes of her parents, used them on herself and is now using them on her children. This is why she has continued to seek academic honors, such as her doctor's degree. Although she has no intention of pursuing an academic career, she is still "a professor's child." And even though she now realizes that her parents were wrong in pushing her to meet their excessive standards, she clings to such standards. Yet in time she may curb the self-belittlement creating her perfectionism—and eventually relax and ease her striving.

Cultural Factors Supporting Perfectionism

One of the subtly confusing aspects of perfectionism is that it seems desirable. We are a nation of doers, accomplishers, strivers, achievers. Thus, our general cultural heritage tends to reinforce the perfectionist's excessive striving. Indeed, everyone seems to approve of the striver's striving, which sets up a façade of achievement that makes its inner emptiness and misery hard to recognize.

Other cultural factors are also involved. For example, the self-belittling aspects of perfectionism are reinforced by our educational system of grading children's efforts, urging them to "do better," and by some church teaching, urging them to "be better." Both tend to support the perfectionistic parent—and his "child of the past."

While a child can win some approval and recognition from his teachers for his accomplishments in schoolwork, this is not true for some church teaching, which holds up as a goal the kind of perfection that can only be achieved by a saint—not a human being. However, this renews and supports the parental demands for perfect behavior, even perfect thoughts and feelings. More important, it contributes significantly to feelings that you are not good enough, that you must feel guilty for seeking any pleasure, and that this self-contempt can only be eased by "doing better." The feeling that God is disappointed in you is a heavy, lonely reinforcement of your self-belittlement. Yet no church expects its human members to become saints.

In considering your own perfectionistic efforts, you should be able to make an accurate estimate of what role these cultural factors have played in supporting parental perfectionism.

What Can You Do About Your Perfectionistic "Inner Child of the Past"?

1. You can identify his belittling and striving phases in your life and keep making the effort to reduce unnecessary striving.

2. You can resolve to treat yourself *in your own way,* by

your own standards, rather than continue your parents' attitude of partial acceptance of yourself.

3. You must tackle and wrestle with your self-belittling in all its forms, even though this requires giving up feeling "at home" and enduring some anxiety until your new attitude toward yourself is established. By reducing your self-belittlement, you will not need to strive so much for an unattainable "perfection." How to help yourself make this effort will be described in Part III, "Changing Yourself and Your Life."

CHAPTER 11

OVERCOERCION—
If you can't stop procrastinating

YOUR INDEX OF SUSPICION: *If you "can't get started," find yourself making extensive daily lists of things you "should" do—and then seem unable to get around to doing them—feel too exhausted to do even things you like to do and end up daydreaming about them, you should consider the possibility that your "inner child of the past" is continuing the pattern with which he reacted to the coercive directions of your parents. Overcoercion is the most common pathogenic parental attitude in our culture.*

Recognizing Overcoercion in Your Past

You can be almost certain that you suffered from some overcoercion as a child because we live in an overly coercive culture.

The parent who is overly coercive constantly directs and redirects the child's activities in an anxious, nagging and pushing way, leaving little or no opportunity for the child to initiate and pursue his own interests and activities. Fortunately, while overcoercion is the most common pathogenic attitude among American parents—as might be expected in a nation of active strivers and doers—it does not create as severely incapacitating personality problems as some other pathogenic attitudes. It is the cause of much unnecessary unhappiness, anxiety, marital and sexual conflict, self-defeat and the inability to achieve a fulfillment of one's potential.

THE PRIMARY SIGNS: If your primary complaint is a combination of chronic fatigue and an inability to achieve your day-to-day goals; if you waste time in daydreaming, and there are no objective reasons why you cannot accomplish your aims, then you are probably suffering from this past pattern of overcoercion. This persisting inability to accomplish what you have set out to do often results in anxiety and feelings of worthlessness. To offset these feelings, you may then, with increasing snarling and barking at yourself, set down an even larger list of "things to be done tomorrow"—and again you are unable to get anything done. You become bogged down and shunted into doing other things—which take you away from your goals. As this inability to act continues, the list of "things to be done tomorrow" grows bigger and longer, becoming completely unrealistic—a list of things which cannot be accomplished tomorrow.

As this kind of slow, daydreaming paralysis continues, you may blame others for your difficulties. Or you may develop a whole series of explanations to yourself and others as to why "it was simply impossible to get anything done."

PEOPLE WHO ARE HARD HIT: People whose work—and through it their self-esteem—depends primarily on their own inner organization are particularly vulnerable to the demands of an overly coerced "child of the past." Among these are salesmen, housewives, composers, executives, scientists, businessmen, ministers, artists and writers. It is critically important for such people to be able to initiate and carry through their self-imposed tasks. Yet often this is the very thing they seem unable to do. They "can't get started," are paralyzed by what at first seems to be indecisiveness and then by what seems to be laziness and self-indulgence. They wish someone would take command of them, tell them what to do at each step, drive them—and ultimately this is what they do to themselves. But this last phase is seldom reached until the pressures on them to produce have reached a maximum, threatening level—and their time to produce has been reduced to a minimum. Thus, instead of being able to do an outstanding or even satisfactory piece of work, they barely manage to get along. The person who is caught in the pattern of overcoercion suffers miserably from his snarling, self-belittling and threatening coercion. He seldom achieves what he has aimed for and falls far short of his potential.

THE PAST HOME ATMOSPHERE: Major clues to the reactions of your "inner child of the past" always lie in your recollections of your childhood home atmosphere. Few of us escaped the influence of parental overcoercion. Indeed, most of us grew up in households in which there was a steady stream of directions, new directions, revised directions, commands and reminders, all delivered in anxious, irritated or threatening tones:

"It's late. Get up this minute! . . . Don't forget to brush your teeth . . . Hurry! Your breakfast is getting cold . . . You'll be late for school. Don't forget your mittens . . . and your overshoes!

"Don't come in until you've wiped your feet . . . Change your clothes, now. This very minute! . . . Go outside and play for half an hour—and I want you to come when I call. Do you hear? Well, show that you hear, say you understand! Don't mumble.

"Now wash your hands. I had to call you twice! . . . Drink the rest of your milk! You don't use a spoon; use a fork. How many times have I told you to come to the table with your hair combed as well as with your hands and face washed? . . . Stand up straight! Do you want to be humpbacked?

"Start your homework. Turn off the radio! No wonder your grades aren't better! . . . Are you sure you've got all your homework done? . . . Now get ready for bed. It's late. You should have been in bed half an hour ago! Be quiet now and go to sleep! Just stop all that, settle down and go to sleep!"

Many of us were exposed to this type of barrage daily. It is a form of parental anxiety about the child—and about the adequacy of the parent. Such parents are often trying very conscientiously to be good parents. In their earnestness they hoe and prune in the garden of the child's psychological development throughout his waking hours, chopping at what they consider "bad weeds." Actually children can do with much letting alone, giving them time to develop and respect their own thoughts, feelings and interests, but many parents fear this is "neglecting" the child. While children need someone "in their corner," backing them up and assisting them, they also need times when, alone, they contend with their environment. In this

93

way they can discover their unique and specific individuality, their powers and capacities and destiny. This helps a child to develop his ability to initiate his own actions and to accomplish to his own satisfaction—an ability he will need in adult life.

THE "COMMAND-RESISTANCE" CYCLE: If the atmosphere of your childhood home followed the overcoercive pattern of constant direction outlined above, you, as a child, probably reacted to this anxious pressure by stalling and dawdling. This would provoke sharper, sterner directions and reminders. Directions would become commands—then threats.

This may have led to active resistance and defiance on your part. However, since active resistance could result in punishment, you probably adopted a form of passive resistance. This would allow you to continue to do what you were already interested in while seemingly complying with the parental direction. What child has not called, "Yes, I'm coming," while still continuing to play?

To the parent this stalling seems purposeless. Many a parent has said to me in irritation about his child's dawdling tactics, "If she was only doing something interesting, something worthwhile, I'd understand." But the child's dawdling does have a purpose. It is to protect his individuality, to insist on it—even though he dare not defy the parent. He is trying to avoid being a puppet who jumps every time the string is pulled. In his memorable book *"Where Did You Go?" "Out." "What Did You Do?" "Nothing."* Robert Paul Smith celebrates this passive resistance. He demonstrates how children need to be left alone in order to grow creatively through such activities as building tree houses and playing mumbley peg.

In this unhappy, nagging battle between the parent's constant directing and the dawdling and daydreaming that is the child's only weapon and refuge, a vicious cycle is set up between command and resistance. Often it spreads to all other fields of life, to school, to work, to suggestions coming from anyone, even oneself. A high percentage of the "bad grades," "poor progress," "inattention," and "not working to capacity" comments of teachers and school authorities are traceable to this "command-resistance" cycle, which may be a clue to the cause of some of your past—and present—difficulties.

If you grew up in an overly coercive atmosphere, you continue as an adult to press parent-like directions on yourself—"Do this! Do that!"—and then resist your own directions, stalling and daydreaming. This is how your inability to act develops. *You paralyze yourself, using the same kind of slyly concealed passive resistance and distractions to your own directions—just as you once resisted the coercive commands of your parents.*

Your Parental Commands

You may not recognize the form which your parental directions and commands take. "I don't go around shouting directions and reminders at myself the way my mother used to do," some people have said on first hearing overcoercion described. Many people, following a pattern established in childhood, set daily goals of work, of social activities, of cleanliness, of earning or even money-saving, that cannot be accomplished in their situation. Aside from the fact that such goals may be perfectionistic, they do not allow themselves sufficient time for their tasks, they overrate their strength and underrate the obstacles and their need to rest. They make almost endless miscalculations as to how much time and effort is required to do anything from reading a book or dusting a room to organizing a committee or going to a dance. Often if a person takes a coldly realistic and objective look at what he is expecting himself to do, he may immediately realize that nobody could possibly accomplish what he expects of himself.

These unrealistic expectations, schedules and programs —lists of "musts"—may be the form that your parental overcoercion toward yourself takes; in thousands of cases they are. Such "musts" cannot be fulfilled. They are often contradictory and inconsistent. Because they cannot be fulfilled, they keep you anxious, striving and pushing—and resisting. Moreover, they subtly belittle your efforts, virtually convincing you that you are lazy, worthless or whatever else you call yourself in a self-derogatory mood.

To be achieved, your goals must be realistic and within your capacities. If your "inner child of the past" has you tied up in a "command-resistance" knot, you cannot achieve your goals.

As you free your energies from such knots, you will be able to begin to meet goals that are reasonable expecta-

*tions. And you will no longer need to belittle and berate
yourself.*

Cultural Factors in Overcoercion

We live in an overly coercive culture. This attitude permeates our homes, running through generation after generation as "the proper way to rear children." It permeates our schools, our work and our organizations. Television and other mass-circulation media constantly hammer away with "Do this! Don't do that!" and the "right way" and the "wrong way" on everything from baking cake to motherhood and being "successful." We are so accustomed to overly coercive attitudes that arm-twisting, demanding commercials on television and anxiety-arousing articles in the press seem right to us.

To the parent, the constant directing and reminding of the child seems to be love and concern about the child's welfare. Often the parent does not recognize that many of his commands are aimed at trying to make up for past deprivations which he, the parent, experienced. The child, because he is a different individual in a different situation, *cannot* experience the feelings of the parent's childhood. "My mother never had the money to give us music lessons, and I want my child to be popular and to entertain people with her playing. That's why I keep after her," such a mother may say.

To the teacher, overcoercion seems necessary for instruction, for clarification, for discipline.

To the employer and the committee chairman, it seems like "the only way to get things done."

Often all these pressures are excessive—and engender the resistance that makes every task harder.

Because our resistance is sometimes slyly concealed even from ourselves, because overcoercion has this pervasive, ubiquitous reinforcement from our culture, overcoercion is often hard to recognize and deal with. We have become so accustomed to it that it feels and seems right, proper, just and needed.

It may seem to you that "shoulds" and "have tos" are needed to keep you from "flying to pieces." Actually they are merely a continuation of your parent's old coerciveness —and what you really need is to be a gentler, more realistic parent to yourself in setting your goals.

Living without this constant pushing of yourself will make you anxious temporarily. You are not "at home" with less inner pressure, just as city people often cannot feel comfortable in the quiet of fields and forests at first. But if you sort out all the coercive pressures, both parental and cultural, that have been blocking your efforts, you will find that this anxiety will gradually ease. This kind of anxiety is really the first sign of a new way of treating yourself. As you begin to function and find satisfaction in your accomplishments, you will develop a new confidence and security in your abilities to replace the old security of the familiar.

How Did You Resist?

In understanding and coping with the resistance of your "inner child of the past" which are balking your efforts, you may be aided by knowing these reactions usually fall into three distinct patterns. Although they may be mixed, applied in different areas in different degrees, these childhood patterns have generally been maintained in adult life—and form your basic way of dealing with your own coercive directions to yourself. They are:

1. *Docility.* If the parent starts coercive control of the child early enough and maintains it consistently, the child generally follows direction docilely, without resistance. Such a child obeys without questioning or resisting the parent lest he lose parental love. As he grows up, he transfers this same unquestioning directional control to teachers and employers. Indeed, he feels lost without it. He needs someone to tell him what to do. He is unable to initiate or act on his own, finding it uncomfortable and even terrifying to assume this kind of responsibility for his actions. Generally he finds his way into a structured job, one with rigid and well-established limits as to what he is and is not to do. He then carries out these assigned functions very well. But he wants and needs to be told what to do at all times and literally cannot comfortably function in any other way. Conflict arises in such a person when someone is not available to tell him what to do.

2. *Active Resistance.* If the parental overcoercion has started relatively late in the child's development, after the child has already developed some sense of his own ability and powers, the child may adopt a pattern of resisting and

97

defying direction. This may provoke still more severe, threatening coerciveness from the parent to force the child to obey. The parent and child may be in frequent conflict, with the adult getting his way only because he is the stronger. The parent also possesses a powerful weapon: the withholding of parental affection and approval, which the child, however defiant, still needs desperately. The child may resentfully give up his own interests and thoughts, but in so doing he says to himself in effect: "O.K., you're bigger than I am and you've got me down, but just you wait until I'm stronger." This pattern may go on throughout childhood—and into adulthood.

The "inner child of the past" of such an adult still smolders with the resentments he felt in childhood. He actively resists direction, often virtually "carrying a chip on his shoulder" in relation to anyone in a position of authority. He almost automatically bucks against anyone's suggestions or orders. However, his own adult understanding serves to modify his urge to defy and it is further held in check by his need to earn a living. He may accept direction but often it is with the same childhood reaction: "O.K., you're bigger than I am and you've got me down (because I need this job), but just you wait until I'm stronger." Still burning with childhood resentments, he is often unnecessarily contentious and resentful toward what in reality is necessary direction.

But if such a person is given the very minimum of general direction and allowed to proceed on his own initiative, he may do an excellent job and find real satisfaction in it. Yet his continuing childhood need to resist actively is often so great that it may unnecessarily distort suggestions and advice from others into coercive threats—which he must defy, creating tension and anxiety in himself and others, the old atmosphere of his childhood.

3. *Passive Resistance.* This is the most common resistance pattern. If the parent has begun overly coercive direction and training after the child has begun to feel some of his power to resist but before he is able to defy the parent actively, the resistance may be passive in varying degrees. The child dawdles and delays in complying with the parent's direction. Told to do something, he replies, "In a minute." When the direction is renewed, he says, "I'm coming"—and still procrastinates, lingering with what really interests him but becoming anxious over the threat of parental disapproval. His dawdling brings forth

still stronger parental demands, frankly coercive, and this "command-resistance" pattern may go on and on, with the parent periodically resorting to angry force.

The command-resistance cycle afflicts most adults in varying degrees and in different areas. On becoming parents to themselves, they continue to resist passively their own directions—dawdling, daydreaming, procrastinating, occupying themselves with distractions. The more they urge themselves on, the more important and fascinating the distraction seems. They give themselves the same type of excuses they once gave their parent and continue their distractions and procrastination until, in many cases, some real threat from the outside arises. Then they resentfully comply. They mutter their defiance and tell themselves they should leave this situation and set up an independent operation. But their own resistance to their active "shoulds" keeps this move in the realm of daydreaming. This is what often happens with the man who is forever talking of "being his own boss" and going into business for himself.

A Case of Passive Resistance

The person who is caught in the passive resistance pattern seldom achieves what he is capable of doing. A young lawyer who suffers from this particular pathogenic attitude tries hard to make headway—but somehow can't get started every morning. He arrives bright and early, fresh and clean, reminding himself he must really get down to "brass tacks." But after he has arranged his papers and gotten the necessary lawbooks, he sits down at his desk and can't seem to get to work. Jack simply can't make up his mind where to start and he begins mentally reviewing what he was going to do.

In a few minutes he stands up. Nothing feels right. He sharpens pencils, smokes, tries to relax by reading the paper. This distraction finally becomes so enormous he abandons it and tries to start again. He sends for more books from the office library, resharpens the pencil. He makes some notes on past cases and rereads old cases. He sees fine points in law and greatly admires the men who made them. But he ends the day with only a few pointless notes—the obvious ones anyone could make on hearing the problem. He goes home grumpy, annoyed with himself, irritated with the senior partner who is being held up by his unproductiveness and who called him just before the day ended to find out if he was finished.

At home he grouches and grumps until the ministrations of his wife ease the damage his unproductiveness has done to his self-esteem. He will really get down to work tomorrow, he promises himself. He tries to think about how he will write that brief tomorrow, and slides into a daydream in which the senior partner gratefully rushes in to congratulate him, the judge is impressed, the client expresses appreciation and the opposition take note of him respectfully. Yielding to Janice's consoling attitude ("Poor Jack, you work so hard with those musty old cases"), he decides that he will do better tomorrow.

But the next day the same thing happens—and the day after that. The question now, as he puts it, is how long Janice, who is busy with an equally complex task—managing the house and their two small children—will continue "to believe me, especially if I lose my job, which may happen unless I snap out of it." These fears, not entirely groundless, have been threatening and coercive, anxiety-arousing—to the point of forcing him to get down to work.

However, in place of the brilliant career he expected to make for himself, Jack is just managing to get along, with much grumbling and discontent, excuses, alibis, anxiety and unhappiness. With all of this Jack is merely repeating a childhood pattern of behavior—resisting whatever is expected of him by his wife or his senior law partner. He is capable and intelligent, but he resists applying himself until some severe threat is made. In childhood he resisted his mother's and his father's directions in just this passive fashion until such a threat was made. In his adult life these same tendencies lead him to run the risk of discharge from employment or the loss of his wife's sympathy and love.

This is the way many people go through life. Unnecessarily miserable, at times anxious, fearful and resentful, unable to attain what they are equipped to do—and want to do—they are dissatisfied with themselves and their efforts. Often their first insight into the fact that something is wrong is that they are passed over when promotions are given out. They know in a vague way that "I'm not handling myself well. This should be easy for me to do, but I just can't somehow get around to it because I'm so exhausted."

Eliminating Physical Causes of Fatigue

Poor productivity is the primary sign—and result—of the resistance of the "inner child of the past." Fatigue is another significant sign. For instance, among housewives, whose work depends upon their inner organization, fatigue is often the main complaint. All persons suffering from fatigue rate a thorough physical examination to rule out anemia, hypothyroid conditions and other debilitating illness. Once this possible physical explanation can be eliminated, the inner command-resistance cycle becomes the prime suspect. I know a woman whose main complaint is chronic exhaustion. She was sent to me by a physician who could not find anything physically wrong with her. From her story of her childhood, it is plain that her inability to do her housework is primarily the reaction of her overly coerced "child of the past." She lets all the housework go, including the washing and ironing, because "I'm too exhausted to lift a finger."

Then her husband runs out of shirts, a church group that she belongs to plans to meet at her house—and she is up half the night, toiling bitterly at the washing, ironing and cleaning. And then she really is exhausted. This pattern of self-resistance and exhaustion will go on until she breaks up the command-resistance cycle that controls her life.

The Woman Who Anesthetized the Drill Sergeant

Your resistance may take the form of symptoms of illness or be overshadowed and complicated by other problems, such as alcoholism. For example, I know a woman who could not do her housework until she had a drink. If she did not drink, she angrily and abusively pushed herself into her housecleaning—and then balked within a short time, feeling exhausted and resentful. If she had a drink, she could fly into her work and accomplish it efficiently.

But she was frightened by her secret drinking—and scolded herself for it. In fact, this is what prompted her finally to come to me. The more she scolded herself for drinking, the more depressed she became, and the less able she was to do her household work. But drinking would overcome her resistance to the work. Once she had in this fashion anesthetized the barking, scowling "drill sergeant" within her who ordered her to work, she could act on her own initiative and get her work done. Yet the drinking plunged her into greater self-scolding and depressed feelings the next day, frightening her with the possibility that she was becoming an alcoholic.

This woman grew up in a home where a stern grandfather ruled with absolute authority. The home, the meals and the deportment of all members of the family, including her parents, were subject to his minute scrutiny, scolding and commands. When my patient grew up, she could wipe out this authoritarian atmosphere—and her resistance to it—only with alcohol. Then she applied her grandfather's attitude to herself all the more savagely the following day.

Areas of Resistance

You may already realize that your procrastination, time wasting and inability to "get started" are limited to certain areas or specific activities which you consider your "duties" or responsibilities. Most parents have put overly coercive demands on the child only in certain areas, areas that were particularly important to them—probably because their own parents put such a stress on these areas. As a result of this selective application, some people are able to function well in some areas of living while in certain other areas they are still involved in a wasteful, unhappy and seemingly uncontrollable command-resistance pattern. On the other hand, severe overcoercion in any area may cause the resultant resistance to spread to many areas.

Often the areas in which overcoercion continues to be applied are important to the full enjoyment of life and to the development of one's full potential as an individual. Area overcoercion can create a crippling handicap, not much different than the crippling of specific joints by a chronic disease like arthritis. The woman who had to take a secret drink to be able to do her housework illustrates this selective overcoercion. Her grandfather's endless scolding about her childhood "idleness" and her "duties" as a

102

maid-of-all-work established a furious command-resistance cycle over housecleaning.

"He couldn't stand to see me playing or sitting reading a book or just doing nothing," she told me. "I spent my childhood dusting things that had already been dusted twice that day. He often made a liar out of me. I mean I would pretend to be working, holding a dust cloth and making an occasional swipe while I tried to read a book," she added bitterly. Even when she really wanted to dust and clean her own home after marriage, she could not do it without a drink until she realized that she was, in effect, continuing her childhood resistance to her grandfather's harsh scolding. Her own parents had been so overcoerced in their childhoods that they followed the grandfather's dictates docilely and thus reinforced his authority.

Generally, parents whose backgrounds include overcoercion either accept and imitate it as the proper way for an adult and parent to act—or rebel against it in some areas to assert their own individuality. For example, the parent who has been forced to "eat everything on your plate" in his childhood either insists on this with his child —or takes pride in his child's finicky impulsiveness at the table. In this manner he vicariously triumphs over the coercive demands of his childhood, even though his child suffers from the failure to develop sound eating habits.

Aspects of Overcoercion

Areas of resistance can exist in any aspect of life, from those which involve health, cleanliness and safety to work, punctuality, sex, religion, scholarship, social status and entertainment. This helps us to understand why some persons cannot get to church, why punctuality is often ignored, why informal and tieless sports shirts and slacks are practically our national attire for both men and women, and why teenagers and college students make sloppy-looking old sweatshirts and blue jeans their characteristic dress. This also helps to explain why absenteeism, which costs us millions of dollars a year in lost production, plagues industries. Particularly hard hit are mass production plants where the worker already feels deprived of his individuality by the character of the work and the constant demands of foremen and supervisors for more production. The "sit-down" and the "slow-down" strike tactics

103

are psychologically firmly based in the resistance of the "inner child of the past" to overcoercion.

Other common areas in which the resentful resistance of the "child of the past" are commonly expressed are:

SOCIAL MANNERS: The person who can't introduce people or adopt ordinary social politeness without embarrassing difficulty is frequently reacting to an insistent, coercive parent who said: "Now, darling, introduce your little friend to everyone in the room—and do it properly! Remember you present someone to a lady, not the other way!"

READING: The inability of many people to enjoy reading for pleasure or the enrichment of their knowledge often arises because some initial slowness in reading prompted the teacher to advise parents to drill a child— and they did so with considerable anxiety and threatening overcoercion.

DRINKING: Much drinking of beer, whiskey and coffee is actually an act of protest and defiance against specific parental coercive attitudes against such consumption. It may also be a reaction to over-all coerciveness of the childhood atmosphere.

PROMISCUITY: In many instances promiscuity arises from the threatening warnings and prohibitions of overly coercive parents. The high school girl who is the "make" of the crowd frequently has parents who are constantly warning and harassing her about the evils of kissing, necking and petting. In such situations the parental command "You must never . . ." is secretly answered with the resistant voice: "I can and I will live my own life." Other aspects of overcoercion in sex and marital difficulties will be discussed in a later section.

EATING: The command-resist cycle is particularly obvious in the food dislikes of many people and in women who are trying to diet. Who has not observed the ritual-like, parental command to oneself: "I really mustn't," followed by an immediate dive into a rich cake or dessert?

MONEY: Children who were made to count each penny and harassed about money in childhood frequently are careless about money as adults. Much "impulse buying," which leads to spending beyond one's means, is a resistant reaction to the continuation of these past coercive attitudes about money. "I can't afford it" is overwhelmed by the powerful impulse to defy at any cost.

ENTERTAINMENT: Much of the partygoing, entertaining, card playing and watching of the late late show on television is based on defiance of strict bedtimes and of overly coercive attitudes against such activities as well as childhood deprivations.

And simply because overcoercion is common does not necessarily mean you had overly coercive parents. All resistance does not stem from the command-resistance cycle—and you may find that you do not treat yourself in this fashion.

In recalling the specific area or activities in which your parents were overly coercive, your best clues will lie in your difficulties today. Areas in which you are slyly resisting your own efforts are usually areas in which you were overly coerced as a child.

You may find that you regard all life as coercive—that you resent and resist many aspects of life, including general customs, particularly if you are expected to do something, to cook, to eat, to be on time, to work, to be clean, to be polite, to marry, to initiate some necessary action, to assume responsibility for yourself and others as an adult. This would appear to indicate that you suffered from severely overcoercive attitudes in childhood and are strenuously resisting even today, long after the original commands of your parents and teachers have faded

Resistance, passive or active, can only follow the command. The command must come first in order to be resisted. In adult life the commands are, except in certain obvious areas like work, nearly always self-imposed. Understanding how this basic mechanism of command-resistance operates within you can help to modify your coerciveness toward yourself—and your corresponding need to resist it.

In coping with the many questions which naturally arise in considering resistance, one must recognize that all resistance is not necessarily self-defeating and that all coercion does not necessarily come from parents. At times resistance may be the only way individuality can be expressed. There are rather spectacular examples of this in the lives of famous people. Glenn Cunningham was badly burned as a child and told he could never walk, yet he went on to become one of the world's famous mile runners because he resisted this dictate. Similarly, Theodore Roosevelt, a severe asthmatic as a child, resisted all efforts to get him to give up athletic activities and went west to build up his physical strength, refusing to accept adult advice that would have kept him an invalid. Again, Franklin D. Roosevelt's heroic resistance to poliomyelitis made it possible for him to become president. In the same fashion, on a national scale, resistance to coercive commands was the heart and soul of the Frenchmen and others whose countries were occupied by the Nazis in World War II. Individual growth and development may result from such defiance.

But when you are imposing coercive commands on yourself, continuing the old attitudes of your parents—and then resisting them, resulting in time-wasting procrastination—you are hurting yourself.

How Overcoercion Affects Sex and Marriage

The effect of overcoercion in the past on a marriage in the present can be bitter resentment and chaos. More often it is a persistent and unhappy feeling of futility, of "getting nowhere," a vague distress and exhaustion because nothing seems to work out as planned. The marriage situation carries within it all kinds of expectations concerning the marital partner and what constitutes the "duties" and "responsibilities" of the man and woman. These expectations have seldom been explored except in the most romantic light. This makes marriage a fertile area for the multiplication of coercive demands, resentments and passive and active resistance. Because overly coercive attitudes permeate our homes and culture, very few of our marriages escape this type of difficulty altogether.

Sometimes these "command-resist" problems are ignored or passed over until children appear. There then may be serious clashes and crises over child rearing—with the children often bearing the brunt of resentments really held against the marriage partner. And often the children are submitted to the same tyrannical direction and redirection that the parent himself is still reacting to. Feeling anxious about his adequacy as a parent, a young father or mother often falls back on the coercive attitudes with which he was raised as a safe way of being a "good parent," which most parents want desperately to be; often they know no other way.

Converting the Partner into the Coercive Parent

Frequently in marriage, the partner whose "inner child of the past" is the more generally resistant to the "shoulds" inherent in marriage tends to convert the spouse into a coercive parent through dawdling and procrastination. Then *someone* actually voices the commands and demands—and the dawdler resists. This may have nothing to do with the actual sex of the partner. In this fashion the burden of responsibility is avoided and, more important, the security of the old pattern of command-resistance is maintained.

Many a husband has been forced in this fashion to be coercive and demanding about the lack of housecleaning, the irregularity of the meals and the unkempt appearance of the children—because his wife's overly coercive mother deprived her of the ability to initiate and carry out household work. Her resistance requires coercive demands before she can function at all. Similarly, many wives have been turned into nagging shrews by the dawdling and delaying of their husbands, who are still resisting their parents' demands to "Do this! Do that!" A request for the repair of a broken blind or the oiling of a door instantly invokes a pattern of resistance and delay which may go on for days. Often wives have had to assume responsibilities normally borne by husbands, either to get these tasks done or to avoid scenes.

The situations in which overcoercion and its resultant resistance play significant roles in marriage are endless. The husband who resists taking responsibility often forces his wife to do so—and then resents her role. In many homes the wife wants to be told what to do and can't move until she is, and then resents it. We all know the woman who buys a hat which she realizes her husband will disapprove of—and then invites his opinion of it. When he tells her his honest opinion, she feels hurt and sulks.

107

EXPECTATIONS BECOME DUTIES: Expectations of what a husband or wife *should do,* always colored and distorted by unrealistic hopes and reactions to one's own parents, are inevitably brought into most marriages. In marriage these expectations often become "duties"—and are particularly susceptible to passive and often to active resistance. In addition, the changing role of women—necessitating a changed role for men—has contributed to the confusion, friction and resentments about roles in many homes.

"If I'd only realized he considered it my job to do everything, I'd never have married him. He leaves everything for me to do!" many wives have protested. Many men, busy with the dishes and dusting, have had similar thoughts. In most such instances people have partners whose passive resistance, daydreaming and procrastination are obvious in youth but are not recognized to be future problems. When the realities of responsibility, of the need to initiate action and persistently carry out functions take grim shape after marriage, these couples are unable to create satisfying lives and are generally distressed and unhappy.

"Sometimes I think my husband is allergic to work. He always has a reason why he can't do something. He will walk by a window that's been broken, and tell me that it's broken. But he won't make a move to fix it. That's my headache. He figures his responsibility ends when he has told me about it," one such woman complained. "If I tell him to do something, he may agree to do it—and then get angry at me if I have to remind him that it still isn't done."

THE INITIAL MOVE: Often the effects of the command-resistance cycle in an individual are more clearly apparent in the sexual aspects of marriage than elsewhere, although certainly many other factors may be involved. Because the person suffering from the overly coercive attitudes of his parents has a marked inability to initiate any action, the question of who makes an initial sexual advance often becomes a focal point in marriage. Such a man, for instance, may be able to function sexually only if he makes the initial advance. If his wife makes such an advance or even indicates that she expects him to do so, his resistant "child of the past" takes over and he backs away. Hidden resentments about her coercive role in other activities, often

108

those in which his resistance has forced her to take charge, may also cause impotence.

In the same way a resented responsibility for contraception may result in diminished sexual responsiveness and satisfaction in either partner. Often the expectations, resistances and disappointments are such that severe-frustration and bitter resentment may cause a withering of the sexual side of marriage.

THE "GOOD WIFE": Perhaps the most widespread difficulty that women experience in this area stems from being taught to look upon sexual intercourse as a "duty" to their husbands, something expected of every "good wife." If a woman looks upon sex in this way, she may comply—but without feeling and with considerable resentment. This resentment, which she often conceals from herself because it jeopardizes her wish to be a "good wife," may cause a splitting headache, a backache or a number of other ailments to develop, thus averting sexual intimacy. Others may resort to elaborate bedtime rituals to forestall sexual advances. In this fashion the opportunity for mutual loving interchange becomes a victim of the resentful "inner child of the past."

Often the marital partner whose resistant "child of the past" is destroying the possibility of sexual satisfactions and affectionate interchange realizes what is happening. But she is confused by both her overly coercive training and the concept of being a "good wife," which she wants to be. Let me tell you of a case in which this happened:

In her mid-twenties an attractive and capable girl, whose mother had been extremely overcoercive in her childhood, meets a man whose thoughtful consideration and attentiveness warms her. She falls deeply in love with him and when he proposes she accepts with delight. She cheerfully and happily provides a comfortable home for him, searching for new ways to cook his favorite foods and listening sympathetically to his accounts of his work. All of this is part of her determination and desire to be a "good wife." Yet she bitterly resents any sexual advance on his part and thrusts him aside, even though she also insistently believes a "good wife" should provide sexual satisfaction for her husband.

On occasion she complies, and "feels nothing," she says. She feels her personality is being wiped out by having to "capitulate," just as it was by her mother's commands.

109

This is not a situation where her husband, who is a patient, reasonable and long-suffering man, actively takes over the commanding role of her mother in creating her resistant frigidity. Her husband's advance or even hint of it inadvertently triggers her intense resistance. She herself takes over her mother's role, telling herself, "Be a good wife! Do it! You must to be a good wife!" In this way she uses the sexual aspect of her life to admonish herself to "be a good wife"—thus creating the resistant reaction.

Her husband, having been rebuffed and denied, feels she isn't very affectionate or loving. He is disappointed, frustrated and considers her reactions to be rather odd and mystifying.

This woman has to learn that commanding or steeling yourself to be a "good wife" has no place in the love between a man and a woman. To attain full sexual satisfaction, you must get outside the command-resistance cycle of childhood.

The Origins of Overcoercion

You do not need to trace your resistance to your own directions back to childhood in order to recognize that command-resistance cycle and to attempt to dissolve it. However, understanding how and why this paralyzing tug of war developed may help you.

All children need the assistance of their parents in infancy in order to survive and grow. They also need—and with relatively rare exceptions, receive—the acceptance and approval of their parents. As the child develops, he needs supervision, guidance and direction. This is important for the safety, health and future development of every youngster.

However, in many cases, this direction and guidance of the child becomes excessive and coercive. One reason for this is the parent's anxiety about the child's development. Another is the parent's anxiety about his own capacity to fulfill the role of parent. Moreover, often this is the only way the parent knows how to act—having had an excessively coercive parent himself. In addition, the coercive pressure behind the directions often arises because the parent has many other obligations and commitments—and anxieties connected with these affairs. Thus, the parent often unwittingly pours out critical comments, redirections, reminders and new directions with sighs of exasperation and disapproval.

What is sacrificed in this process is the child's ability to initiate and to accomplish through his own efforts. He develops no feelings of being able to direct himself along lines in which he is interested. He has no opportunity to increase his self-esteem through his own accomplishments Inevitably he responds to directions which take him away from things he is interested in by dawdling, daydreaming and procrastination as a way of asserting his individuality.

When does this dawdling response begin? There is, as yet, no evidence that could be applied to every case. However, it is generally clear that the child first discovers his power to balk the parents' constant directions in the course of eating and, particularly, toilet training. It is this command-resistance cycle, rather than the Freudian idea of "anal fixation," that has made toilet training a point of emphasis in child rearing. In toilet training the child, rather than the parent, controls what will happen. If the child does not respond to the parent's request for a bowel movement, the parent becomes increasingly exasperated, annoyed, demanding, disapproving—overcoercive. The child, discovering bit by bit that he can really defy the parent, goes from toilet resistance to a more general use of dawdling as a way of combating parental direction and of asserting his individuality.

By the time the child reaches school age, he has learned to apply dawdling to many situations—and to daydreams. This protects him momentarily against the excessive pressures of the parent. To resist actively would mean loss of parental approval, which the child cannot stand without severe anxiety. By dawdling the child resists the parent but avoids a direct clash. (If the parental coerciveness were reduced, the child would no longer need to resist and could express his individual interests without loss of parental approval.)

Thus what is established at a relatively early age is the command-resistance cycle.

This pattern is continued in adult life—with self-imposed parent-like directions now being resisted by the same person. What such a person has learned to do in life is to resist. In this he finds the security of the familiar.

The Question of Motivation

When we consider anyone's ineffectual efforts, the question of motivation arises. A person may genuinely desire to achieve his goals. But in using his parents' exasperated and critical tones of disapproval, calling himself lazy, insincere and worthless, he sets in motion the resistance which defeats him. All this tends to be damaging and is no solution to his unproductiveness.

Productiveness is a natural state of man. Human beings are naturally productive—and it hurts us to do nothing. It damages our feelings of being worthy, of being needed and useful—upon which our adult self-esteem and inner confidence depend.

Mother's carping or father's order can never be adequate motivation—it is only carping or an order. In the same way commands and carping at ourselves cannot adequately motivate adult activities. They are merely echoes of the past.

If you will remember that the commands must come first to set up the command-resistance cycle—and reduce them —you can automatically reduce your need to resist. However, the tendency to command yourself is your old "at home" pattern, and at first you will feel strange in trying to live without it. But when you abandon the habit of setting up lists of "shoulds" and "have tos" and can establish what you really want to do, you can make the first preliminary steps toward your achievable goals. As you begin to find satisfaction in your ability to act without coercive threats to yourself, your resistance will further decrease— and your confidence and ability to act will grow.

CHAPTER 12

OVERSUBMISSIVENESS—
If you are demanding and impulsive

YOUR INDEX OF SUSPICION: *If you have a tendency to fly into temper outbursts, if you like to drive fast and do impulsive things on the "spur of the moment," if you find making persistent efforts at work and other activities "not worthwhile," and feel unloved if people don't give in to you, you are probably still reacting to the oversubmissiveness of your parents.* Next to overcoercion, this is the most common pathogenic parental attitude in America. Often the effects of overcoercion and oversubmission, despite their contradiction, coexist in the same person. This dualism may develop if one parent is overly coercive while the other is overly submissive toward a child. In being a parent to yourself, you may have continued this dualism, swinging from moods of overcoercion to oversubmission toward yourself.

Recognizing Your Own Oversubmission

The individual whose parents were overly submissive toward him in childhood is generally an attractive, bright, warm and friendly person who "lives for the moment."

If you are impulsive, generally unable to resist "acting on the spur of the moment" because "it feels so good" —even though you may recognize it to be shortsighted, you are probably continuing the oversubmissiveness of your parents to your immature whims and demands. "But it seems so natural, so spontaneous," impulsive people some-

113

times complain when they recognize their impulsiveness as a source of unhappiness. "How else can you act?"

Impulsive behavior is natural in a child; his immaturity and lack of knowlledge make it impossible for him to act in any other way. But it is self-defeating and often cruel to others in adult life, which, in our society, must be guided by long-range goals rather than immediate satisfactions. In becoming a parent to himself such a person submits to his immature whims and demands in the same way his parents did. In a certain sense he has never had the opportunity to learn that to achieve desirable goals, the adult must control and guide his impulses. As an impulsive man once put it in a moment of introspection: "I feel as though I have been trapped in childhood all my adult life."

People suffering from their own oversubmission are fickle, driven forever to find some place where "the grass is greener." They are inclined to overeat, drink too much, drive too fast, philander, waste money and ignore vitally important matters. They have temper tantrums if their impulsive demands are not met. If something requires patient, persistent effort, they find it "exhausting" and "tiresome." They have seldom learned to find satisfaction in accomplishing things through their own efforts and expect others to provide for them. If expected to provide or to maintain constancy, the impulsive person becomes angry and resentful. In psychiatry this type of person has long been particularly recognized because of his tendency to break off treatment. Therapy requires such people to work with the psychiatrist, to face their lack of consideration for others and to establish limits to their impulsiveness. By setting limits to their impulsiveness, therapy cuts down on their immediate satisfactions. They feel strange, "not at home" and deprived, and this causes many of them to end treatment.

TYPES OF DIFFICULTIES: Broadly speaking, two specific kinds of difficulties plague the impulsive person—and these brief summaries' may be clues to establishing whether parental oversubmission was a significant factor in your childhood:

1. Impulsive-driven people frequently infringe on the feelings and rights of others. Accustomed to following their impulses unreservedly, they are often astonished to find others have been hurt by their temper outbursts, infidelity or lack of consideration. Because they "live in the mo-

ment," they actually tend to be blindly unaware of the feelings of others. In love they tend to be dictators and their partners only slaves; mutuality is not recognized, understood or even considered desirable. Their overeating, drinking, philandering, temper tantrums, reckless business ventures and spending infringe on the rights of others. Often they are frankly exploitive toward others.

2. Because they are impulse-driven, they are frequently unable to move consistently toward adult goals—even though they may sincerely want to achieve them. They are easily distracted and diverted from their goals. Their impulsiveness endlessly sidetracks them because it prevents recognition of the distraction as something which can prevent achievement of the adult goal. The most obvious example is the flirtation which jeopardizes a durable marriage. But most distractions are not so obvious—the impulse to telephone a friend, the stop for a snack, the "impulse-buying" of novelties which prevent a more important purchase. While these distractions are always accompanied by rationalizations which seem to justify them, in the end the impulsive person seldom achieves his long-range goal.

Because they are easily diverted from finding satisfaction in the persistent application of their efforts in the slow, often difficult progress toward adult goals, such individuals are endlessly hunting immediate impulse-satisfactions. Others may call their behavior "childish," but often living by impulse is the only way they know how "to feel alive." Persistency and constancy make life seem bleak and drab to them.

SPECIAL CHARACTERISTICS: People who have been submitted to in their childhood have certain special characteristics which make them particularly attractive. They are frequently physically attractive. And their impulsiveness itself is most attractive. In our society, particularly in the Age of the Organization Man, the spontaneity and impulsiveness of an individual often make him exciting. People are drawn to him. He says the forbidden words and acts as we wish we could. At any meeting or party the person who acts impulsively wins attention, friends and admiration—though what he says and does may be foolish.

Secondly, such people, acting impulsively, are often very creative and confident. They do not doubt their feelings, which helps to make them confident and successful in certain areas.

Thirdly, impulsive people have an ability to form close personal relationships quickly and easily. When they want to win love and approval, they can be extraordinarily winning, charming and admirable, with a certain unerring sense of timing, saying and doing the right thing at the right time with the right tone. Other people, particularly those who have difficulty in forming close relationships —and therefore especially value closeness—are often "swept off their feet." They are delighted to find themselves so intimately involved with so little effort—only to find that when someone else appears, they are abandoned without a thought. In this fickle fashion the impulsive person often hurts people close to him. Because he forms such relationships quickly and easily, a close relationship has less value to an impulsive person than it does to persons who form such relationships with difficulty, and then often cling to him, inviting exploitation in their desperation.

THE WEAPON: The impulsive person has, in addition to temper tantrums, a standard weapon which he uses to force others to submit to his immature demands: "You don't love me," he cries. "If you did, you'd do what I say." This is, as a later section will show, a very old weapon for this type of person, and one that has been found to be successful in childhood. But it is a difficult weapon to contend with, as many a spouse has found, because nothing will satisfy its user short of full submission to his demand. *While equating love with giving in can easily appear to be foolishness itself, what is often not understood is that the impulsive person really deeply feels unloved and unwanted if his demands are not met.* This creates a trying and often severe problem, but it cannot be solved by others. It can only be solved by changing the attitude of the impulsive person toward himself, establishing limits on his impulsiveness.

All of the above special characteristics can frequently be noted in theatrical personalities. In the theater the impulsiveness, the uninhibited ability to form an immediate close relationship and a keen impulsive sense of timing may make a great actor or comedian. Many such theatrical personalities have a continuing close relationship with their mothers. These mothers have often taught their children to look upon themselves as "special" and "unusual," and in many instances have provided the inspiration and drive to create spectacular careers. But they have often also made

themselves slaves to the children's impulsive demands—
and their careers. The mothers of such people constitute a
special base throughout their lives. While these impulsive
persons have been spectacular successes on stage and in
the movies, they have often been spectacular failures off
stage in life itself.

The Case of Fred

Most impulsive people never live up to the initial impression they make. Fred, for example, has always been
known for his intelligence, bright wit and general poise.
His conversation is brilliant and people immediately warm
to him. Their first impression invariably is "that person will
go far because he's so bright, unusual and charming."
Often however, before the evening is over their picture has
changed, because Fred, with his bright wit, can't resist the
impulse to be "truthful." He slyly drops biting sarcastic
digs at the people drawn to him, sometimes hurting them
painfully. They begin to see some of his limitations.

But that is not the end of his difficulties. He inherited
his father's business. But its annual gross has been dwindling ever since his father's death because Fred, caught up
in impulsive distractions, cannot apply himself persistently
to necessary details of the business. He also cannot resist
his impulse to use a caustic tongue with employees and
even customers—and has lost some of both to competitors.
His secretary lives in constant anxiety because he pounds
on his desk and "wants what he wants when he wants it."

He eats and drinks too much, which further complicates
his business affairs because he often isn't there when de-
cisions should be made. If things aren't done to his satisfaction, he usually blames an employee or his wife—and
impulsively solaces himself with another drink. At times
he is abusive toward his wife. Even in this he is following
a childhood pattern. When Fred was growing up his mother
felt that he could do no wrong and that he was destined
for greatness. She gladly complied with his whims because
he was such a special person to her, even when he abused
her. Her feelings would be hurt but she would not set limits
on him or correct him. Instead she excused his behavior
—and continued to submit to him.

His wife has grown resentful and angry with Fred's
attitude, threatening to leave him. But what alarms Fred

even more is the obvious dwindling of the business which he inherited. He knows that he should pay more attention to its details, that he should be out seeking new business in an active way. But he is unable to make this kind of persistent effort. Sometimes he is distracted by pleasant conversation at lunch and lingers until late in the afternoon; sometimes someone proposes golf or tennis, at which he excels—and he must play *then*. He tells himself he must "keep in shape" and that he will probably pick up some business at the club. But he never does and his anxiety about the business and what he can do to check its downhill slide grows, making him nastier toward his wife and employees. He is vaguely aware of the fact that he hasn't lived up to people's expectations—or his own. But he goes on expecting other people to do whatever is necessary to make him successful—and blames them because they somehow do not. "Why the hell must I do everything?" he whines to himself.

The Case of Connie

The child whose parents have been oversubmissive faces a difficult problem in adult life because nothing can match those childhood days when he or she ruled like a monarch. Such a woman can make life miserable for her husband. This is the case with Connie, who demands living on a scale beyond the family means, insisting on a maid, elaborate parties and vacations. She often finds her children more annoying than enjoyable—and is sometimes jealous of their privileges. She expects every attention from her husband and believes that by virtue of being a woman she is entitled to have all doors opened for her, all chairs pulled out and no questions asked.

She pursues pleasure avidly, often to the neglect of her family. She indulges in rich foods and complains because she puts on weight. At parties she sparkles and likes to flirt. She makes friends easily but is quick to be offended if the bridge club doesn't agree with her views. Her temper is explosive—and when she still doesn't get her way, she cries. She often rebuffs her husband's sexual advances to force him into capitulation to her immature whims. Her snippy and catty remarks have so alienated other women that she was forced out of one social group by their frank hostility and cold ignoring of her attempts to "sparkle."

Much of the time she is lonely, dissatisfied and unhappy. She can't understand why her husband can't make more money and why they can't move to a nicer neighborhood, "away from all these awful people." She bitterly resents her housework, which she never had to do as a young girl; her mother always told her, she likes to remind her husband, "Connie, you'll marry a rich man and live like a lady." Then she adds, with some bite in her tone: "And look where I ended up—on my knees scrubbing floors!" It is one of her favorite stories—and she loves to tell it at parties, sometimes to amuse others, sometimes to embarrass her husband, sometimes because she feels abused. In a sense she is alway seeking the atmosphere of her impulsive childhood, and she does not understand why her quick friendships evaporate.

Two factors make it difficult for people to accept those who are overly submissive to themselves. 1.) They are hurt by the impulsive person's riding roughshod over their feelings and draw away from such individuals. 2.) They grow weary of having to comply excessively with the impulsive person's mood and begin to show their resentment; nobody can be excessively compliant without developing resentment toward the person who demands his compliance. As a result impulse-driven people find themselves forced to make successive attachments—or else live with a person who complies with their wishes with growing inner resentment. This is the story of many unhappy love affairs and marriages.

People Particularly Susceptible to Oversubmission

Whatever troublemaking attitudes our parents may have had, we are inescapably influenced by them and, on becoming parents to ourselves, use them on ourselves. However, in some instances, circumstances of birth may place extra emphasis on some already excessive attitudes. For example, the first child is more likely to suffer from overcoercion than later children because new parents tend to "push" their first child as a result of their anxiety about being good parents; with later children they feel more relaxed, more confident about themselves as parents and less disturbed by the various developmental phases of behavior.

But the first child, because he is the first at every stage, often meets overcoercion from birth through adolescence to maturity.

Circumstances of birth particularly influence the overly submissive attitude of parents toward a child. Thus, a first child may also be overly submitted to by his anxious parents. Similarly, parents with an only child or a handicapped child often have a difficult struggle to avoid submitting to the child's demands. The same may be said of the last child in a family, a child born after the death of another child, or any child who is "special," such as an unusually gifted child.

The Origins of Oversubmission

The pattern of impulsive behavior, which so often defeats attractive and talented people, originates in childhood. At that time, instead of placing limits on the child's impulsiveness, the parents submit to the child's immature demands. At each significant stage in his development no one can say "no" to his demands and successfully establish limits to his impulsiveness. Not having learned such limits as a child, he has a difficult time forcing them on himself as an adult. If he tries, he loses both the security of the old familiar "at home" feeling of childhood and the immediate satisfactions provided by letting his impulses control him.

Why do parents submit to the whims of a child? Why do they permit this immature youngster to be their master?

The parents answer that they do this out of "love." In this "love" two important factors, which may operate singly or may be combined, are usually involved:

One is that the child occupies a special position in the lives of the parents, particularly that of the mother. As indicated earlier, he may be a first child, an only child or a child "born late" in a marriage or following the death of another child. Often such parents have desperately wanted children and, at last "rewarded," they equate giving in to the child's whims with loving him.

Such parents, seeking the child's happiness and welfare, try to give him "everything his little heart desires." They are most anxious to keep the child's love. With this kind of anxiety, they cannot bear to see a scowl, a look of annoyance or irritation on their baby's face, for it threatens them with the loss of the child's affection. Anxious submission to the child's whims becomes their way of handling him. The child quickly learns that he can get his way if he fusses and fumes. At later stages, when the need for firm limits may be clear to the parent, his temper tantrums force the parent to surrender, even if it means the parent must make great sacrifices and give up his own way of life and his rights. It is in these years that the child learns to use what is a sure-fire weapon with his submissive parent: "If you loved me, you'd do what I say." This forces the parent into proving his love—and nothing counts but full submission to the child's immature demands.

The second factor may also be a primary cause of oversubmission in a parent. The parent may, in some cases, be preconditioned to a submissive role to the child. One such type of submissive mother has a powerful maternalistic nature and tends to "mother" everyone. Even outside their family roles, such women like to serve others and seek constantly "to do" for others, baking pies for next-door neighbors, staying up all night to make cookies for church bazaars, doing a sick friend's housework and cooking. In addition, they like to see everyone happy and smiling, with everything going smoothly, and will make almost any sacrifice to avoid scenes of disagreement.

In their maternal role, they willingly become servants to their children, unwilling to deny them anything—and the children take advantage of them. They cannot set limits on their children's impulsiveness because their satisfaction in life depends on the children's approval of them and their affectionate appreciation.

There are two other types of overly submissive mothers:

1. Those who were reared by very demanding parents who permitted them no rights as individuals and trained them to serve their frequent parental demands. In motherhood such women automatically serve their child with no thought of themselves. Submitting to the child's immature whims is the only way they know of responding to any demanding person within the family.

2. Others have so consistently and persistently belittled their own feelings that they believe they have no rights. They place their children's whims above any needs of their own. While they may see the need to limit the children's impulsiveness, they cannot respect their own rights

sufficiently to stand firm in the face of the children's tempestuous demands.

These parents confuse submission to the child with providing love and security. Loving and respecting the child does not mean capitulating to his every demand. By submitting to the child's demands, his impulsiveness is encouraged and his security is actually jeopardized—because his intense feelings frighten him. He expects and wants his parents to set limits on them.

The Impulsive-Submission Cycle

When the parent confuses submission to the child's whims with giving him security, the foundation is laid for continued impulsive behavior. As the child develops, he finds he can get what he wants by being increasingly impulsive and demanding. Often the parent becomes irritated with these impulsive demands, because his feelings and rights are being stepped on. But instead of his irritation resulting in limits on the child's impulsiveness, it makes him feel guilty. Acting from guilt, which tells him he isn't really a good parent and doesn't really love this "special" child, he redoubles his efforts to give the child love and security—through submission to him. And the child, feeling the parent's irritated withholding of approval, redoubles his efforts to get it in the only way he knows—by increasing his demands.

This cycle repeats itself until the parent at last "blows up" with accumulated irritation and resentment over some minor point—for which the outburst is excessive. At this point both the parent and the child recognize the outburst to be unfair. The parent then feels guilty—and may be accused by the child of being mean and unfair—which results in the parent's redoubling of his efforts to give the child love and security by submitting to the child's demands, and the whole cycle then starts over again.

If you recognize yourself to be an impulsive adult, this understanding of the early origins of your impulsiveness may help you to realize that you must be prepared for a long, arduous effort to check it. In becoming a more useful and helpful parent to yourself, you must refuse to submit to your own impulses as your parents once did. What you need to establish is not a blanket wiping out or denial of your impulses, but a selective control of them.

122

Cultural Factors in Oversubmission

One of the major reasons why impulsiveness is so difficult to check in the adult—and why oversubmission is one of the most common troublemaking attitudes among American parents—is that it is solidly reinforced by cultural influences. This is also why it is not unusual to find parents being both overly coercive and then trying to make up for their constant nagging and pushing by being overly submissive in other directions. Thus, many individuals are coercive toward themselves about their work and impulse-driven in drinking, eating and sexual affairs. Many people give free rein to their impulsiveness in driving—and such impulsiveness in driving nearly two tons of steel at sixty miles an hour on our highways accounts for a high percentage of our accident fatalities.

Much of the confusion among mothers about their children's need for love stems from these cultural influences. In the last twenty-five years thousands of often well-intentioned magazine articles, radio and television programs, dealing with everything from child-rearing and marital problems to our appalling crime rate, have attributed all difficulties to the failure of mothers to give their children "love and security." This material has rarely made it clear that giving your child "love and security" does not mean submitting to his whims.

As a result, mothers have been made so anxious to provide their children with "love and security" that they will make any sacrifice to keep them smiling and happy—or, to put it another way, to avoid establishing limits to their children's impulsiveness. They do not understand that establishing limits is a necessary ingredient in making the child feel secure, that he wants limits established for him and is constantly "trying out" his parents to determine these limits, to see "how far he can go." Establishing limits can be done firmly but respectfully, without harshness or punitiveness.

Threatened with the possibility that they may be raising the next generation of juvenile delinquents if they fail to provide sufficient "love and security," many mothers do not fully understand that in submitting to their child's whims they are creating the pattern of unlimited impulsiveness which forms a major, driving component in delinquent behavior, adult and juvenile. Limits imposed by one's parents create the basis for the self-control which all adults need in order to function and to fulfill themselves. Without such control, the individual is most vulnerable, forever driven by impulse, unable to adapt himself to the situations he will encounter as an adult.

In our culture the adult who is trying to put a brake on his impulsiveness has a difficult time because many of our social customs and other elements in our society are aimed at breaking down such controls and unleashing impulsiveness. For example, much of our advertising is not based on detailing the particular merits of a product but on the theme: "Give yourself a break . . . treat yourself." Whole industries are based on "impulse-buying"—and stores are laid out so that the customer will not buy only what he needs but also what impulse dictates. Everything from the item itself to its packaging and display is aimed at prying loose the impulse to possess. Often the item itself is neglected. The impulse-appeal is made to anxieties, to hopes and dreams. What is implied is that if you own this item, you will be safe, comfortable, healthy, able to take pride in yourself, loved and "somebody."

Our credit buying, with its enticing low, low down payment for everything from table radios and clothes to cars and vacations, aids and abets the impulse to spend, to "give yourself a break." As a result of impulse buying, many families are spending next year's income, according to *Fortune* magazine.

Romantic and sexual impulsiveness is stimulated by all our mass media. Our magazine and newspaper stands appeal to virtually every area of impulsiveness, but particularly stress sexuality. Our songs make impulsiveness seem worthwhile and attractive. Our literature in general, our theater, movies and television dramas—from the Westerns to the more serious efforts—celebrate the impulsive character who "takes a chance." The drive-in theater is often a vast arena of impulsiveness, from what is portrayed on the screen to sexuality in the cars. The snack bar, with its insistent appeals to "treat yourself," thrives on impulsiveness and often provides a major portion of the drive-in theater's income.

If you understand how your impulsiveness is stimulated and exploited by these cultural factors, it will help you in your efforts to establish limits for yourself. This means, inevitably, that you must deprive yourself of some immediate satisfactions and pleasures; it will make you uncomfortable, restless and anxious. Having a long-range goal is necessary to help you feel these minor deprivations are worthwhile. Without such a goal, you will feel the effort is not worthwhile and "backslide" into your old attitudes.

Areas of Impulsiveness

Impulsive people are generally impulsive in most of their activities. It is the way in which they "feel alive." However, many of us have acquired, either through our parents' efforts or through our own experiences, controls and limits in some specific areas—and yet have none in others. And often we do not recognize the impulsive character of our actions because they may have an aura of social approval and, more important, the immediate impulse-satisfaction "feels so good."

The following areas are some of those in which over-submission to one's impulses commonly takes place:

TEMPER TANTRUMS: Impulsively giving vent to one's irritation and anger, often in unduly harsh and abusive terms, on being balked or frustrated in some way is common, even among those who do not consider themselves impulsive. Often cruel and damaging things are said which are later regretted, but cannot easily be repaired. The temper tantrum arises when an impulsive person cannot get his way. He seldom considers the circumstances, but storms and rages against the person he blames for these circumstances. Such temper outbursts show no consideration for the feelings of others, who have often made strenuous efforts to comply and cannot for reasons beyond their control. These outbursts are often the cause of much unhappiness and misery. Many people have learned to use all kinds of devices, from counting ten to taking a walk around the block, to limit their own tendency to indulge in temper outbursts. The temper tantrum must be recognized for what it is: a furious outburst—not a genuine deep anger over some prolonged wrong or infringement. Recognizing this will help you control your expression of anger and irritation over accidents and the occasional frustrations inherent in all living.

Some people use psychiatric concepts of repression to excuse their tempers. "Had to get it off my chest," "I had to explode, I was all bottled up," "I didn't want to repress this feeling so I expressed it" are examples of this. But people do not necessarily function on the same principle as steam boilers. Healthy repression is a good idea when the rights of others are involved.

OBESITY: Many persons who suffer painfully from their obesity are unable to establish limits to their food consumption. In childhood such a person often had a mother who catered to his food whims in an anxious effort "to get food into him." In other instances actual deprivation in other areas, such as loneliness, poverty or lack of status, causes people to overeat. Others, without being deprived, cannot curb their impulse for "a treat." Obesity clinics such as those established in New York City by the late Dr. Norman Jolliffe have revealed that unless a person has a strong motivation to reduce, efforts to curb food intake are often of the same impulsive character as overeating—and invariably fail. These alternating patterns are common among women. According to the New York City studies the strongest motivation for women to reduce is the desire to look more attractive. For men, it is fear of a coronary attack.

Efforts to establish limits are often broken down by our social customs and holidays. "It's Christmas—forget your diet," or "It's Jackie's birthday, you must have another piece," undermine the intentions and efforts of many impulsive people. Fear of offending one's host also contributes its mite—and often all it takes is a mite.

If you are troubled with overweight and are endlessly trying diets, you may be emphasizing the results of being an overly submissive parent to yourself, rather than trying to change this old parental pattern. You must ask yourself what kind of a parent you are being to yourself, rather than what diet will take off weight most quickly.

OVERDRINKING: The impulsive, uncontrolled drinking of many alcoholics may originate in the failure to establish limits in this direction in childhood. Much social drinking, bordering on alcoholism, has this impulsive character. Almost anything can become an excuse for a drink with an impulse-driven person. The tragic lives that have ensued from this inability to say no to one's impulse are too common to merit description. Not having had limits established on his impulsiveness in childhood, the person

126

who drinks too much often flounders helplessly in adult lift without a sympathetic understanding of what his problem really is—a lack of limits, not what is in the bottle. But his inhibitory control is chemically weakened with the first drink.

Many people who have a drinking problem scold themselves—and invite others to scold them too. They do not understand that limits can only be established in a respectful atmosphere that recognizes the struggle. If you understand you are limiting the impulsive child you once were, it will help you be respectful—and this in itself will help create the atmosphere in which you can develop controls.

Alcoholics Anonymous helps an impulsive drinker by establishing group controls until his internal controls are sufficiently strong to take over. This is done in an atmosphere of deep-seated respect. Only in such an atmosphere is the development of firm internal limits possible. By providing a scaffold of "steps" on which internal limits can develop in a respectful atmosphere, AA has helped many people.

SPENDING: Impulsive spending has become more pronounced in recent years with full employment, more leisure time, and with the social security act underwriting some of the costs of old age. At times impulse spending can be constructive and satisfying. But when it makes fulfillment of more serious obligations impossible, it is obviously the cause of much trouble.

The repeated parental submissiveness to the child's impulsive desire for material things, demands that may be backed up with embarrassing temper tantrums in the store, often lay the groundwork for such spending. According to numerous studies and the repeated statements of many marriage counselors, impulsive spending is a leading cause of discontent and quarrels in marriage. Often these quarrels are so bitter they culminate in divorce. Suburban families commonly scold themselves for having "champagne tastes on a beer budget."

When we are children our money is controlled and limited by our parents. If they were submissive to your demands for novelties, you may now be submitting to yourself in the same way. Ask yourself whether, in being a parent to yourself, you continue to spend as a child spends. Are you buying because you need? What is the nature of your need? Is it a genuine need? Or an impulse that may

127

hurt your ability to meet your real needs? Impulsive spending may even fritter away money you need for genuine recreational needs.

GENEROSITY: One of the attractive characteristics of impulsive people is that they are usually generous. Because so much has been given to them by others, they have a great deal to contribute in a psychological sense—and they freely give it. But they are as fickle in their generosity as they are in other impulsive ways. Their generosity cannot be counted upon. Their impulsiveness often leads to failure to reckon on what they owe others—and their generosity may suddenly change to a cold, unknowing stare. Often they impulsively make pledges—and then are astonished to find other people expect them to keep these pledges. In much the same way they form close relationships and abruptly leave them.

"HAVING A BALL": This informal, often spontaneous episodic socializing is the most purely impulsive custom in our society. In it every kind of impulsive behavior, from excessive spending to overdrinking, overeating, expansive generosity and philandering, is not merely condoned but widely admired and approved. People often try to outdo one another in their reckless impulsiveness and it is the subject of endless social conversation, envy and pride. Historically, the "binge" has become "having a ball," and we have given social impulsiveness a form of approval that would have startled an older generation. Because it involves group impulsiveness, because it involves so many areas, because it has won social approval, the true price that many people pay for such episodic impulsiveness is concealed from many of them. The popularity of "having a ball" is a significant indication of the free rein which we are increasingly giving to impulsive behavior.

How Oversubmission Affects Marriage and Sex

Impulsive people rarely marry impulsive people. Both tend to make demands on one another and to refuse to accede to the other's demands. In a way they are blind to the satisfactions of serving and helping others; other people exist, so to speak, to serve them as their parents always did. Impulsive people, if they are initially attracted to one another, quickly discover in courtship that they are expected to serve their partner—and they break off the relationship. Neither is sufficiently tolerant or considerate of the other to sustain the relationship.

This provides some clues to the character of the relationship impulsive persons form in marriage and the types of difficulties that develop. The impulsive person, with his spontaneity and easy ability to form a close relationship, often marries an inhibited and restrained person who is willing to submit to his demands in order to achieve a close relationship. It is the more restrained and inhibited person who sustains the relationship, often with the hope that in time he will acquire the warm, impulsive spontaneity of his partner. But in actuality this hope is seldom fulfilled and the restrained partner finds himself dangling, going up and down with the moods of the impulsive partner and inevitably feeling used by him. "Living with my husband is like living on an emotional roller coaster," one woman said. "He doesn't care anything about how I feel. It's only how he feels that counts—and I am expected to go along for the ride and be happy about it."

Often what holds the more inhibited person in the relationship is his need for a close and affectionate tie. The impulsive person, being always able to count on his parents' submissive love, which is what enables him to make close relationships easily, has no such need. What is life-sustaining to the more inhabited partner is often not very important to him. Puzzled and hurt by his inconsiderateness, the more inhibited partner may try to make demands on the impulsive partner which then are met with temper outbursts or a fickle turning to someone else, abandoning the partner who does not submit to him. These weapons force submission on the more restrained partner. Yet excessive compliance gradually builds up powerful resentments that can result in bitter wrangling and battles. The complaint against the impulsive person is almost standardized: "I'm being used." The complaint of the impulsive person: "He won't do what I say."

What is very difficult for the impulsive person to do, even when he tries, is to find satisfaction in serving others. It is an almost total reversal of his entire childhood experience. If he does anything, he expects to be magnificently rewarded with total submission. It is startling for such persons to find that they can take satisfaction in helping others. "I did something today for someone I've never seen and I can't possibly get anything out of it," an impulsive man once told me, "and it really took some trouble. But what astonishes me is that I feel good about it. I really helped someone other than myself."

The complaint of being "used" is made most frequently in the area of sex. A woman married to an impulsive man often complains: "He is inconsiderate of me and my feelings. He is rough and doesn't appreciate me as a person. He thinks of only one thing: his satisfaction." Another woman says, "My husband treats me like dirt all day, demanding this and that, and then expects me to jump joyously into bed with him at night. I do love my husband but my feelings are too bruised to feel that I owe him anything."

The impulsive woman is similarly inconsiderate of her husband's feelings and uses sex as a weapon. If he does not obey her dictates in other areas, she refuses and rebuffs his sexual advances. As one husband describes his wife: "She gets sore at me, pouts because I don't make enough money to buy every little thing she sees. And sexually she says 'No!' to me unless I do what she says. I sometimes feel I will have to buy her a diamond bracelet to get her to make love with me." Often these marriages are stormy and tempestuous. "If you loved me" is volleyed back and forth with anger, in tears, in rage, in sadness and in plain unhappiness.

To the impulsive person, sex is a sensation to be "lived up" and the partner is only a tool used in attaining the pleasurable sensation. However, because such people are spontaneous, generously giving and showing that they are enjoying the sexual intimacy, the experience itself often may be gratifying to the partner who wants to serve. But because the partner is fickle and impulsive, this intimacy and closeness is not sustained and in time the more restrained partner feels "used." This complaint if voiced directly to the impulsive partner only puzzles him. He lives in his moment-to-moment sensations and he expects others to do the same.

CHAPTER 13

OVERINDULGENCE—
If you are bored and can't "stick to it"

YOUR INDEX OF SUSPICION: *If you are generally bored and listless, unable to become interested enough in activities to participate in them, find yourself "not wanting to do" what others find satisfying, notice you are always complaining, and cannot establish or move toward genuine goals but seem to drift and depend on others to provide for you, you should consider the possibility that your life is being dominated by an overly indulged "inner child of the past."* Overindulgence differs significantly from oversubmission and causes a different type of problem in adult life. While oversubmission results in an active, demanding child-adult, overindulgence creates a bored, passive but discontented child-adult. Many of us have been overindulged in some areas.

Recognizing Your Overindulgence

If you have been subjected to a primary attitude of overindulgence by your parents, you will not have a difficult time in recognizing the effects of this treatment. Such a person has two marked characteristics:

1. He is tired and bored, affecting a blasé and even jaded manner, yet lonely, discontented and restless. This boredom does not come from sophisticated knowledge or experience, but from childhood. Unable to take an interest in most of the activities around him, he often takes a dim view of another's enthusiasm.

2. He expects others to provide for him without his

stirring a finger and yearns for someone to rescue him from his lonely inner boredom, sullen discontent and lack of interest in life. His voice often has a whining undertone of complaint.

In addition, the person suffering from overindulgence cannot initiate and carry out any persistent effort; any effort he does make, however slight and even though it may be self-serving, exhausts him. Often such a person has no recognizable or achievable goal. Yet he wants something, is discontented with himself and the life about him, but cannot find what he wants and move toward it.

Often such people may be intelligent and attractive, but their passive attitude and bored inability to take an interest in life tends to isolate them. In a new environment, such as college or a new job or new town, they may, like everyone else who is new, find themselves stimulated and on the periphery of activities. Unlike more active people who tend to move into such activities, their passive attitude toward life holds them on the periphery, hesitating and delaying as their momentary interests dwindles and dies. Soon they are overtaken by their boredom; they have seen and felt it all before, "know in their bones" that "nothing will happen." They affect a blasé attitude: "It's the same old thing." They see others move into friendly, warm, close relationships, often jealous and discontented but still feeling unable to say the words, make the smiles, take the steps that will lead to such relationships for them. They wait, excusing themselves—indulging themselves— finding reasons for their passivity in everything from politeness to the customary role of the sexes and lack of money.

AN IMPORTANT CLUE—DRIFTING: Sometimes such people, sensing what seems to shut them out of life, make resolutions to change themselves—to seek people out, to smile, to be friendly, to be enthusiastic, to "plunge in." But trying to adopt such an attitude is so exhausting to them that often the effort itself is inadequate. Their general air of tired, dull boredom tends to push people away and often they cannot overcome their seeming inability to take the initiative. In their lonely, discontented and detached way, they wait and watch while life passes them by and they drift on, unable to anchor themselves to anything or anyone. This characteristic drifting is an important clue to an overly indulgent childhood.

People suffering from overindulgence tend to keep mov-

ing on, from job to job, from love affair to love affair—
even from husband to husband, from house to house or
town to town. This process often serves both to keep alive
their expectant hope of finding some way to participate in
life and to conceal from themselves and others their inability to make progress or achieve any satisfying relationships. As they grow older, they tend to become bitter,
complaining and hypocritical about their passive dependency on others.

In a certain sense what the person who has been subjected to overindulgence as a child seeks is not the usual
goal, but "someone who will make life interesting for me."
These people tend to allow others to become responsible
for them—and make the others feel responsible for them.
They are often unable to believe that they can do anything
themselves which would provide them with any satisfaction.
In their loneliness and passivity they cling to others who,
realizing this, feel guilty about wanting to leave them,
though the overindulged person provides little to sustain
the relationship.

CONVERTING FRIENDS INTO PARENTS: In a way, the person suffering from an overly indulgent childhood tries to
make the people who become his friends play the overly
indulgent role of his parents—having them supply everything he needs and wants without his being obliged to
supply anything in return. Such persons have trouble—
and may often confuse themselves and people who try to
help them—with seemingly plausible rationalizations about
objective difficulties which excuse their inability to make
progress. And often, as a result of this prolonged process,
their objective problems have become serious. They are
mired in the bored passivity and dependence that characterized their childhoods. Overindulgence is the only attitude
toward themselves that they have known and often they
frankly wish for the childhood days when they were not
expected to do anything—and could expect others to anticipate their wishes. In psychotherapy, for example, it is
characteristic of such persons to break off treatment because they are expected to modify their dependency on
others through their own efforts. Unless they can recognize their own potential in this direction and are willing
to make that effort, psychotherapy threatens their security
in the old "at home" feeling of childhood—overindulgence.

The following cases may provide you with some insight

133

into the many forms overindulgence may take and help you determine to what extent your own life has been affected by it.

Daddy's Little Girl

At twenty-eight, Linda is an intelligent, seemingly poised girl who, when she is not bored, borders on panic. Born nine years after her brother—which in effect made her an only child—she was constantly overindulged by her gracious mother and lawyer father in their midwestern suburban home. She says that she "had a very, very happy childhood," although she also says that she learned "to perform"—to put on spurts of activity which brought greater rewards from her parents.

When she reached college age, she was mentally bright, equipped with well-polished social manners, but somewhat obese. At college she maintained excellent grades for the first two years, but she was unable to make any close friends; in childhood her suburban home itself and her older parents tended to isolate her from children her own age; in college she couldn't understand the other girls' lack of clothes and money or their working. On the eve of final exams in her junior year she felt it wasn't worthwhile and did not go to the examinations.

Instead she went home and, in tears, told her mother she hated it, hated the other students, the professors, the whole school. She had been bored with the work and couldn't see that it was worthwhile. For the next three years she sat around at home, enjoying the active social life of her parents, spending her summers at a nearby beach. She had few dates because she refused to take much interest in boys she met at the beach—and her overly chubby figure did not attract many of them. What she enjoyed was the gossipy excitement of the "young crowd" and the splendid dinners her mother gave. Often her father brought young lawyers home with him for these affairs and everyone said "bright, interesting things." Otherwise she was mostly bored.

One night, when her father complained of a secretary's resignation, she volunteered her services, learned typing and thereafter went with him each morning to his office. There she was bright and cheerful and acted as a "special secretary" for her father. Because she was "Daddy's little girl" she did not have to punch a time clock, could run out on shopping errands and had no regular duties beyond some of her father's correspondence and extra typing. She "got along" with the other girls in the office but formed no close friendships with them. She generally went to lunch with her father and met more young lawyers and learned enough about law to "laugh and smile at the right time" as they told stories. A few dates resulted, but her bored manner and inability to be impressed kept these relationships from developing beyond occasional theater or dinner dates. Thus six years passed.

Meanwhile, her few young women friends from the beach club had married—and when one of these girls had her second child, Linda had a panic reaction. She was getting nowhere and stormily blamed her parents for not sending her to a better college while having "lavished" money on her brother's professional education in dentistry. She impulsively decided to leave home, get a job, become independent and self-supporting, meet a nice professional man and marry him. With this in mind she moved to a big midwestern city.

There she quickly got a secretarial job and found a girl who needed a roommate to share an apartment. But after her first flush of success faded, she did not like her job. She hated punching a clock, being expected to lunch in an hour, not being allowed to run out on shopping errands. Moreover, the work was a constant pressure and her salary did little more than cover her essential expenses. She was lonely in the big city crowds and at night she was especially lonely. Her roommate was often not home—out on supper dates with her "steady," whom she planned to marry soon. Linda spent her evenings reading and writing letters —often to ask for funds. Sometimes she went window-shopping, which filled her with longing.

Linda hated having to do her share of the bed-making and cleaning up, which her roommate insisted be done "so that Joe won't think I'm a lousy housekeeper when he comes up here." She particularly hated doing her own laundry. All of these things had been done for her at home, either by the maid or her mother. She liked to listen to the disc jockeys' patter and to wait up for her roommate. Then she wanted to be told all about the date, acting very much as her own mother had done. But the roommate, after the first time or two, brushed aside her queries—and wanted to know why the breakfast dishes still weren't done. At other times her roommate happily discussed her plans to get married. In either case Linda, feeling unutterably sorry for herself, would either spend a sleepless night or cry herself to sleep.

Invariably she would be late for work. At the office the personnel manager came down hard on her tardiness, which caused her boss to look into her problems and to view them sympathetically at first. He suggested she try to meet other young people through churches, dances, social organizations or just by going wherever young people were, taking a girl friend along for company. She made some efforts to make friends among girls in the office, but each of them was involved in living her own life. She was bored with their excitements and thought they ought to invite her to their homes; when they didn't, she gave up trying to become friends. They were boring, she said, because their conversation was not interesting like that of the people at home.

Her insomnia—and resultant tardiness—grew worse after her roommate announced she was getting married and moving out. At first this pleased her because it meant no one would harass her about cleaning up the apartment or doing the dishes. Then she realized she would have to get another roommate—and when this proved too difficult, she turned back to her parents for sufficient money to maintain herself "without that stupid girl or another one like her."

Initially she also cheered herself up with fantasies of how she would redecorate and would have young men up for dinner and "interesting talk"; this would keep her awake until dawn—and then she would be late again. She could not hear the alarm clock and when threatened with being fired she had her mother telephone her every morning. This was a forty-cent call—but her mother's voice restored some of the atmosphere of childhood and for a while she got to work on time. However, when her efforts to meet young men collapsed because she refused to acknowledge the existence of "any but professional men," she took to going back to bed after her mother called because she was "exhausted."

She took her dismissal from her job stolidly. It was a stupid place anyhow, she said, and she went back home to another summer of boredom on the beach, with panic and loneliness at night. She blames her parents and the crowd at the beach, and clings to her few married friends who feel sorry for her. "They and their stupid kids bore me," she says, "but I don't know anyone else and they invite me—what can I do?"

The Story of Sue

A good-looking and intelligent girl who dresses casually in expensive clothes, Sue reports on herself as follows: "Two years ago I dropped out of nursing. I thought I might like taking care of people, being of real use to sick people, but I just couldn't go on with it. I mean, it was endless. I felt tired, real tired all the time. After I quit, I decided to study liberal arts.

"Then I met this boy, Ralph, on campus one day. I had known him since high school and gone out with him a few times. Well, he called me up and I started going out with him. He'd call me and I liked him all right because he was someone to talk to—you know, about people we knew. He wanted to marry me and at first I thought that would be nice. But during the summer I thought it all over. I didn't think I loved him enough and I'd have to entertain his friends and family and do all those things. So I canceled our wedding plans and decided to quit college. I stayed at home and while my parents are always worrying and trying to do for me, I just felt more and more bored. When Ralph came home for Christmas he came to see me and we talked. He had been worrying about me, blaming himself for my quitting college, and he got me to go back and take music.

"I still see him but, well, they aren't regular dates or anything. I mean, nothing romantic. He still like me very much and can't see why I called off our wedding. He is very nice to me and does what I want him to, but the truth is, I'm bored sitting around with him. I sometimes wish he'd say or do something exciting. He just tells me what other people told him. Or how he did this or that and what do I think of that. Well, most of the time I just don't care so I just say, 'Mm-mm' or something like that. I realize that I would be awful lonely if he didn't come around but still he really bores me.

"One thing I've noticed is that other people expect you to be all excited over this or that, the team, what somebody said, something new. That's the way Ralph is, everyone is. But I'm not really interested in these things. I'm not interested in whether I study music or not, or even whether I finish college. It's just a way of putting in time instead of sitting at home and putting it in there. I don't want to marry and have all that fuss and be tied down to a home and kids. Years ago I was pretty happy, but it seems the older I get the more tired I get and the less interested I am. I get up in the morning because . . . well, it's another day. But I don't really care. I don't practice my music lessons because it's too much work and the instructor would crab even if I did practice. The only thing I like is sitting in one of the booths listening to music with earphones on. I just shut my eyes and am very still and this makes the notes seem different, so that you really hear each one, but after you've heard a symphony a half-dozen times it bores you too."

Vincent

Vincent was once a physically attractive man who is now somewhat paunchy from overeating and drinking. A quiet man, his obvious loneliness at a company picnic attracted the attention of a chatty, bright girl who had a good job in a subsidiary company. She sat down with him for a few moments, then gaily asked him to dance with her. With a blasé but indulgent air, he said he couldn't see the point—civilization had ruined dancing. He quoted anthropologists and philosophers. The girl, whom we shall call Edie, was impressed—and almost shocked to find he had an unimportant, almost menial job.

On learning he had been to college, she asked why he didn't get a better job. He said he believed you couldn't get anywhere in this company or the business world, for these areas were controlled "by you know whom—and I don't care to know them. And anyhow they are all sheep people, playing follow-the-leader." Edie stayed on, listening, impressed by his blasé answers and provoked in some ways by his indifference to her—for most young men were not so indifferent. When the picnic ended she was both fascinated and determined to polish up this "diamond in the rough," as she thought of him.

She invited him to her apartment for dinner and took pride in the way she drew him out about his lonely childhood as the only son of a well-to-do widow. To her suggestions that he seek a better job, he had endless objections—but she had an answer: she would solve the problem. Thus, when he objected to a better job she had found for him because he didn't have a car, she got him one. When a girl friend suggested that she would be afraid to invite a man she didn't know any better than Edie knew Vincent to her apartment, Edie scoffed. "Vincent was a perfect gentleman," she declared—and he had not made any passes.

This process went on, with Edie solving the problems, until she married Vincent. She even got him to prepare for a career. He decided to become a chiropodist. When he opened his office and his practice developed, Edie was to quit her job. In due time he finished his course, but his practice never developed. "The doctors are all against it because you're not an M.D.," he complained. He decided, while waiting for patients, to take up flying. "Aviation's going to be bigger than ever," he said. "They're going to fly everything that moves by freight."

Edie went on working while he trained to become a pilot; it seemed very exciting to her. But when he had a license, he didn't like the rules and regulations and complained, "They hold my age against me." He then decided to take up air conditioning and heating, but in the end he never went into that business. "You need capital," he said, "and these big companies won't give the little fellow a break."

At this point Edie, who had worked hard and supported him through years of studying, now recognized that he could not persistently carry out any of his plans. She felt bitterly that she had been used by him. She wanted to leave him but she couldn't imagine him existing without her. He sat at home, eating and drinking, going down to "see the fellows" at the tavern in the evenings. He was indifferent and full of excuses about everything. "You have bored me for years with your chattering about this and that. Who cares? Not one word you say is of the least importance to anyone," he would tell Edie if she complained about his going out in the evenings. Yet inwardly he felt very lonely and anxious. He wished at times that he could "just disappear," but he also needed, he couldn't exist without, Edie's comfortable support and sympathy.

The Outlook of the Overindulged

From these glimpses into the lives and problems of persons whose passive, expectant, overindulged "inner child of the past" still dominates their adult lives, you may find clues to help you determine whether your difficulties arise from this pathogenic parental attitude and your continuance of it. Many of us have been overindulged in childhood in some respects, but not in the total way in which these people have been.

The overly indulged person has a whining, complaining attitude toward life and toward being expected to do anything. In World War II many of our young soldiers were accused of "Momism" because they had been overindulged and overprotected in childhood and complained bitterly of everything they were expected to do as soldiers.

Because he expects everything to be done for him, the overindulged person works himself into a self-defeating form of complete paralysis. He tends to view everything that would require any effort from him as impossible or beyond him. Not long ago a young man who has been subjected to extreme overindulgence all his life by his parents wrote out how he felt about life, himself and his problems. Here is what he wrote:

> I am an organism that possesses Life. I am the product of American society. I must conform to certain standards of living because they are deemed necessary and even mandatory by society, i.e., I would not walk down a street without clothes on because society deems clothes necessary. The goal of Life is happiness. How happiness is achieved by different people or is approached by them is different for each individual.
>
> The goal of an individual's life is happiness for that individual.
>
> One therefore must decide what it is that will give him or will help him to achieve happiness.
>
> Happiness to my way of thinking is impossible in this century.
>
> Complete happiness cannot be achieved in this century; only compensatory partial contentment.

Why am I paralyzed? It has to be because I know that it is impossible for me to achieve my goals.

Paralysis might be alleviated therefore if the end-goals are changed.

To achieve any of my goals regardless of how they are constantly modified, education plays a prominent role. I have decided that self-education for me is impossible and the mechanics of receiving guidance in learning from public institutions renders this method impossible, also.

At this point the activity that should be in progress to achieve any end-goals is one of employment. This to me is impossible.

An alternative would be a stay in the ———— State Hospital. This would be difficult but not impossible.

I can only stay at ———— for two months or so.

I am apathetic. My life is hollow, empty. I don't feel like typing any more so I will stop. There's no reason to, really.

This is almost a classic statement of the way the overly indulged person sees life. Anything that would require some effort on his part is "impossible." Yet only making such an effort will change the emptiness of such a life into a feeling of satisfaction and make the achievement of goals a possibility.

Origins of Overindulgence

As is the case with most other troublemaking parental attitudes, overindulgence seems to the parent to be the only way of expressing his "deep love" for the child. He constantly showers the child with toys, goods and services, generally before the child has any real need for these items or expresses any interest in them.

Overindulgence differs significantly from oversubmission. The overly submissive parent responds to the child's demand or whim—and gives in to the child's demand. The overly indulgent parent does not wait for the child to make any demand but provides goods and services long before they are demanded. As a result, the child of overly submissive parents is impulsive, demanding and *active* in pursuing his wants while the child of overly indulgent parents tends to be *passive*, expecting things to be provided, and bored and uninterested because so much is provided.

The cornucopia of the overindulgent parent tends to obliterate any need for the child to make an effort—even a demand—and deprives him of the opportunity to learn to take satisfaction in his own efforts. Such a child never learns to take the initiative or to make persistent efforts, but instead is kept in a dependent, passive state. The child has so much provided for him that he becomes bored or surfeited with what is given to him and is unable to sustain any interest or effort for long. He expects everything to be provided by others and gets along poorly with other children who will not cater to him. Because he cannot sustain his interest in things, he is incapable of amusing himself and expects others to provide entertainment. In adult life this dependent, bored and passive attitude of expecting others to provide for all his needs is continued. When thrust into unfamiliar surroundings where he is forced to rely on his own resources, anxieties and fears may result. But often he is merely puzzled and disappointed that his friends have not provided for him. He tends to "write off" such friends as not being "true."

Certain types of parents are particularly inclined to be overly indulgent:

1. Those who have had deprived backgrounds themselves and are determined that "my child will not have to suffer the way I did" or "go through what I did." Such parents are attempting to fulfill their own childhood yearnings through overindulgence of their children. Often this type of parent has only recently "made it" in terms of material wealth and showers everything from elaborate toys and expensive clothes to summer camps, convertibles, fur coats and vacations abroad on his child. The child drifts passively without having to make any effort, bored and indifferent. He may eventually feel guilty because he has not earned these comforts, i.e., "not suffered the way my parents did." He may also become hypochondriacal, using aches and pains to force others to cater to him.

2. Wealthy parents whose means make it possible to provide everything without any effort on anybody's part —except possibly those of servants. In this social stratum, overindulgence may easily become a way of life because the need for satisfaction through effort is diminished.

3. A third type of parent feels guilty, often without reason, about himself, his past, his marriage or the child,

142

and overindulges the child as a means of assuaging his guilt feelings. Such guilt feelings are often part of the parent's "child of the past," particularly when they relate to sex, or to some circumstance of the marriage or pregnancy.

4. Still another type of parent—and often grandparent —have excessive needs to mother and to give affection, resulting in overindulgence and the surfeiting of the child with affection, goods, services. "Doting," overly affectionate admiration of the child leads to anticipation of all his wants and needs and his overprotection from the usual hazards of childhood. Often incompatibility and sexual difficulties between the parents turn the mother's attention more fully toward the child, resulting in overindulgence and overaffection.

Overindulgence is a way of gratifying very diverse parental needs. But it prevents the development of the child as an active individual who is capable of initiating action and gaining satisfaction from his own efforts.

How the Overindulgence Cycle Operates in Adult Life

While overindulgence in the parent may arise from many different causes and circumstances, the cycle it follows tends to be the same.

The child, when prematurely provided with toys, presents, goods and services which he has neither desired nor sought, becomes passive, bored and expectant. What satisfaction the child might have had in these items if he had desired or struggled for these things is, in effect, sacrificed to the parent's feeling that he is "providing everything" and demonstrating his own deep love for the child. Also sacrificed is the child's need to learn to take the initiative; instead, he learns that everything will be provided by somebody.

Despite his momentary interest in new toys or presents or clothes, the child feels restless, bored, discontented and dissatisfied in a vague and uncomfortable way. The parent, noticing the child's lack of interest and restlessness, tries to meet this dissatisfaction—by more overindulgence. This further develops passivity and indifference in the child. He feels no need to seek anything actively or to make any persistent effort in any direction. Yet he remains dissatisfied and bored in a whining, discontented way. Thus the cycle continues, and in time it becomes very difficult for the child to take the initiative or make any persistent effort.

As an adult, the person who has been overindulged continues this pattern. While this can take the direct form of overindulgence in a certain area, such as eating, its main characteristics include passivity, a dependence on others to provide everything for him, and an inability to carry out a program of work or study. Such a person has, for example, little or no ability to take the initiative. He cannot find a job; he complains and depends on others finding employment for him. On the job he generally does poorly, gaining little saticfaction in it and complaining about everything he is asked to do. His dependence on others is often expressed as a disbelief that he can find any satisfaction in achieving something himself. Boredom, loneliness and discontent pursue him and he blames others for not providing for him—for not rescuing him. He expects everyone to look after him.

"Mind Reading" Complaints

One of the striking characteristics of the overindulged "inner child of the past" in the adult is that such an individual expects others to "read his mind," to know what he wants—and to provide it. When his wishes and desires are not anticipated, as they were in childhood, he complains bitterly—often only to himself initially because he has not learned even to make complaints or demands. Often the person who is expected to provide in this fashion has no inkling of what is expected, but the overindulged "child of the past" expects his wishes to be anticipated and provided automatically.

The complaints of such people have this "mind-reading" character:

"My wife ought to know I like something different for breakfast every morning. It ought to be a pleasant surprise . . ."

"My husband ought to send me to Florida for a few weeks. After all, lots of husbands do that . . ."

"My wife ought to know I like to have my head massaged if I have a headache; my mother always did that for me and I told my wife how my mother used to do it . . ."

"My husband ought to kiss me and tell me how he loves me in front of people . . ."

"My husband ought to do the dishes and let me go to the movies with the girls. He knows I am always tired after cooking and I just hate to clean up . . ."

The overly indulged person who makes these "mind-reading complaints" actually feels he isn't loved because as a child his wants were anticipated by his parents—and this was their standard way of demonstrating their love. Thus, as an adult, he feels unloved if this same pattern is not followed.

Because these expectations are seldom met, such people live in an inner aura of discontent. Unable to act for themselves or even to maintain a passive interest, they are never happy for long. They are unable to achieve any significant satisfaction through their own efforts because effort requires discomfort and at times anxiety. By maintaining their passivity, however discontented, bored and complaining they may be, they continue the overindulgence of childhood. Such persons inevitably whine if forced by circumstances to act. Often, simply by listening to yourself, by "playing back," so to speak, the words and tones you used in critical moments, you can determine whether your "inner child of the past" has been over-indulged. For the voice of the overindulged "child of the past" has a whining, petulant tone that is unmistakable.

When the overindulged child grows up, he has difficulty in coping with the demands of reality. He tends to blame others for his being deprived of the cornucopia of childhood. Because of the close relationships existing in his childhood, he tends to be attractive and charming, moving quickly and easily into close relationships. But he expects as his automatic right the unlimited goods and services he had in childhood. When the relationship requires that he contribute, he cannot comply easily and often turns against the partner in his disappointment. Often the indulged person hurts those closest to him.

Areas of Overindulgence

Nearly all of us overindulge ourselves at times in some areas. However, not all such overindulgence is necessarily the result of overindulgence in childhood. For example, deprivation may cause adult overindulgence whether the deprivation occurred in childhood or in current adult life. The overindulged parent, in attempting to make up the past deprivations of his childhood by indulging his child, is another example.

Generally you can determine whether your overindulgence has its origins in some past deprivation or in the parental pattern of overindulgence in your childhood because the deprivation is clearly discernible and real. For example, a girl who was raised on a farm spent her childhood dreaming of having really decent shoes instead of "hand-me-downs." By the time she had reached adolescence she was determined to have beautiful shoes—and lots of them. When she finished high school, she got a factory job, and every week bought a new pair of shoes until she finally had twenty-odd pairs. This is overindulgence based on a real deprivation.

On the other hand, the overly indulged "inner child of the past" in an adult feels deprived all the time but can rarely point to any genuine deprivation. Moreover, he is not willing, as this girl was, to work in order to indulge himself. He simply expects others to provide for him.

The existence of this over-all attitude may be revealed in certain areas and activities, in addition to difficulties in achieving one's potential and in maintaining stable relationships. The most common areas of overindulgence are:

EATING: While they may have other causes, both obesity and "finicky" eating frequently result from a childhood pattern of parental overindulgence. Many parents, often not overindulgent in other respects, feel that indulging their child with food, sweets, treats and "seconds" in desserts is a way of showing their love. The child's likes and dislikes are catered to and he is often permitted to neglect nutritionally sound foods in favor of treats.

Because food likes and dislikes and eating habits are generally established early in childhood, this form of overindulgence is difficult to control and often reveals the general parental overindulgence of the childhood home. In many cases, because they easily feel imposed upon, persons with such backgrounds use "treats" to "make up" for their assumption of responsibility and their efforts to work persistently. Such efforts make them feel deprived —and overindulgence flows as a natural result.

Unless such persons recognize that their burdens are really no different and no heavier than those borne cheerfully by others, the feeling of deprivation—and its resultant overindulgence—may be unlimited. In many instances, people who have been overindulged in childhood may gain insight into their unwarranted feelings of deprivation in a structured situation, such as the Army, where they can see they are not any more deprived than anyone else and must carry their share of the work as a matter of self-respect.

DRINKING: Alcoholism can be a form of persistent indulgence toward oneself. While it is often complicated by other factors, drinking can be a way in which the person who was overindulged in childhood attempts to overcome his boredom, loneliness and passivity. He then may become dependent on alcohol to "feel alive." However, this effect is only temporary and alcoholism exacts a heavy toll for its momentary alleviation of restless boredom.

SPENDING: The adult whose "inner child of the past" was overindulged is often extravagant and unable to handle money in a realistic way. His interest in new things quickly fades, to be replaced by boredom and discontent. Treating his discontent as his parents did, he attempts to quiet his restless dissatisfaction with new purchases. However, since his ability to work persistently is often severely limited, his earnings are likewise limited, and he must often depend on others for his funds. If they curtail his unrealistic indulgent spending, he becomes embittered toward them. Characteristically, he fritters away money on novelties to satisfy his ever-present discontent rather than preserving it for a long-term purchase.

CLOTHES: Many women, who may not be overly indulgent toward themselves in other respects, can't resist buying clothes. The general cultural attitude that "a woman can't have too many clothes" tends to support such overindulgence as a female trait. Costume jewelry and other novelty accessories are created to cater to this general attitude. By creating the feeling among women that they are deprived if their clothes are "out of fashion" this year, the fashion industry depends almost as much on overindulgence as it does on the need to clothe oneself adequately.

CARS: The average automobile owner actually travels only about 10,000 miles a year, according to transportation studies. From the viewpoint of a transportation engineer, a luxurious 200-plus-horsepower car is not needed for this purpose. Cars are probably one of the more conspicuous examples of overindulgence in American life and one which is only now, with the advent of the small foreign and compact domestic cars, beginning to be questioned. However, so many complicated factors enter into this picture that it would be difficult to decide, except on an individual basis, when childhood overindulgence is playing a significant role in this area.

How Overindulgence Affects Sex and Marriage

We have seen that overindulgence in childhood creates a passive expectancy in the individual that others will lovingly provide for him and that he need do nothing to retain this outpouring of affection, gifts and services. This attitude—if continued in adult life—causes much inner anguish, loneliness and unhappiness in marriage and sexual relationships. In fact, it often results in nothing—neither marriage nor sex.

For example, a man who was subjected to overindulgence in his childhood always took flight the moment it was obvious that his girl of the moment expected, to quote him, "something more than a one-night stand." He wanted love desperately but beyond asking a girl for a date, he could not take the initiative. She had to call him, even arrange where they would go. When the girl took the initiative sexually, he enjoyed it—and then fled. "All these girls want to call it love," he complained. "I hardly know them." Yet he complained bitterly that no one loved him —if they did, they would not expect anything of him.

The intimacy and involved emotional character of marriage and sexual relations often create embarrassing and intensely painful difficulties for both such a person and his partner. In a love relationship, the overindulged "inner child of the past" in the adult expects the same unlimited outpouring of affection, goods and services that he received from his parents. It is in this relationship, above all, that he expects his partner to "read his mind," to know what he wants and to provide it—from meals and other "creature comforts" to sexual caresses.

And, again as in childhood, he doesn't feel any need to provide anything in return. This was not expected of him in childhood—and he doesn't feel or acknowledge his partner's need for attention and affection, either quantitatively or qualitatively. If his partner fails to fulfill his expectations, he is disappointed, annoyed, restless and "frustrated." The person still dominated by his overly indulged "child of the past" is filled with complaints about his partner's failing to give him love, his favorite foods, money, all kinds of ease and comfort and, almost invariably, sexual satisfaction.

He waves aside the fact that he disappoints his partner as "not my business," and may even claim it is something about which he can do nothing. If the partner demands that he contribute emotionally to the relationship and take some responsibility for its maintenance, the person suffering from overindulgence finds his partner "tiresome" and "boring," and seeks ways and means of escaping the effort to make such contributions.

Inevitably his partner, feeling he carries more than his share of the burden and has been cheated and used, may desire to end the relationship—but cannot do so because the overindulged person has become so desperately dependent on him that the thought of terminating the relationship arouses powerful guilt feelings. This is, in brief, often the exhausting and unhappy situation in which both partners find themselves. Such a relationship may continue for years, a kind of mutual enslavement painfully empty of satisfaction and affection.

Or it may end. The "provider," who is capable of taking the initiative, may decide to terminate the relationship. But more often the overindulged person, disappointed at the paltry offerings of the partner and coerced by the partner's expectations, slides away, seeking a new partner who will truly "love" (provide for) him. This phantom partner may be pursued in casual, lonely sexual relationships and shallow socializing. But it is passive pursuit which is doomed from the start because the overly indulged person can rarely take the initiative.

"The honeymoon is over" is the popular expression demanding—or lamenting—the end of overindulgence and the acceptance of adult responsibility. Does the widespread use of this expression mean we all were overindulged in childhood? The answer is no, but nevertheless in nearly all marriage and sexual relationships there is a tendency to seek indulgence. Because affection is generally involved, as it was in childhood, this is an area in which the role of the overindulged "child of the past" can be clearly distinguished from transient indulgence by paying attention to the following aspects:

INABILITY TO INITIATE: While overindulgence in childhood does not explain all forms of passivity, which sometimes arises from factors as diverse as fatigue, fears or even preoccupation, it does significantly affect the ability to take the initiative emotionally, particularly in the giving of affection and in sexual situations. As a result, the adult subjected to overindulgence in childhood is forced to depend on others taking sufficient interest in him and being sufficiently aware of his needs to assume this initiating role and provide him with love and affection—which he desperately needs because his whims in this area are over-developed and pass for necessities.

He may develop, within his generally passive attitude, many winsome, wistfully appealing ways of attracting people willing to take the initiative in this respect. He becomes an artist in attracting sympathy, in explaining how his plight is the fault of others. However, often his general passivity, air of boredom and lack of interest in others cause people whom he likes to move away from him; they feel he is not interested—because he doesn't respond to their overtures. Moreover, the more the overly indulged person is catered to, the more passive he becomes.

Overindulgence in childhood creates the passive expectation that others will, always and automatically, take the initiative in providing love and affection and without anything being expected in return. Often you can determine whether your "inner child of the past" was subjected to overindulgence by your inability to take the initiative emotionally and sexually and by your persistent assumption or expectation that the initiative is always your partner's responsibility. If you depend on your partner in this fashion and feel annoyed if you are expected to assume some responsibility or to contribute equally to the relationship, you have a significant clue to the possibility that you were overindulged in childhood.

DEPENDENCE: Interdependency is characteristic of most stable marriages. However, the person who has been overindulged in childhood has never felt responsible for anyone or recognized any need to consider anyone except himself, and he dislikes the expectation that he should do so. At the same time, his dependence is frank, open and demanding. He blames his partner for whatever happens and takes no responsibility either for himself or for making any contribution to the relationship. Such a person will make a date and then not keep it because he cannot break away from a luncheon where he is surrounded by office friends. The reason for this is that the overly indulged person so desperately needs warmth, affection and approval—and in his view gets so little of it—that he cannot pass up any opportunities for it. His need is so great that in a certain sense he cannot distinguish between the friendly warmth of casual acquaintances and the person to whom he is married. If the marriage partner expects him to return love in like measure and assume responsibilities, the overly indulged person will prefer the casual friends who expect nothing of him but laughter.

Despite such conduct, the overindulged person clings to the partner whom he thus uses by making his dependence keenly felt. "But he needs me so badly, he'd go all to pieces if I left him," has been the closing line of many a woman after a long account of how her partner has exploited their relationship. Overly indulged persons often become expert in the manipulation of others by making them feel guilty or sorry for them. This is the art of the "free-loader," as can be witnessed in any cocktail bar.

You can, by some honest reflective thought, establish the extent to which you are dependent—and whether your attitude toward yourself permits you to assume some responsibility for yourself and consideration for your partner's needs and satlisfactions. But dependence, by itself, is not necessarily the result of overindulgence.

DRIFTING: Overindulged persons, unable to take the initiative—which would give their lives some direction—tend to "go along for the ride" in their relationships with others. Taking no responsibility for these relationships, in a certain sense not really caring about them, they "pass through" many shallow relationships without recognizing that their persistent unhappiness and bored discontent lies in their continued overindulgence of themselves.

Often such persons say they are "merely putting in time." The overly indulged male often has such severe conflict over his masculinity that he may decide he is a "born bachelor." Both sexes have extreme difficulty in maintaining a continuing and meaningful relationship.

As a result of such difficulties, such persons may reduce their sexual relations to casual affairs and give up any attempt to form a close relationship. Disappointed, bored, annoyed with the expectations of others who may try to be affectionate with them, they drift into a lonely, empty existence—simply watching others live. Some may, if circumstances permit, fill their lives with social activities which are essentially meaningless to them. They may never recognize what the overly indulged "inner child of the past" is doing to their lives. Sylvia, for instance, is like this.

SYLVIA AND THREE HUSBANDS: A small but exquisitely beautiful woman who has been married three times, Sylvia creates a first impression that it is impossible for anyone to be so delicate, so fragile and—inevitably—so "doll-like." Her dark eyes and hair and somewhat full, pouting lips give her a hurt, smoldering look that has, in the past, sent high school boys, then college boys, then businessmen, brokers, salesmen, contractors and actors scurrying in pursuit of her with lavish gifts.

Sylvia always expected everything to be done for her. When her first husband, struggling with his career, expected her sympathetic understanding and support, she could not provide it. Her parents, who had disapproved of her marrying, because her husband was not already a successful businessman and because it deprived them of their "pride and joy," subtly undermined both her first two marriages. They backed up Sylvia's overindulgent ways as her "right." Belatedly, her mother realized that Sylvia could never be happy if she continued to depend on her parents. As a result her second marriage lasted longer than her first. But eventually her second husband grew tired of being called upon to admire her, to excuse her from all duties and effort and to supply the emotional content of the marriage—which Sylvia looked upon as "making me happy." Making her husband happy was something she did not think of; people existed to make her happy.

Used to "nothing but the best," Sylvia is extravagant. It was on this score that her first two marriages broke up. Her parents, now growing old, are worried about this and so is Sylvia. Together, without a word being said about it in a direct sense, they have contrived a way of trying to prevent its happening a third time—by making her husband her father's business partner. While this has served to relieve certain economic aspects of Sylvia's marriage, it has not altered or prevented her overindulgence toward herself. Her husband is irritated with her continual whining boredom. Within the family business he has no real power.

Her childhood was not much different from this. Her parents, well-to-do and successful, provided everything they could think of for Sylvia and her sister. Her sister, without Sylvia's startling beauty, did not have their rapt attention; she has never attracted men and lives a tired, bored existence alone. In school and later in college, Sylvia, who does not like to work and in fact does not know how to, got either her parents or boys to do everything for her, from carrying her books to doing her homework. She barely passed through college, shamelessly copying her examination answers from boys who were wild about her. She didn't want to go to college anyhow, she says, except for the social life.

She has used her small physical stature to emphasize traditional conventions such as that which calls for men to open doors. Pretending to be much weaker than she really is, she tries to avoid lifting a finger. The only activity she likes is dancing; although she barely comes above waist height, she simply collapses dreamily and hangs onto the man. She likes best of all to sit at a table on the edge of a dance floor and be waited upon, admired, catered to, obliged—and to watch the effect of her beauty on others. Her face has, with all its beauty, a delicate but indelible expression of discontent which sends those about her, particularly men, hurrying to do for her, hoping to win her affection.

All three of her marriages have been unhappy, mainly because her husbands have indulged her. Her present husband increasingly feels he has been "taken." He talks to

Sylvia of their setting out on their own in another town; she discards this as foolishness, something not to be thought of because "this is where all my friends are." He is also tired of carrying the entire burden of the relationship. For instance, while initially he was sympathetic to Sylvia's story of the breakup of her first two marriages and classed her husbands as mean, demanding brutes, he now says, "At last I understand why the hell they got out!"

Sylvia tries to get her husband to "relax and enjoy yourself," by which she means "indulge yourself as I am doing." Despite this encouragement from her, he still strives "to make something of myself." But if his self-contempt for his role as a "gigolo" continues to grow, he may yet walk out. Sylvia knows this, but "Ken and his complaints bore me," she says. "He never had it so good." What really worries her is her fading beauty, and sometimes she wishes she would meet a man "who would absolutely make me do everything he wants and beat me if I didn't." As a bored, overly indulged child, she used to have similar wishes to be made to do things. But no one did so then—and no one is likely to do so now. Although her life is now filled up with meaningless social activities and her main satisfaction is the narcissistic watching of the effect of her beauty on others, she continues to hope that someone, even if he beats her, will make her live. She still looks to others, rather than her own efforts, for satisfactions.

Changing the Pattern of Your Overindulged Child of the Past

It is difficult to feel much sympathy for people like Sylvia who have been overindulged, unless you realize that this pattern of overindulgence was something imposed on them in childhood by their parents. They had nothing to do with it. Nevertheless, and in spite of the passive clinging role they may play, they are discontented and often filled with contempt and hatred of themselves and their passivity.

When they come to realize that they are indeed continuing the old overindulgent attitude of their parents toward themselves, they face a difficult and anxious inner struggle. They must not yield to the impulse to give way to fruitless self-criticism and self-contempt, but learn to accept in a respectful way the dissatisfied demands of the overindulged "child of the past" for more indulgence.

Then, taking the role of a kind but firm and really helpful parent, they must impose strict limits on their tendency "not to bother," to overindulge, to depend on others. They must struggle to participate actively in their relationships with others—to return what they get, rather than to lapse into the old bored passivity.

By proceeding patiently and persistently, just as a parent teaches an infant to walk, without harsh self-criticism or self-belittlement, they can begin to find deeper satisfactions than they have known in their old passive and dependent role.

In adopting this new parental attitude toward themselves, a difficult struggle cannot be avoided. In it they lose the security of the familiar old "at home" feeling they had in their passive, dependent role—and must assume responsibilities and make efforts which in the past have always seemed "tiresome" hardships. They must recognize there are no quick rewards in this inner struggle. The initial satisfactions may be long in coming.

But just as a child who has always been carried can learn to walk, it can be done.

CHAPTER 14

HYPOCHONDRIASIS—
If you worry constantly about
your health

YOUR INDEX OF SUSPICION: *If you cannot participate in activities because you do not feel well, are easily fatigued and are constantly "doctoring" yourself even though your physician cannot find a basis for your complaints, and you connect your body's sensations and functions with the possibility of illness, you should strongly suspect that your "inner child of the past" was subjected to parental hypochondriasis—a disabling preoccupation with aches, pains and disease.*

A large proportion of the millions of dollars which Americans spend on patent medicines, vitamin preparations and laxatives each year is really paid in tribute to the complaining "child of the past" who continues the fearfulness of his parents toward "germs" and the possibility of disease. But the financial aspects are minor compared to the misery and unhappy incapacitation of thousands who, although seemingly well, feel so weak, sick and tired that they cannot enjoy life.

Such preoccupation with disease and self-"doctoring" can lead to genuine illness. In Denmark, for instance, the consumption of pills, sedatives, tranquilizers, headache powders and other medications had reached such proportions by 1962 that a Danish medical journal* reported it second only to heart disease in causing hospitalization.

* *The New York Times*, January 27, 1962.

Recognizing Hypochondriasis in Yourself

In determining whether your complaints are realistic or hypochondriacal, the first step is to have yourself examined thoroughly by your physician with special attention to your specific complaint. This establishes a base line against which your complaint can be objectively evaluated.

If you have any tendency to be hypochondriacal, you have probably already done this—perhaps several times—without establishing any organic cause for your complaint. You may even believe the examination wasn't thorough. It is not unusual for patients, found free of physical signs of illness, to demand time-consuming tests, medications and even surgical intervention. Unfortunately, as Dr. R. L. Faucett of the Mayo Clinic has pointed out, "Physicians frequently allow themselves to be coerced into collaboration with the patient's wishes and demands."* When this happens the doctor is yielding to his own anxiety to be a "good" doctor and his frustration at being unable to find the cause of the mysterious and usually vague symptom.

How You Treat Yourself: How you feel is fundamental in determining how you treat yourself—what kind of a parent you are to yourself. The person who has been subjected in childhood to the anxious, fearful "sick room" atmosphere created by hypochondriacal parents can rarely escape exaggerating his minor aches and pains. He is full of complaints—his head aches, his stomach rumbles, his bowels didn't move on time this morning, his hands are cold, his feet hurt, his back is tired, his eyes bother him, his knee feels strained, his nerves are on edge, he feels a draft. Most of all he feels sick and tired.

Because he believes he is either sick or about to get sick, such a person treats himself gently and tenderly. He worries anxiously over his entirely normal organ functions, exaggerating the importance of any seeming irregularity, warding off possible illness and his chronic fatigue with tonics and pills. On growing up, the person subjected to hypochondriasis remains the child he once was, taking care of himself in the same anxious, fearful way his parents

* R. L. Faucett, *Minnesota Medicine*, 41:691, 1958.

did. As a result, such a person feels he "can't do" very much, often lamely abandoning many activities which others consider life itself, including work, sex and recreation.

WHAT SETS THE HYPOCHONDRIAC APART: We all have times when we are not feeling well or "up to par," when we are plagued with colds, headaches, muscle pains and fatigue, and when we feel worn out and sorry for ourselves. Despite this, most of us try to keep going. But the person subjected to hypochondriasis in childhood both exaggerates his aches and pains *and* gives in to them. He surrenders himself to his vague symptoms, allowing them to force him out of participation in life's activities.

It is this acceptance of minor aches and pains as incapacitating that markedly sets the person subjected to hypochondriasis in childhood apart from persons whose parents were not overly fearful of disease—and health. In time fearfulness of health becomes an important component of persistent hypochondriasis because, if actual organic disease or malfunction can be ruled out, the person suffering from this attitude then develops anxieties about his ability to function as a healthy individual. He feels weak and helpless because he has to assume responsibility for himself which, as a child, he never had the opportunity to do. Therefore, he often develops new and different but nearly always vague symptoms as rapidly as the old ones are shown to be without any organic basis. The reason for this is that he has learned from the emotional atmosphere of his childhood home to expect himself to be sick—and not to expect himself to be healthy and vigorous. Thus, feeling sick and ailing and constantly ministering to these feelings seems much more comfortable than participating in normal activities—and health becomes a threat.

If you find yourself expecting yourself to be ill, looking for aches and pains or other symptoms which will make it impossible for you to attend some social function or take a job, you have a strong indication that your "child of the past" was exposed to hypochondriacal influences.

Often the person who is hypochondriacal realizes his aches are exaggerated—and he is ashamed of his pills, powders and inability to function. We have all seen, in cartoons, movies and television shows, satiric caricatures of the fears and complaints of the pill-swallowing hypochondriac. While these complaints may be objectively baseless, what is often overlooked is that these exaggerated aches are real and painful to the hypochondriac. Unless he understands their origins in the attitudes of his parents and the mechanism by which he continues these attitudes, the person so afflicted has little chance of either escaping or combating them. Generally he must give in to them and "take care" of himself.

Because their aches and pains are real to them, many people are relatively unaware of their hypochondriacal tendencies and how they use them. Only by taking note of how many things they "can't do"—and how often they attribute this to ill health—can they begin to realize the total effect this old parental attitude is having on their lives. One woman described her realization of this as follows:

"I just listened to myself one day—listened to all my complaints, what I told myself when I got up, what I told my husband, what I told my neighbors, what I told my aunt, what I told my children—and that evening I wrote them all down on a sheet of paper I titled, 'The Day's Complaints.'

"I listed everybody I spoke to—and what I complained about. When I then went over the list, I realized I was exaggerating. Why, I even found that I had told the postman I have been having trouble with my eyes. I realized that if all these things were wrong with me, I belonged in a hospital.

"Yet if anybody had said to me, 'Geraldine, we're taking you to the hospital,' I'd have been startled—and refused to go. I wasn't *that* sick!"

Why, then, are the lives of so many physically well people filled with a kind of murmur of complaint of "poor health," vague aches, operations and misery? In most cases, this murmur merely re-echoes the atmosphere of their childhood home, comforting them with the security of the familiar, the old "at home" feeling. In addition, because illness is actually common and deserves to be respected, the person who complains gains the sympathy and indulgence of others. Yet these satisfactions are small compared to the gains in self-esteem which can be achieved through one's own efforts.

If you suspect that you exaggerate your aches and pains you need to examine two specific phases of your life:

YOUR CHILDHOOD: What were the attitudes of your parents toward illness? Did they enjoy good health? Did they complain of poor health? Did they require you to take special precautions against cold or rainy weather, precautions that exceeded those of your schoolmates? Did they often keep you home from school because they thought you were sick? Can you recall specifically how they told you about "germs" and what measures they took to protect themselves and you from them? Do you recall using your parents' concern about your health to escape from chores, schoolwork or social obligations? A physician may properly be said to be preoccupied with the struggle against disease, but his children are not necessarily hypochondriacal. Would you now, as an adult, characterize your parents' concern about health—their own and yours—as being excessive?

YOUR PRESENT LIFE: Are you beset with aches and pains which seem to have no organic basis? Are you always worried about your health? Do you make dates with the reservation "if my health permits" in most instances? Do you take better care of your health than most people? Do you worry, when you learn of someone you know having a disease, that you may also have contracted it? Does your "poor health" keep you from doing things you would like to do? Do you complain a lot? Are you regularly taking any patent medicines? Is your medicine chest stocked with remedies for all sorts of ailments? Do you imagine, on reading an article about some disease or seeing television shows about some aspect of medicine, that you have the problem described? Do you "doctor" yourself with folk remedies?

If from your answers to the questions about your childhood you realize that your parents were overly concerned about health and persistently preoccupied with the hazards of disease, you will probably find that you have continued their hypochondriacal attitudes—and the evidence will be in whether you answer affirmatively most of the questions dealing with your present life.

Hypochondriasis in a Famous Family

Intelligence, social status and economic security can neither prevent hypochondriasis nor alleviate it. In fact,

160

when these aspects of life are free of anxiety, fear of ill health may become somewhat exaggerated. In a general way life consists of conflicts and problems. When economic and status stability are assured, these conflicts and problems often center about health, increasing the relative amount of attention paid to it.

This is clearly documented in the history of the family of Charles Darwin. It demonstrates how parental hypochondriasis can be passed from generation to generation even in a family that is included in all familial studies of genius. Darwin, whose brilliant studies of evolution made him one of the outstanding scientists of the nineteenth century, was markedly hypochondriacal. Even when his health was good, he constantly wore a shawl to protect him against drafts. He and his wife had ten children, of whom seven lived to adulthood. Of five sons, three had careers of brilliant distinction and a fourth was a leading geneticist and president of the Royal Geographical Society. Yet of the seven, only two escaped hypochondriasis and nearly all of them, adopting the household symbol of ill health, took to wearing shawls in adult life years before they died. This "inheritance" of hypochondriasis has been documented by Dr. Douglas Hubble in a series of articles in the British medical journal *Lancet.** From diaries, letters, autobiographies and a biography of the family, Dr. Hubble has provided a clear picture of the transmission of this pathogenic attitude.

Charles Darwin was the son of a well-known Shrewsbury physician, Robert Darwin, an authoritarian man whose confident manner made him a wealthy practitioner at a time when scientific medicine was just beginning. Although kindly, he brooked no opposition to his views and he liked to talk for hours—with no replies expected or ventured. Charles was his fifth child and Mrs. Darwin died when Charles was almost nine years old. Charles's education was handed over to his sister and Charles reports that he would stand outside her door asking himself: "What will she blame me for now?"

In his benign but highhanded way, Dr. Darwin decided his sons should be physicians. He sent both Charles and his brother Erasmus off to medical school in Edinburgh although neither wanted such careers. From all accounts, it may properly be inferred that they grew up in an at-

* Douglas Hubble, *Lancet*, 2:1351, December 26, 1953.

mosphere which was overly concerned with disease, at a time when little was known about it scientifically, and in which there was a constant checking for symptoms. A visiting cousin wrote of the air of restraint about the Darwin household: "We dined at half-past one, dressed afterwards and sat about three hours expecting the tide to come in about dark, and a rather stiff and awful evening it was." (The "tide" presumably was Dr. Darwin and his two-hour monologue on life, death, patients and disease.)

The death of the Darwin mother doubtless contributed to the children's feeling of helplessness and fear. While both Charles and Erasmus dutifully finished their medical schooling and were qualified to practice medicine, neither ever did so. According to Dr. Hubble, "each was deterred from strenuous effort by knowledge that Robert [their father] intended to provide for them." Upon graduation, Erasmus retired into quiet bachelorhood. Charles, in a passage revealing the family's preoccupation, wrote of him: ". . . his health from boyhood has been weak and as a consequence he failed in energy." But it was not so weak as to prevent his living for seventy-two years.

After medical school Charles's curiosity and reflective mind, untroubled by the need to earn money, led him into the study of geology and nature and eventually to the question of how the various species originated and evolved. This, in turn, led him to the now famous voyage of the *Beagle*. In his autobiography Darwin reports that while waiting for the *Beagle* to sail, he developed heart palpitations. Although thoroughly frightened and miserable, Charles did not give in to his alarming symptoms. He kept them a secret and decided against seeing a physician lest he be told he could not make the voyage. Thus, he forced himself to go in spite of his fears—and the voyage provided him with observations that were to lay the basis for his famous work on the origins of the species.

After his successful voyage, he somewhat confidently married his distant cousin, Emma Wedgwood, whose family was already a well-established fixture of the English upper middle class with a fortune made from the fine china bearing its name. Charles turned happily to the study of the specimens gathered on his voyage.

But when his wife became pregnant, Charles became ill. He complained of insomnia, stomach aches and drafts. He took to his bed and for the next two years was incapable of any sustained work. Everything wore him out. Emma sympathetically ministered to his aches and pains. Because of his ill health they withdrew from all social activities. As Dr. Hubble points out, "Thus early in their married lives, the lifelong roles . . . were determined. He was the invalid incapable of social activity . . . and she was the perfect nurse."

Darwin's physician father decided that Charles could regain his health only by years of living quietly in the country. This advice prompted the family to move to a country estate, Downe House. With money provided by both the Darwins and Wedgwoods, this refuge offered seclusion from friends and callers, quiet, and full indulgence of Charles's twin preoccupations—his scientific work and his health. In this lonely situation, comforted by his wife and delighted with his children, Darwin slowly regained his strength. He read, studied, classified and thought a few hours each day, working in a small laboratory. On days when he felt strong enough, he was able to walk in the garden.

But he was rarely able to abandon his shawl and the question of his health dominated the household. He looked well but he constantly complained of sleepless nights, upset stomach, and of feeling "seedy," weak and fatigued. He never ventured a trip to the scientific circles of London or to visit anyone. His friends, believing his robust appearance better evidence of his health than his endless recital of agonizing nights, diagnosed his difficulties as hypochondriasis. "Everyone tells me that I look quite blooming," he wrote, "and most think I am shamming."

But his wife never complained. Although she was frequently pregnant and carrying the burden of running the increasingly large household, she sympathized with his difficult struggles with "poor health." Mrs. G. Raverat, an American who married one of the later Darwins and has written a biography of the family, *Period Piece*, has said, "I have sometimes thought she must have been rather too sorry for her family when they were unwell." Dr. Hubble sums up their relationship in this way: "The perfect nurse married the perfect patient."

During his sleepless nights Darwin occupied his mind with scientific speculations and organized his theories and then checked them against his laboratory observations in the morning. He read and he wrote, but his fatigue and general feeling of ill health kept him from participating in

the active discussions of scientific groups.* Scientific friends
came to see him; he never felt well enough to go to see
others. He finally put together and published his monu-
mental work only after a friend, who had been urging him
to do so without success, revealed that another scientist
was about to publish similar ideas. His isolation from others
made Darwin both innocent and insensitive; he was unaware of the controversy his ideas would provoke. When
his work was attacked, he made no attempt to defend it;
he left its defense to scientific friends like Thomas Huxley,
who fought furiously for him against bitter opponents.

As a father, Darwin was affectionate and overly indulgent. If on occasion he spoke brusquely to one of his children, he could not sleep in his regret. He once astonished
his eldest son by begging forgiveness for a reprimand. In
contrast to his wife, who was sympathetic but calm and
practical, Darwin had an excessive wish to love and be
loved and was in all respects a doting and sentimental
father.

Darwin's constant complaints about his health, fear of
drafts and germs were absorbed and imitated by his children. So great was his anxiety when one of the children
became ill that the child begged he be kept out of the
sickroom because his hand-wringing distress was harder
to bear than the illness itself.

Only two of the children escaped obvious hypochondriacal fears. Annie, the oldest girl, died when she was ten
years old. After that all the children were tremendously
influenced by their father's attitude. Four years later, Henrietta, then aged twelve, became ill with an undiagnosed
fever. She was sick a year, convalescent another year,
and an invalid the rest of her life. Her doctor recom-
mended breakfast in bed, a suggestion she followed until
she died at eighty-six.

The two children who seemed to have escaped hypochondriasis were Elizabeth and William. Elizabeth was
mentally retarded and dependent on others all her life in
any case. William, apparently because he was sent off

* Dr. Jay Tepperman comments: ". . . Darwin used the illness to
insure himself the kind of privacy he needed in order to concentrate
on his great problem. He sat on no committees, mowed no lawns,
washed no dishes, attended no Cub Scout pack meetings. He worked
—only two or three hours a day, according to many accounts. But it
is hard to believe that he didn't spend the rest of his waking hours
brooding about some facets of the species problem." (*Perspectives in
Biology and Medicine, 4*:445, 1961.)

when he was twelve years old to a boarding school where other attitudes toward health prevailed, never developed the family's disabling preoccupation.

George, later a professor of astronomy at Cambridge, "inherited" his father's hypochondriasis and symptoms—"a constant strain of ill health of a most wearying nature." According to Mrs. Raverat, he married an American girl "who did not enjoy ill health, wanted him to get well, and he did get very much better." Another son, Leonard, went to Woolwich Military Academy, which lessened the influence of his father; nevertheless he resigned from the army at the age of forty because "his health was not very good." Yet he lived to be ninety-three years old. Sir Francis Darwin, knighted for his brilliant scientific achievements, suffered from depression all his life, "his form of the family hypochondriasis," according to Dr. Hubble.

Sir Horace, who founded a famous scientific instrument company, was frail and so slow to develop that he was initially considered retarded. Of Horace, later president of the Eugenics Society, Leonard said, "Of all my brothers, Horace was the one whom I should have thought the least likely to make a success in life." The general hypochondriacal attitude of the family is revealed in what his mother wrote of Horace when he was recovering from an illness when he was *thirty-eight years old:* "I have seen the dear old man. His poor hands are very transparent." And Henrietta, a lifelong invalid, took a genuine delight in the management of illness. "Anybody being ill is like champagne," she once wrote.

William, whose health was sound and who had escaped the disablement of hypochondriasis, nevertheless shared the family fear of drafts. At his father's funeral in Westminster Abbey, he felt a draft—so he sat through the service with his black gloves covering his bald head!

Commenting on this remarkable family, Dr. Hubble says: "Here was economic security to the degree which makes the modern eye envious, and here was love in abundance—man's plenty and God's plenty. Security and affection, psychologists of whatever school are agreed, are the twin needs of growing children; with these endowments all evils are abated, and when they are lacking, no gifts can take their place. The records of Downe House show once again that children can have too much of a good thing. Affection in excess arouses anxiety and security in itself breeds a fear of insecurity."

Superficially, there might seem to be some truth in Dr. Hubble's closing generalizations, but actually he is making the same mistake that many parents make—that of calling an excessive parental attitude "love and affection." What really plagued the Darwin household and its children was an attitude toward disease that was in itself unhealthy and pathogenic, based on fear and the disabling indulgence of symptoms. In addition, it was coupled with overindulgence, both in the case of Charles and his brother Erasmus and in that of his children too; in the case of Charles and Erasmus, it was further complicated with overcoercion, which forced them into an unwanted medical education.

When one speaks broadly of "too much of a good thing," as Dr. Hubble does, one beclouds the problem and prevents recognition of the specific pathogenic parental attitudes, attitudes that are bound to make trouble. When these specific parental attitudes can be discerned and sorted out, they can—with genuine effort—be reduced, modified, controlled and altered to permit a fuller participation in life and the real development of an individual's full potential. The real question is whether you will continue the pathogenic attitudes of your parents when you become a parent to yourself.

It is not a question of "too much love and affection" creating anxiety, as Dr. Hubble implies. Excessive and pathogenic attitudes usually appear to the parent as a form of "love and affection," true concern for the child's well-being. This is the guise which perfectionism, overcoercion, oversubmission, overindulgence and other such troublemaking attitudes often take. Failure to recognize specific pathogenic attitudes results in confusion and often in a breast-beating attack on the problem which does not alleviate it.

For example, an attack on "love and affection" seems to deny these human needs without clarifying either what is wrong or what can be done. In this country, during World War II, our young soldiers were accused of being "Mom's boys." Oversubmission, overindulgence and hypochondriasis were popularly lumped together as "Momism" and attacked as evil. Thousands of bewildered young soldiers and anxious mothers were stunned and hurt by these charges. The attack neither clarified the problem nor helped them to understand there was something they could do about these specific attitudes—both as soldiers and as mothers.

166

There is nothing wrong with love and affection—except when these terms mask troublemaking attitudes.

Areas Affected by Hypochondriasis

Hypochondriasis tends to disable to the extent to which the person suffering from it permits it to do so. The capacity for work is perhaps hardest hit, but the ability to function socially and sexually is usually involved.

We have only the faintest glimmerings of what hypochondriasis costs us or its true extent. But nearly every physician knows patients who have invalided themselves for "heart disease" which cannot be found. One of the great educational efforts of the American Heart Association has been to teach physicians not to utter a meaningless "M-m-mm" while applying a stethoscope to a patient's chest because so many patients immediately decide this means they have heart disease and that the kind doctor doesn't want to tell them the truth. Often on the strength of that "M-m-mm," sometimes because they also have palpitations arising from anxiety and tension, many patients have restricted their activities, given up work and settled down to hopeless lives.

What is often difficult for the healthy person to understand is that the person suffering from hypochondriasis is not "shamming," as Darwin puts it. His aches and pains and other symptoms, such as fatigue and dizziness, are real to him and cannot be overcome with scoffing or pep talks.

Some of us, while generally free of disabling hypochondriasis, suffer from this type of attitude unnecessarily in specific situations. This, too, is a result of hypochondriacal fears expressed by parents about such situations. For example, some people are fearful about getting their feet wet and cannot go out in the rain without rubbers, raincoats, umbrellas, feeling certain they will contract pneumonia. Others have similar fears about washing their hands before eating, about insects, about wearing hats, about exerting themselves to the point of perspiring.

While such precautions may be generally sound, they sometimes restrict actiivties unnecessarily or form a block against enjoyment. For example, it is a sound health procedure to wash one's hands before eating. But at times

167

this may be very impractical or even impossible, as on a picnic. But for some people the absence of this ritual is disturbing. If they do not eat, they are hungry—and if they do, they are uncomfortable, "woozy," and their stomachs may actually become upset.

Because hypochondriasis drastically limits the amount of energy available, it hits hardest in the following three areas:

WORK: The person suffering from hypochondriasis has his greatest difficulty in working. He feels so sick, weak and fatigued that he either is absent from work frequently as "sick" or does barely enough to retain his job. He rarely performs in an outstanding way although occasionally there have been scientific and literary masterpieces turned out by hypochondriacal persons like Darwin and Proust who, by creating an environment that accommodated their hypochondriasis, were able to work. Generally speaking, however, such a person cannot sustain a daily work routine.

Because it is necessary to earn a living, many persons suffering from hypochondriasis try to save their energies for work. Then, equipped with patent medicines and often demanding sympathy from their fellow workers and their families, they struggle along. But because they do poorly and generally regard work as a terrible burden, they rarely feel any satisfaction in their efforts. Instead work is regarded as a daily agony that must be endured, and just as they exaggerate their symptoms, aches and pains, they exaggerate the hardships of the work.

SOCIAL ACTIVITIES: Because of his poor health, the person suffering from hypochondriasis cannot satisfactorily participate in social affairs. He often wishes he could but he "can't count on" his health. Therefore, the social life of such persons is restricted. However, if other people will take the initiative and come to see them—and listen to their recital of misery sympathetically—they find it very satisfying. Many hypochondriacal men and women never leave the parental home on attaining physical maturity. They seek to remain under the protection of their hypochondriacal parents. Yet often the rationale offered for their continuing to live at home is that they are "taking care of" their parents.

How Hypochondriasis Affects
Sex and Marriage

In many instances hypochondriasis prevents marriage. Potential partners, listening sympathetically to the complaints of the person suffering from hypochondriasis, dimly realize that in marriage they would be called upon to play the role of sympathetic nurse rather than that of mate. Moreover, the hypochondriacal person's passivity and inertia, while "explained" by the complaints of ill health, make it plain that he cannot be expected to take the initiative and carry his share of the relationship. All this tends to push the potential partner toward a search for a less complaining and more capable person. However, the "nurse" role frequently appeals initially to the maternalism of many young women, and to the gallantry of young men. Later, when they are burdened with a hypochondriacal partner and realize how it affects their own opportunity for happiness, they may feel deprived of normal marital satisfactions and exploited.

Thus, within marriage, hypochondriasis in either partner generally results in a deterioration of the relationship, often including the complete curtailment of sexual activity. The hypochondriacal woman, with her endless complaints of "not feeling well enough" to participate in social affairs, of headache, backache and fatigue, may also find sexual intercourse painful, even intolerable. Or she may consider it her "duty" and comply without pleasure or satisfaction. Her husband, cast in the role of tormentor by her martyr-like compliance, feels frustrated, inadequate, unhappy, and may become resentful and embittered. He wants her "poor health" cleared up—but no amount of "doctoring" seems to help, which causes further deterioration in the marriage.

Often the hypochondriacal wife may be unable to do her housework, cooking and shopping. This, too, causes deterioration of the marriage relationship. Often the husband is forced to take over the housework. Similarly, the wife of the hypochondriacal man may be forced to earn the living.

The chronic, inexplicable and apparently unrelievable character in the shifting symptoms in hypochondriasis creates a situation which, except in wealthy families, differs significantly from that created by a genuine organic illness or crisis. The impact of a genuine illness can be met, as thousands of people are demonstrating daily, by both partners without any significant deterioration in the relationship.

In a marriage in which one partner is suffering from hypochondriasis, guilt often plays an important role in continuing the relationship. The hypochondriacal partner realizes the heavy burden and denial of satisfaction placed on the partner and feels guilty and depressed about it, adding to existing strains. Similarly, the healthy partner may want to abandon the relationship because of his frustration and the unequal burden placed upon him, but he does not do so because he feels guilty about wanting to abandon someone who is "sick." Thus, such marriages, although often hotbeds of festering frustration, misery, guilt and unhappiness, may continue for years.

If the man is hypochondriacal, his complaints and fatigue not only prevent him from providing a secure home and helping his wife, but he seldom performs satisfactorily at his job. He often is not advanced, is frequently "dropped." In many cases the hypochondriacal male maintains only a very tenuous grip on his job through the constant sympathy of his wife—and his fear that he will lose this support if he should lose his job. He expects and demands that he be given extra consideration at home.

In some respects hypochondriasis is a form of overindulgence and resembles it. The hypochondriacal person's passivity and expectation that others will provide for him are duplicated in the pathogenic parental attitude of overindulgence. However, in place of the boredom and lack of interest characterizing the overly indulged, the hypochondriac uses the possibility of disease as an excuse for his passivity. He seeks sympathy constantly, manipulating others by stimulating guilty feelings in them. But he does not suffer from the inability to sustain his interest which is characteristic of the indulged person, and feels keenly his incapacitation.

The Case of Mrs. Rae

What is easily overlooked in hypochondriasis is that the pains, aches and fatigue are felt as acutely as they would be if they actually were caused by some organic disorder. This is clearly demonstrated in the case of Mrs. Rae, a delicate, tense young woman of twenty-five years, who told her story in these words:

"I've been sick for about eleven months. I have had a thorough physical examination and many X-rays and laboratory tests, but none of the physicians have been able to find anything wrong with me. I am now getting very upset . . . well, this seems to be all in the mind or something like that, and I really must get over this. At times I feel very sick. I get dizzy spells. I cry a lot. I am very low in my spirits. I just have to lie down when I think about myself. I get so depressed. Am I losing my mind, thinking I am so sick? I sleep a lot. I'm afraid and nervous all the time, but I don't know what I'm afraid of. I'm always tense and nervous, a bundle of nerves, like they say.

"For the last few months I have been taking B$_{12}$ shots to help my nerves, but I don't feel they have helped much. My husband agrees that something must be done. I just seemed to collapse a year ago. I got very tense. My nerves just seemed to draw me taut as a fiddlestring.

"I was in bed for three months, just helpless. I couldn't do a thing but cry. I have been up for eight months now, but I'm so weak I can't do a thing. I can't do my housework at all.

"This all started about a year ago. I had the flu. But when it cleared up and I started to get up, I started to itch and I felt very weak. The itching got worse. The doctor gave me a shot for the itching and then I really collapsed. Things just got worse and worse. For four months I couldn't get out of bed without getting dizzy. My nerves were just shot. Then my husband insisted that I have this physical examination and all those tests. Nothing was found wrong with me, but I still feel sick and weak.

"Every time I get outside my own home I feel scared. I start to get dizzy. I'm afraid I will get dizzy and collapse on the street and no one will know me. I just haven't any peace of mind. I worry and worry. I go to bed, but that doesn't help.

"I've been married for five years. My husband is a construction foreman. Until this happened I worked as a file clerk. I liked my job, but I wasn't happy. I think I worked much, much too hard. I worked hard at the office and then tried to keep my house spick and span, and it was just too much for me.

171

"I can't think of anything, of any one thing that upset me before I got the flu. Just before that, a cousin came to visit us. In a way she was pleasant company, but it was a responsibility, having her visit us, extra meals and all that sort of thing.

"We got married just after my husband went into the service. When he got out of the Army, he took this job. Up until then I lived at home. Then we set up housekeeping. We both worked hard, especially Carl. He'd help me out and he still does. In fact, all these months he's been doing most of the housework. But he's getting disgusted with me. He is more moody now, just sits, not saying anything. He used to try to cheer me up, but I guess I'm such a drag on him that I got him down too. Whenever I try to talk to him now, he just says, 'I see,' and nods and then goes on doing whatever he was doing, even if it was only sitting there. I am getting to be a terrible drag on him. I'm no wife to him. Everyone likes him and usually he's cheerful and affectionate, but I seem to be getting him down. I really must get over this sick feeling."

In Mrs. Rae's story of her childhood there were strong indications that hypochondriasis was a prevailing attitude of her parents. She spoke of her childhood experiences in this way:

"I was sick quite a bit until I was about ten. I had all the childhood illnesses, and was hospitalized with pneumonia. Later I had a ruptured appendix with peritonitis.

"My parents were very affectionate people and so are my brother and sister. The whole family was very kind to me when I was sick. In fact, I was pampered. Everyone would do everything for me—anything I wanted. I really had a happy childhood.

"My mother is a wonderful person—very kindhearted. She always deprived herself to give to her family. She was happiest when she was doing for one of us. We always turned to her. She worried about my health all the time.

"My father was sick a lot. He was quite nervous, jumpy and grouchy. He still depends on my mother, always has. He used to say he could never go on living without her. He used to worry about my health too. I could always get my way with both of them."

Some of the pertinent clues to hypochondriasis in this woman's story were: ". . . I have had a thorough physical examination and many X-rays and laboratory tests, but none of the physicians have been able to find anything wrong with me . . . I'm always tense and nervous, a bundle of nerves . . . when it [flu] cleared up and I started to get up, I started to itch and I felt very weak . . . I still feel sick and weak . . . I was sick quite a bit until I was about ten . . . The whole family was very kind to me when I was sick . . . She [mother] worried about my health all the time . . . My father was sick a lot . . . used to worry about my health too."

Can you pick out similar clues in your own story of your childhood experiences with sickness and your parents' attitudes about illness?

There is no question that Mrs. Rae worked hard at two jobs—at an office and as a housekeeper and wife. She sternly silenced her hypochondriacal "inner child of the past" until she came down with the flu. At this point her somewhat pampered "child of the past" took over her life —and when she tried to get up, she developed an itch, and then collapsed when treated for it.

Once she recognized that she was actually continuing to use the old worried, hypochondriacal attitudes of her parents toward herself, Mrs. Rae began a determined struggle to free herself from these old parental attitudes. It has not been easy. At first she literally dragged herself —and her shrieking, complaining "child of the past"— from one household chore to another. She has now reached the point where her husband's assistance is not required in doing her household work although he still does the shopping. She is preparing for that task by forcing herself to go out every day in spite of her tendency to feel dizzy and her fear that she will collapse. She says, "I just stand still and shut my eyes and say I am just acting the way I did when I wanted to be babied by my parents, and I understand that because that is the way my parents treated me, and I say to myself, there is nothing wrong with you and you will be all right, but I am not going to criticize you or give in to you. By the time I have done this the dizziness has passed and I can go on."

Her progress has given her much satisfaction. She no longer is depressed and low in her spirits. Her husband, encouraged by her efforts, has resumed his old cheerful, affectionate manner. Their sexual relations have been resumed. "My husband can see I'm getting better and his pride in me makes me more determined to do more for myself," says Mrs. Rae. "I'm still worn out if I try to do too much, but I try to do just a little bit more each day because I am determined to live a real life."

By recognizing and accepting her "child of the past" and making up her mind that she did not need to treat herself as her pampering, hypochondriacal parents did, Mrs. Rae established the basic foundation on which she could build a new, more satisfying life. The actual building—the day-by-day, pot-by-pot, dish-by-dish, room-by-room development of this life—has required heroic efforts. But today, instead of complaining that she "can't," Mrs. Rae is accomplishing more every day.

Let no one underestimate the effort the hypochondriacal person must make. The complaining "child of the past" will always exaggerate minor aches and pains, bumps and bruises, turn up new symptoms with howls, demanding tender care, sympathy and indulgence. In being a parent to oneself, the hypochondriacal person, recognizing the origin of these complaints, must respectfully set them aside and proceed with his search for adult satisfactions. If these complaints are angrily or contemptuously thrust aside, ignored or denied, they will build up—and then when a real illness, like Mrs. Rae's flu, develops, they will be insatiably demanding. The old childhood pattern will be re-established—and it will be very difficult to overcome.

The Origins and Mechanism of Hypochondriasis

We must carefully distinguish hypochondriasis as a pathogenic parental attitude from all others in order to deal with it.

In its persistency hypochondriasis differs from a psychosomatic symptom, such as a headache, heartburn or fatigue, which may develop in an otherwise healthy person as a result of some inner conflict, frustration or resentment. Nearly all of us have had such psychosomatic symptoms at one time or another without being the least bit hypochondriacal.

However, the person suffering from hypochondriasis may develop exaggerated, even alarming symptoms, on attempting to venture into activities from which his hypochondriasis has kept him. These symptoms are the protests of your hypochondriacal "child of the past." Darwin's heart palpitations while waiting for the *Beagle* to sail are an example of this type of symptom.

Often the hypochondriacal person's pleas and demands for sympathy and indulgence are so obvious and their symptoms so trivial that it is difficult for others not to believe their ailment is a total "sham," to use Darwin's expression. The "enjoyment of illness" often arouses irritation and resentment in the persons who are called upon to provide for the anxious hypochondriacal person. This may cause an outright accusation of "shamming," which deepens the hypochondriac's feeling of helplessness and already existing feelings of guilt. It does not overcome the hypochondriacal attitude. Similarly pep talks are of no avail and sympathy adds to the person's belief in his sickness.

ORIGINS: Hypochondriasis originates, in most cases, in the fearful attitudes toward disease expressed by parents and heard by a child. The child, helplessly dependent on his all-knowing parents, absorbs and adopts as his own the anxious attitude of his parents, imitating them. It helps him to feel close to them and secure—literally like them, the only adults he knows and his protectors. On becoming a parent to himself as an adult, he continues these old parental attitudes because this is the way he has learned to take care of himself and to feel secure.

Because it is transmitted, like other attitudes, from parent to child, hypochondriasis often expresses fears that were current many years ago when little was known about disease in a scientific sense and when such fears were more common than today. This attitude is secondarily supported by the gains in sympathy and indulgence which the "ailing" person obtains from those around him.

What Can Be Done About a Hypochondriacal Child of the Past

To be overcome, hypochondriasis must be dealt with by the person suffering from it. He must become aware of his exaggeration of his aches and pains. He must feel, deeply and strongly, that he is missing a great deal of satisfaction in life through his passive and restrictive "surrendering" attitude. He must be determined in his struggle not to give in to his fatigue and be prepared to cope with new symptoms as he respectfully sets aside old ones.

In order to carry out this struggle successfully, he needs to do the following:

1. Accept the objective findings and evaluation of his symptoms by his physician as reasonable and scientific. He must satisfy himself with the aid of modern medical science that his complaints are really based on fearful attitudes.

2. He must locate in his childhood the hypochondriacal persons who influenced and developed these attitudes in him—his parents, grandparents or other adults who played significant roles in his development.

3. He must then be prepared to recognize the *exaggeration* of his symptoms for what it is—the continuation of hypochondriacal attitudes absorbed in childhood. We all have minor symptoms most of the time. We cannot, for example, exert ourselves strenuously without feeling tired. We know and expect this, but do not let it incapacitate us. The exaggeration is what incapacitates the person suffering from hypochondriasis.

4. He must be prepared to struggle against indulgence of symptoms and try hard to participate actively in achieving adult goals.

5. He must, on detecting them, abandon efforts to win the sympathy and indulgence of others with his complaints. Such efforts increase feelings of guilt. He must recognize that satisfaction in actively achieving goals which he sets for himself will be greater than the sympathy and indulgence of friends.

6. He must recognize that this is going to be a prolonged struggle, that he will have setbacks at times in stressful situations. He may need the understanding support of his physician, who can recognize the character of new symptoms as they arise in making this effort to overcome the hypochondriacal inner atmosphere of childhood. If the person suffering from hypochondriasis recognizes that he is dealing with the fears of a child who found security in childhood in absorbing and imitating these fears, he can, as an adult, be a better parent to himself than his fearful parents were able to be.

The most difficult aspect of learning how to be a better parent to your "inner child of the past" is developing *respect* for these childhood feelings. Because we want to be mature, we may be ashamed or contemptuous of the part of ourselves we call "childish." We may attempt to bulldoze, intimidate or ignore these feelings. If you do this you are on the road to unhappiness and alienation from yourself. Instead, you must realize that you could not—then or now—determine your childhood. Whatever your parents' attitudes were, whether hypochondriacal, perfectionistic or overindulgent, these attitudes were beyond your control and they will always play a role in your life, in what you fear, what you feel, what you hope for.

Because of this, your opportunity for achieving satisfaction in life lies in accepting your "child of the past" respectfully. What you can change are the parental attitudes you hold toward yourself which currently cause you pain and unhappiness and limit your efforts to find satisfaction.

CHAPTER 15

PUNITIVENESS—
If you constantly seek revenge
for the past

YOUR INDEX OF SUSPICION: *If you frequently feel you
are "no good" or "bad" and find you are punishing yourself—or being punished by others, if you tend to seek
work that requires a capacity to "take it," and you are
often filled with hateful desires to "get even," you have
strong indications that your "inner child of the past" lived
in a strict, harshly punitive atmosphere.* Few of us escaped this attitude altogether; it has prevailed in schools
as well as homes. This stern, punishing attitude accounts
for much of the guilt felt by adults about their leisure
and pleasure, the guilt being the continuing reaction of
the child who expects to be punished if he casually enjoys himself. Similarly, much of the bitter, generalized
desire to "get back at" the world, which scorches the lives
of many people, can be traced back to excessive parental
punitiveness and the child's desire for revenge.

Recognizing Your Punitiveness
Toward Yourself

Do you constantly "beat yourself up"? Many people do
not recognize the punitive, scolding attitude which they
have toward themselves. Raised in a culture that believes
parents spoil the child if the rod is spared, they continue
to apply the rod to themselves as adults. This is the way
they were taught to treat themselves as children—and the

"child of the past" feels anxious and guilty without the excessive punishment characteristic of his early home.

Such punitiveness need not have been physical. It could have been endless, strict moralizing—the creation of guilt and feelings of utter worthlessness in a child because of his immature behavior at an age when he is naturally immature. The child, acting on impulse and forever curious and exploring to discover himself and his environment, cannot "stay out of trouble" in a punitive home. He neither recognizes his impulses nor can he understand the need to control them, lacking both adult knowledge and perspective. The harsh scoldings, angry beatings and solemn moralizing tend, in a cumulative way, to convince him that, deep down, he is really very "bad." Is he not always guilty? Is he not always "in trouble"? Could his conduct not always have been better?

Invariably some love and affection is mingled with this harsh punitiveness. Punishment, even severe and brutal beatings, can become a form of security for a child, his way of knowing the world and himself in it.

As a result of all these factors, and of the deep roots of childhood security and affection attached to them, it is often very difficult for people punitively treated as children to recognize their own continuing punishment of themselves and how it destroys their capacities to enjoy life. Such persons may complain bitterly of how hard they work, how cruelly they were treated in childhod, their inability to give or receive affection, how uncomfortable they are in social situations and their inability to relax. Yet they do not connect their difficulties with the fact that basically they continue to treat themselves as their punitive parents did. "You say I'm punishing myself?" such a patient may say. "Of course I punish myself. I deserve it. But I can't understand why I have these blue spells."

Your best clues in recognizing whether you are being punitive toward yourself lie in your feelings as an adult today. The most significant of these feelings are *guilt, revenge, fear:*

GUILT: Parental punitiveness imbues the child with the feeling that he is "bad," a "little devil," a "bad actor," someone who is constantly misbehaving and needs "a good licking to straighten him out." As an adult, such a person constantly feels guilty without having done anything wrong

—and especially if he enjoys himself. If he finds pleasure or relaxation in anything, his "child of the past" feels he is being "bad." Therefore, as a parent to himself, he must be strict, moralizing and punitive. He tells himself, just as his parents once did, that he is "bad," shameful, a disgrace, "no good" and utterly worthless. Although actually free of wrongdoing, he feels guilty—and must "pay for it" by punishing himself.

Often this punishment takes the form of grueling work. The housewife who carries out an exhausting, unnecessary housecleaning routine is frequently punishing herself. Why? She has done nothing wrong but she feels guilty. At the moment she may attribute her guilty feelings to "loafing," to neglecting her work, missing church services, spending her husband's money on a trifle. Yet objectively none of these items will account for the depth of her uncomfortable guilty feelings. Only her punishing daily routine gives her relief. Only then does she feel at ease. She's been bad —but she's punished herself.

Similarly men who have been punitively treated as children often cannot feel satisfied that they have "done a day's work" unless their knuckles are skinned, their muscles strained and their joints aching. Otherwise they feel that they have been loafing, cheating the boss— guilty. The forms this kind of self-punishment takes vary enormously, from unnecessary deprivations to the laceration and physical wounding of oneself.

Deeply imbedded in childhood by everything from beatings to comments like "You make me sick," such feelings of guilt in adults often take the form of self-belittlement: "I'm such a nuisance . . . I'm so sloppy and ugly . . . I'm a lousy wife . . ." Objectively such statements are rarely true. They are usually self-punishment. The guilty person has little or no self-esteem. He focuses on his weakness or shortcomings and disregards his accomplishments because this is the way his punitive parents looked at him. If people praise his accomplishments, his guilty "child of the past" reminds him that they don't really know how "bad" he is. Often such a person belabors himself to the point of exhaustion to stave off guilty feelings that stem from childhood.

If you blush and feel uncomfortable if a person compliments you, it is usually because your "inner child of the past" denies you any feeling of satisfaction with yourself. Often this childhood feeling of guilt is so sweepingly and deeply ingrained that many persons feel they are "no good" for anything. They must punish and abuse themselves because any feeling of satisfaction frightens them. Many married women call themselves "whores" if they enjoy sexual intercourse, if they feel momentarily attracted to men other than their husbands or if they desire attractive clothes. In both sexes this childhood guilt may paralyze sexual responsiveness and only patient reassurance from some adult whom they respect will ease these guilty inhibitions.

Often these childhood feelings of guilt take the form of anxiety in the adult. The anxiety arises because the adult, freed of the strictness and forbidding punitiveness of the parental home, tries to accept himself as an adult and to enjoy life as one. But this makes the "child of the past" feel guilty and anxious, expecting punishment. Anxiety about what the neighbors will think, about money, about sex often is a form of punitiveness toward oneself.

While these anxious and guilty feelings are particularly attached to whatever was forbidden in childhood, the major devastation wrought by parental punitiveness is that it creates such a profound feeling of guilt and worthlessness that nothing can be enjoyed. Thus, it severely restricts many lives and causes much depression.

A person with such a "child of the past" may be unable to enjoy simple pleasures like a day off, a holiday or an evening of socializing. He may have a difficult and uneasy time learning to accept his own creative abilities. A woman suffering from childhood punitiveness may decorate her kitchen—but to be praised for it and feel satisfaction in the praise may frighten her. In such a moment her abusive, punishing "child of the past" has control of her—and makes her feel guilty for her satisfaction in that praise.

RETALIATION: If you were excessively punished as a child, you probably have already found that one of your greatest problems is controlling a burning, generalized hatred that flares up within you. This may express itself as criticism, protest and furious complaint, as jealousy or envy, or an overwhelming desire to "get even" with the world.

Children can generally accept correction and punishment that is just from loving parents. They can gradually accept the need to control their impulsiveness and the need for rules governing behavior.

But the child's response to unjust and excessive punishment is a fierce desire to retaliate, to strike back. He learns to hate the punitive parent. You can abuse me now, he says in effect, because you are bigger than I am but just wait until I'm stronger and I'll get back at you if it's the last thing I do. The more unjust the punishment, the more fiercely do these retaliatory fires burn. He learns to lie—to avoid punishment—and has destructive self-contempt for himself because he lies, because he is not yet big enough to punish the parent. A severely punished child dreams of revenge. He is unable to see the need for correction, for rules, and he feels no tenderness.

As an adult, he may still be driven by a deep desire to get back at those who punished him so unjustly and cruelly. Because his parents have generally disappeared from the scene of his adult life, his desire for revenge may be released in many ways. It may, for example, be directed toward others smaller and weaker than himself, whom he punishes as he was punished. It may take the form of disappointing and hurting his parents by violating every rule laid down in the parental home, from stealing to promiscuity. Often it is an impulsive desire for whatever is forbidden, regardless of who or what does the forbidding.

The person who as a child is filled with retaliatory hate cannot easily find satisfactions in adult life. His life is given over to the desire of his "child of the past" to "get even." Often such people find they really are incapable of giving or receiving love; it does not satisfy their demand for revenge. Not recognizing the origins of their retaliatory and often cruel impulsiveness, they often cannot maintain more than a fragmentary control over these drives. Their punishing attitudes alienate others, who fear them and avoid them. In close family relationships, these attitudes often may "bring the roof down." The story of Eleanor, which is related in the section dealing with the effect of punitiveness on marriage, demonstrates the destructiveness of these retaliatory impulses.

Probably the most conspicuous and clear-cut examples of retaliatory drives are to be found in the lives of young criminals. Initially, their crimes are often vengeance-driven blows for the excessive and cruel punishment they did not deserve in childhood. In their blinding hatred of their parents, they see society and its rules as a kind of universal parent—and they thirst to "get even." But their crimes, like most retaliatory blows, often make them feel more guilty rather than satisfied. Such crimes confirm their "badness," deepen their feelings of guilt and make them hunted men. Sometimes such criminals betray themselves, seeking in effect the public branding of themselves as "bad" to relieve their guilty feelings and the need to control their retaliatory impulses.

These retaliatory impulses express themselves in many ways—in sassy impudence, in criticism and self-righteousness, in a punishing attitude toward others, in jealousy and envy, in flirtations and extramarital affairs. Much energy that might flow into productive efforts that would genuinely enhance one's self-esteem is wasted in fulfillment of the retaliatory dreams of childhood.

FEAR: A person raised in a punitive atmosphere grows up feeling guilty—and fearful. He cannot trust anyone. He fears he will be found out—and punished. He fears his own dreams of retaliation (which also increase his feelings of guilt and worthlessness) and he fears the discovery of these retaliatory feelings. Moreover, his desire to "get even" is so powerful and so murderous that he fears a loss of his ability to control it, which would bring still more powerful authorities to punish him.

Thus the person constantly punished as a child for his immature impulsiveness, although he may put up a show of defiance and bravado, is often internally paralzyed with fear. From trying to control and conceal all these impulses, fears and feelings of guilt, he also suffers from a nearly unbearable tension and anxiety.

Because basically, from childhood on, he has been convinced by his parent's harsh punitiveness that he is "bad" and "no good," his only relief is in punishment—and self-punishment is not only the safest course but often the only one he can follow in being a parent to himself. But he also knows that he is *not guilty,* either as a child or an adult, and that the punishment is excessive. His desire to retaliate grows and his tension and anxiety over not being able to control his vengeful impulses really expresses his increasing fear.

If you recognize these hidden feelings of guilt, desires to "get even," fear and tension, as being ones which constantly contend within yourself, you have evidence of punitiveness within your childhood home. You can still wish to strike back at your parents for their harshness and strict rules, but you can begin now to be a kinder parent to yourself.

Sometimes, the child treated punitively seeks parental approval by slavishly adopting his parent's attitude, punishing himself and trying desperately hard to be good. As an adult, he becomes self-righteous. His retaliation is to look down on others as "bad." His constant moralizing alienates others because he makes them feel guilty—in the same way their parents did.

But most of all, punitiveness destroys spontaneity. The severely punished cannot be spontaneous easily because so much of their energy is tied up in feelings of worthlessness and guilt, their desires to strike back, and fear. Spontaneity requires an ability to trust onself and others. But punitively treated people are afraid of spontaneous impulses; in childhood such impulses brought punishment. In general, the spirit of life and its spontaneous enjoyment has been crushed by their punitive upbringing and their continuing self-punishment. Only by being a kindly and understanding parent to their harshly punished "child of the past" can they begin to regain their ability to trust and to feel and move spontaneously.

The Case of a Woman Who Married Twice

Until you realize that you are still punishing yourself for the ordinary and natural acts of a growing child—call them misbehavior if you *still must*—you cannot free yourself from this punitive childhood prison of guilty feelings. As an adult, acting as a parent to yourself, you can recognize what caused you to act as you do, and so help yourself come out of your darkened room.

No one should underestimate the difficulties of this kind of an effort with a "child of the past" who has been belittled, made to feel worthless and guilty. I know a woman who was beaten physically practically every day of her childhood. When her father came home in the evening, her nervous and anxious mother would accusingly report the "bad" things she had done—and her father would beat her "to teach her better." Yet, as is usual with punitiveness, she never learned—and the beating and harsh humiliations went on into her teens.

Finally her long-dreamed-of day of revenge came. A

man spoke kindly to her, called her "good looking" and asked for a date—something especially forbidden by her parents; she had been beaten for merely talking to boys whom her mother called "no good." She had no experience with men and this one seemed heaven-sent to rescue her from her punitive father. She slipped out to meet him secretly several times and dreamed of announcing dramatically to her stunned parents that she was leaving them forever. On her dates, however, she felt so guilty and fearful that she trembled. But the man told her he loved her, which made her feel triumphant and vindicated; her parents never told her they loved her. She was terrified of their dates being discovered. So, at the age of seventeen she eloped—being too frightened of her father's power to make her dramatic retaliatory announcement.

She and her husband settled down in a small apartment in a midwestern city. She soon found out that her husband, though he said he loved her, could be just as cruel and mean as her father. He would beat her, then be sorry, beg forgiveness and then, after a while, beat her again, calling her all sorts of names. For a long time the names he called her seemed to fit. They were the names her father would have used for a girl who met a man secretly and then ran off with him. Thus she punished herself. But gradually she realized that she was not any of those names—and that the only reason she went on living with this cruel and punitive man was her fear that she was no good, a cheap tramp. Finally, after living with this man eight years, she recognized her own innocence and that he was incapable of being a kind and loving husband. She left him and got a divorce amidst a great flurry of abuse.

For two years she worked as a department store stockroom helper, later as a clerk. Attractive but quiet and subdued in her manner, very anxious to please, she punished herself both at her job and in her tiny apartment by doing extra work; she scrubbed the floor of her apartment every night. She also punished herself by refusing all invitations to social affairs, dates for movies or lunch. If she felt like accepting an invitation for lunch or a movie, she felt forced to refuse it in spite of her desire to go, and punished herself with all the names her father and husband had called her.

But her loneliness was painful and her life empty. She realized she did not want to spend her life this way.

Gradually she resolved that she would accept some dates and that if she ever married again, she would marry a man who would treat her kindly. She began to go to lunch with fellow employees and through them met other people. After a while she decided that the man she liked the best was one who was mild-mannered, industrious and considerate of her feelings. He often asked her casually but sincerely if he could take her to supper or to the movies. She accepted these invitations and became certain that he surely was not like either her father or her husband. Because he treated her with love and respect, she married him when he asked her to.

However, after living with this man for six months in a comfortable, cheerful apartment, she became increasingly depressed. She same to see me in the depths of depression, describing herself as "no good," a bum, a cheap tramp, an utterly worthless creature. She particularly felt that she was unworthy of her husband, who was so good and kind to her, never spoke angrily to her or "slapped me around."

As you can see, this woman has been compelled by the feelings of worthlessness and guilt of her "inner child of the past" to recreate the circumstances of her punitive family background again and again, either by marrying a punitive man like her father or by being a punitive parent to herself. Her self-punishment has been extreme. Even when she was living with her first husband, who often beat her, she punished herself severely. When she lived alone after divorcing him, she was also punitive to herself in her extra work and her evenings of scrubbing even though at the time she decided to leave her first husband she had "established her innocence."

When she married a man who did not punish her, she did not feel "at home" inside. Because he was kind, considerate and loved her, she felt utterly unworthy, so much so that she felt sad and depressed. She felt she could never be good enough to deserve someone so good. The old guilty feelings of childhood tell her she is a fraud.

What most of us seek in a marriage partner is someone who helps recreate some of the feelings of security we knew in childhood. In deliberately selecting a man who was respectful and considerate, kind and loving, this woman eliminated an emotional element, punitiveness, that had always been significant in her life. So she punished herself—by belittling herself to the point of becom-

186

ing completely depressed about herself. The better she found her husband, the more she felt she was worthless.

Until she learned to value and respect herself, she had a difficult struggle with her punishing self-belittlement. She did not recognize for some time that her depressed feelings were a form of punishment. Nor did she understand that in "establishing her innocence" as she had done while living with her first husband, and in seeking a man who was not punitive, she had made great positive steps forward toward releasing herself from the childhood pattern of feelings of unworthiness and guilt created by her punitive upbringing. When she came to realize that she had made that step alone and in misery, she began to respect herself and to put aside the feelings of worthlessness of her "child of the past." This has made her feel less depressed about herself. She now knows that she uses her husband's kindness and love to set in motion her own punishing self-belittlement. Gradually she has come to see that she really merits and deserves the respect and love which he gives her.

Origins and Mechanisms of Punitiveness

It will help you to understand how you punish yourself and how you can check this harsh, self-defeating treatment if you understand its origins and basic mechanisms in yourself.

WHAT IT IS: Punitiveness is an excessively strict, stern and harshly punishing viewpoint toward a child on whom a parent consistently vents his own recurring personal hostility and aggressive feelings. Just as "love" and "hate" are opposite sides of the same coin, the punitive parent usually loves and cares about his child. He may see his punitiveness as necessary to "teach" the child how to behave for his own safety and good. "I'm doing this for your own good," he may shout as he rains verbal and physical blows on the shrinking child. Dependent on his parents not only for food and shelter but also for their loving approval, this is damaging to the child's self-respect and capacity for growth. Punitiveness assaults him as being worthless, no good, bad, not worth loving. It does not respect his feelings or interests and often forces him to lie

187

and deceive to escape punishment for activities which are immature but natural at his age.

There are, as will be shown later, sound alternatives to punitiveness. But in our culture punitiveness is generally approved or at least condoned as a parental right and legally sanctified. It is important for you to realize that your parents' punitiveness and your abuse was not an individual affair. Your parents probably were similarly abused and so were millions of other children. What we are dealing with is a cultural attitude toward children. The parents serve as the "carriers" of the attitude.

How It Occurs: Punitive action by the parent generally occurs in two ways:

1. It may occur when the parent, often because of some disappointment, hurt to his pride, frustration or some unsolved problem in his own personal life, directs his hostility and aggressions toward the child in the name of discipline. The child may trigger the punitive action by some immature behavior, at times to get the attention of the preoccupied parent, and then become the target of the adult's pent-up rage. Or the child may do nothing initially. Some incident in the parent's life, such as marital discord, an annoyance at work, increasing taxes or even a newspaper account of delinquency in a distant city, may set off the parent's hostility in the form of new and stricter rules—which may cause protest and defiance in the child, bringing on the punishment itself.

Many parents are filled with hostility toward their children because they are not convenient, may cause embarrassment, require much attention, prevent the parent from doing things he wants to do. This is why the child often becomes the target of the parent's hostile feelings. Also, the child cannot defend himself. Utterly dependent, he is a "safe" outlet for the parent's own ugly feelings. Often the parent, seeing the child as an extension of himself, is deeply embarrassed by any sign of immaturity and punishes him furiously—as though he himself had been discovered urinating on the front lawn. "This hurts me more than it does you," he may shout as he belabors the child.

Young parents are often immature themselves, may resent the problems and responsibilities of parenthood, and frequently resort to punitiveness. Often their punitiveness is a direct retaliation for the punitiveness visited upon them by their parents.

2. While the above type of punitiveness may occur more

or less spontaneously depending on the inner feelings of the parent, punitiveness may also result from the parent's belief that hurting the child is the necessary duty of the parent and the proper way of rearing him. This belief, quite mistaken, holds that painful lessons are good ones because the hurt is remembered. Usually raised this way themselves, such parents are excessively strict. They may try to be impersonal in their punitiveness, saying in effect, "You know the rules. You know the punishment. You broke the rules and now you must get the punishment. It hurts but that's your fault." Actually, usually the child is too immature to be expected to follow these rules. But the rules are rarely scaled downward—and the punishment is rigorously enforced. In such a household the mother often reports the day's infractions to the father, who carries out the punishment. Often such homes are little more than prisons in a psychological sense.

Regardless of how punitiveness arises, it is nearly always called "teaching." And the hurt, deprecated child is told he will "have to learn to behave better." He is no good as he is. This verdict, reemphasized in recurrent punishment, is one of the foundations of the self-belittlement with which many people belabor themselves all their lives in self-punishment.

When punitiveness occurs because of some dissatisfaction in the parent's life, it may be less frequent than it is when the parent believes punitiveness is necessary. But it is often explosive in its excesses. Often the parent immediately recognizes the child's offense was trivial and his punishment unjust. He may then overindulge the child to ease his own guilty feelings about abusing the child.

Punitiveness rarely dominates a home the way perfectionism or overcoercion does. Although very common, it is usually a secondary pathogenic attitude, coexisting with others. When something goes wrong from the parents' view, it comes into play. For example, it may be the end result of overly coercive or perfectionistic attitudes, resorted to if the child balks at excessive demands or used to drive the child to greater efforts. It may be combined with overindulgence as noted above. Or it may be a belated revolt by the overly submissive parent against the child's demands. Usually overly submissive or overly indulgent parents feel very guilty about punitiveness and then renew these already excessive pathogenic attitudes. Punitiveness may also be combined with rejection, in

189

which case the child is viewed as a nuisance and burden; he may be punished for merely existing.

Punitiveness arising from some disappointment or frustration in the adult's life is frequently very inconsistent. Its severity depends on the ups and downs of the parent's inner life, rather than on the child. The child's misbehavior may be laughed off one time or even considered cute—and the next time it may set off a scalding verbal and physical assault. Because its severity has nothing to do with the child's offense, it is nearly always excessive.

Parents who believe in hurting the child as a method may be more consistent. They try to make their strict rules plain and they rigorously enforce them. Many try to make the punishment "fit the crime." However, despite such efforts, their own personal ups and downs invariably influence the severity. What is often overlooked by such parents is that they themselves have been raised in this fashion and see the world only as a grim, strict "do-your-duty" place. Their restrictive rules and excessive punitiveness are often retaliation for the punitiveness of their own parents.

Many of their rigid, unnecessarily restrictive rules are detrimental to the child's potential development. For example, a child may be forced to be in bed by 9 P.M., long after he needs such a bedtime. Social and athletic activities may be banned altogether or permitted only under such restrictive rules as to be considered undesirable by the child. In short, the child's needs, social and emotional, may be seriously short-changed.

While consistency does not permit the child to know when he is doing something for which he is punishable, his growth constantly pushes him toward forbidden areas —and into deceitfulness, lying and guilt. One of the common examples of this is an unreasonable parental ban on dating—which often results in promiscuity.

Some punitive parents proudly declare that they "never laid a hand on a child." This type of parent practices a pernicious form of punitiveness—excessive moralizing. Attaching moral values to the child's behavior, calling his immature actions "bad" and "evil," has the same effect as beating him. In fact, many children will tell you it is harder to bear—for the punishment immediately becomes self-punishment and may be carried on endlessly by the child within himself. Thus, it is invariably excessive—and why "a talking to" is dreaded. Such moralizing creates a profound self-belittling distortion in the child's feeling about himself. Often moralizing is resorted to by parents who also physically punish their child.

The effect of all punitiveness is to create in the child an excessive guilt and feeling of being no good, worthless, contemptible, not worth loving. The "good-bad" formulations of morality are too inflexible a framework to permit healthy development and sound self-esteem. In his moralizing, as in other forms of punitiveness, the parent vents his own feelings of hostility and projects his own feelings of guilt onto the child. Often religion and the child's desire for approval are misused to give the child a vicious psychological beating.

Walter Lippmann, the famous columnist, once described such an incident in his own life: "I can remember a birthday 'party' for two or three chums which developed into a 'rough-house.' In the excitement we used cakes as ammunition, leaving the carpet in a shocking state. This angered the maid who was responsible for the tidiness of my room to such a pitch that only religion seemed adequate for the occasion. In the late afternoon she began to talk to me in a solemn voice. I would have preferred a thousand beatings to that voice in the wretched gaslight which used to darken homes before electricity reached the middle-class. The flickering shadows on the cake-strewn carpet were unbearable and accusing shapes full of foreboding to boys lost in sin. I burst into tears at the impending wrath of God. And for years God was the terror of the twilight."*

I am sure you will agree God is not an instrument to be used to create guilt in children and to terrorize them. Yet this is the way God is used by many punitive persons. Not once as would seem to have been the case with Lippmann, but daily. And severe and cruel as the maid was, had this been done by Lippmann's own parents the punishment would have been still harder to bear. What echoes in the lives of millions of people is Lippmann's line: "I would have preferred a thousand beatings to that voice . . ."

THE PUNISHMENT-RETALIATION CYCLE: You may be able to pick out from these brief summaries the type of punitiveness the child you once were had to endure. Now that you are acting as a parent to yourself, you can perhaps find in these patterns some of the ways in which you con-

---

* Walter Lippmann, *Drift and Mastery*, New York: Mitchell Kennerly, 1914.

tinue to punish yourself. You will tend to punish yourself in the same manner that your parents did. If they were inconsistent, you will be. If they set up strict rules which disregarded your needs, you will do so—and then be forever pushed toward violation of these rules by your own needs, causing you to further punish yourself. You may continue the pattern of punishing yourself, then overindulge yourself—which many obese persons do in dieting.

But what may be clearest is how your self-belittling, a form of self-punishment, was created by the punitiveness of your childhood home.

What is also established in childhood is a punishment-retaliation cycle. Studies of the effects of punishment on children show that the child responds to it with one or a combination of the following:

1. Behavior which invites punishment.
2. Retaliatory desires for revenge against the parent.
3. Self-punishing guilt and feelings of worthlessness.

In adult life, crippling self-devaluation and feelings of guilt and worthlessness are major characteristics of the person who punishes himself. This self-punishment sets in motion his retaliatory desires for revenge, which are often still fired by his resentment over past punishment. Often his life is dominated by retaliatory desires, leading him to be abusive and cruel to others, hurting them as he once was hurt. As a parent to himself he both punishes himself and retaliates against this punishment. His self-belittlement, if particularly severe, may lead him into situations where others punish him.

In being a parent to yourself, any reduction of these forces will help you reduce your own punishment of yourself. If you can recognize that your own retaliatory desires derive much of their fierce heat from punishments you suffered as a child, you can reduce your need to lash out at others—and at yourself. If you can understand how your own feelings of guilt and worthlessness were really created in childhood by punitiveness and how they constitute a form of self-punishment, you can begin to develop a new esteem for yourself based on what you have accomplished and can do—and this, in turn, will help you reduce your retaliatory desires to "strike back."

And these efforts will help you reduce your need to punish yourself or seek situations in which you must prove once again that you can "take it."

Areas Commonly Involved in Punitiveness

While punitiveness can take place in many areas of living, and people punish themselves for all kinds of things in many different ways, the basic punishment-retaliation cycle is always the same. However, certain areas are more commonly involved than others. Among them are:

WORK: Probably the most common way in which people punish themselves is with work, and some persons punish others by driving them hard to satisfy retaliatory feelings created in childhood.

Many people attempt to wipe out the recurring feeling of their "inner child of the past" that they are bad and "no good" by hard, dirty, muscular work. The housewife with the unnecessary and strenuous cleaning routine is one such example.

Certain occupations attract men with punitive backgrounds. These jobs provide some of the hit-and-be-hit atmosphere of their childhoods. For example, the so-called "rock salt" jobs, such as sandhogging, mining, longshoring, truck driving and laboring attract men who have frequently been found to have been severely punished —often brutally beaten—in childhood. Professional football and boxing also attract such men. Through their work they continue the punishment they knew in childhood.

Many businessmen release their retaliatory feelings in ruthless driving to "beat down the opposition." These feelings often lead them to select their present business. They are more interested in crushing the opposition than in salaries, careers or service. Just as in childhood they lay awake with dreams and schemes of humiliating and striking back at punitive parents, they now lie awake with dreams of smashing the competing companies. In our competitive business world such men often rise to commanding positions.

The pressures of past punitiveness often push people toward work where such pressures can be "safely" released. For example, persons who have been strictly and punitively treated as children are often attracted to police jobs, to the armed forces and other jobs which have disciplinary functions. Their resentments from childhood cause them to retaliate against those whom they can intimidate, humiliate or abuse—just as their parents acted toward them.

Many persons with punitive backgrounds tend to be drawn into work where they are both exploited and abused. While often they have lacked opportunities for education, the real cause of this situation is their continuing self-belittlement and feelings of unworthiness. They feel that they are no good, that they have no rights, that abuse is their lot in life—just as they did in childhood. Many migrant laborers and farm workers are thus trapped by their low self-esteem, which is used by others to exploit and abuse them. In place of true self-esteem, they take pride in their ability to "take it."

HOME: Many people who are not at all punitive in their work or relations with others away from home become punitive the moment they enter their homes. The reasons for this, and other aspects of punitiveness in marriage, are discussed in the section on marriage.

MORALIZING: Sometimes a child raised in a strict, moralizing home adopts his parents' standards and attitudes; he is by their standards "good." In this way he secures the warmth and security he needs as a child because he cannot stand their disapproval. However, in adolescence, when others begin to date, his self-righteousness sets him apart from the others. He takes pride in denying himself ordinary social satisfactions and pleasures and he makes those around him feel guilty—in retaliation for his parents' unreasonable restrictions.

His hostile self-righteousness not only alienates others, but often it conceals, even from himself, his interest in the other sex, an interest which his parents' attitude disapproves of. Their self-righteousness has taught them to look down on others' "foolish behavior." In retaliation, they destroy others' pleasures and satisfaction by their carping criticism and self-righteousness. Often they punish themselves with hard work, which fills them with retaliatory hatred and meanness. They feel all honors and attention should come to them because they have been "very good." They often become very jealous of attention given to others who are, in their view, cheap, common, bad, no good.

Betty was like this, for example. She looked down on

the girls in her office because "all they talk about is boys, dates, that sort of thing."

She worked hard at the office of a large insurance company and her diligent, conscientious work initially won the praise of others, including her superiors and the girls who did similar work. When others praised her she felt quite happy. But her self-righteousness alienated others and the general isolation in which she soon found herself hurt her deeply. She became very jealous of certain other girls who were not so careful in their work but who, because their general cheerfulness contributed to office morale, were often given attention by superiors.

Betty had been raised in a strict and religious home where punitiveness took the form of constant moralizing. All entertainment was "run down," to use her own phrase, as foolishness and wasteful, if not "bad for you." She was not allowed to go to the movies except under parental supervision—and these movies were specially selected and usually on religious themes. Girls who dated were similarly "run down" as wicked, foolish, "loose," and "shocking" by her parents. Betty grew up proud of the fact that she was a "good" girl.

At school she had achieved good grades but her aloof and righteous attitudes made her very lonely. She was very much afraid of boys and when one of them took any interest in her she drove him away with her disapproving prudery about movies, dancing, "wasting time" in the school hangout. If she was attracted to a boy she sternly fought "the devil" inside her.

As she grew older, she realized her attitude was driving people away from her. It seemed to her that she was being "punished" for being good. She retaliated by moving out on her parents, whom she blamed for having caused her loneliness. She then tried to meet other young people and socialize in a casual way. But she could not quiet her self-righteous attitude and for a while, having lost the warmth of her home, she was lonelier than ever. She did not like casual dates; she wanted formal invitations for formal meetings. If she went to the movies with a boy she was sternly critical and moralizing about the story and the behavior on the screen, mainly because she "didn't know what else to say." Of course, the boys soon lost interest. She grew more stern and more proper. But at the same time she grew more serious in her search for companionship. She began, with help, to recognize slowly that it was her "child of the past" who interfered with her opportunities to find companionship and affection.

Betty's experiences can be duplicated in the lives of thousands of other men and women. Many are bewildered. Have they not been "good"? They do not realize that the attitude of the parental punitiveness with which they view themselves and others is the main factor in their "goodness"—and the main obstacle to their being able to make and hold friends.

If punitiveness in your home took the form of moralizing righteousness, you need to examine whether you continue to punish yourself in this way, shutting yourself off from others and from many of the pleasures and satisfactions of adult life.

How Punitiveness Affects Sex and Marriage

One of the peculiarities of punitiveness is that persons who may be quite reasonable at work or outside the home are frankly punitive and hostile at home in their relations with their spouses and children. In such people the punishment-retaliation cycle appears to be limited to the home.

Often what has happened to such persons is that after being raised in a punitive home atmosphere, they escape its punitiveness and restrictions either to go to college or to work. In the new atmosphere the retaliatory desires to strike back lose their strength because the chafing restrictions have disappeared and the punishments are not constantly renewed. They also have the freedom to establish their own rules and to satisfy their own interests and impulsiveness. Establishing such rules requires some consideration of one's needs and one's likes and dislikes, as well as some adjustment. Recognition of the need for such rules also produces a new respect for the parental role one plays toward oneself and this too tends to reduce retaliatory feelings. Unless the individual establishes for himself the same restrictive and punitive rules his parents had, his retaliatory feelings may seem to disappear altogether.

However, when such a person marries and establishes a home an entirely new situation is created—one that closely parallels the old home. All the old emotional chords are sounded, including not only those of affection but also the retaliatory ones that strike out against restrictive attitudes. What is considered desirable or undesirable in behavior in the home or in the role of the partner often duplicates what was known in the childhood home. Indeed, such attitudes are often really those of the "inner child of the past" who seeks the security of the past home. If stringent rules and punitiveness were part of a person's past home life, they are sought again by his "child of the past."

Often a person with a punitive background feels "at home" only when he is burning with retaliatory desires —against rules or attitudes which, as a parent to himself, he has established. Similarly, his "child of the past" may feel guilty and worthless because he violates these rules to satisfy his retaliatory impulses. The man who says he must go to church, then defies his childhood training by not going and then feels guilty is a common example of this. What frequently happens is that one partner tries to get the other partner to establish the rules or attitudes concerning what is desirable—so that his "child of the past" can rebel and retaliate against them. Thus, one marriage partner often plays the role of the restrictive, punitive parent of the past.

Sometimes the very affection and love involved in marriage seems to rekindle the old hurts, resentments and retaliatory desires of childhood. The child feels keenly the sharp contradiction between loving and excessive punishment which, in effect, says that he is not worthly of love. As an adult, his "child of the past" demands loving to make up for past punishment. Yet because in childhood love and punishment were combined, he always feels something is missing—harsh punitiveness and his own retaliatory feelings.

Many adults lash out at their spouse over trivialities in satisfying the abused feelings and retaliatory desires of the "child of the past." These desires may take many forms. One woman may, for example be a sloppy housekeeper because floor-scrubbing was a constant punishment in her childhood. Thus, she retaliates by not cleaning. But this lack of tidiness invites her husband's growling rage and reminds her she is "no good," just as her mother constantly did. She then scrubs the floor and cleans up the entire house in a furious, exhausting and punishing effort, which relieves her of her guilty feeling of being "no good," and she then resents her husband's excessive remarks. The cruelly punishing character of her husband's remarks comes from his own retaliatory impulses stored up for the day when he would be "boss."

What all this punitiveness and retaliation often adds up to is spat after spat, row after row, quarrel after quarrel, with excessive punishment on top of excessive retaliation until at last the marriage is on the verge of a breakup. In a divorce court one hears one tale after another of the punishment-retaliation cycle operating. One can hear how cruelty followed cruelty, what he did, what she did, how he struck and she threw. Yet one never hears any consideration of how past punishment and past retaliatory desires created these blast furnaces of excessive punishment over trivialities and misunderstandings.

The Invited Slap

In some instances women with punitive backgrounds invite a slap from their husbands by impulsive and provocative remarks or behavior. Often this is a form of self-punishment. These women often know very well what will bring a slap from their husbands and they may deliberately provoke it. Then they say, "What have I done?" They seek to re-establish the old punitive home atmosphere in which they depended on others to control them as their parents once did.

In many cases exercising mature control of oneself seems to be an intolerable burden. Instead such persons permit the impulsive, retaliatory "child of the past" to take over their words and deeds. Then they feel guilty about satisfying their impulsiveness, whether it is buying some frivolous thing or being sassy or rude. The punishing slap, although they may complain bitterly about it, relieves them of their guilty feelings and, in effect, assumes parental responsibility for them. But the slap does more than just that—it refires the retaliatory desires and once again renews the deep childhood feelings of being guilty and unworthy.

I know several men who were quite cruelly treated in their childhoods, and who now regularly use their wives as punching bags to work out the retaliative feelings of their old home backgrounds. These feelings couldn't be expressed when they were children but can be now that they are physically stronger than the person who is "at home" with them—their wives.

198

Why is the wife the target? Because she is the only adult closely connected to the "at home" atmosphere.

After striking their wives, these men may feel very guilty. They call themselves every foul name they can think of. They punish themselves, reminding themselves daily of how really bad they are, how unfair and brutal. They give themselves extra chores and go out of their way to be nice to reduce their guilty feelings. Gradually over a period of time this self-punishment builds up the old retaliative feelings—and then they again strike their wives. In many of the cases I have seen, the wives had also had punitive childhoods. Slapped, they may seem to forgive and forget but they get in their retaliatory digs in little cutting remarks which are subtly undermining, provoking and belittling. Usually it is one of these little "innocent" teasing remarks which provokes the retaliatory slap. Then it starts all over again.

Retaliation can take the form of reckless spending or even reckless driving, alcoholism or flirtations; much marital infidelity is occasioned by these resentful desires to "get even." Inevitably marital relations deteriorate unless someone learns to limit his retaliatory desires.

However, even when cruelty is met with cruelty, some marriages nevertheless continue. I have noticed that many times a woman who complains bitterly about her husband's abusiveness and cruelty nevertheless goes right on having one child after another, making it economically impossible for them to separate. And many a neighbor who has intervened in an abusive quarrel has been chased out by both husband and wife. Often what is at stake in such situations is the chance to retaliate—which would be destroyed by separation.

Punitiveness in Sex

This tendency to hurt and be hurt often plays a significant role in sexual relations. Freud and other psychiatrists and psychoanalysts have written extensively about this tendency in terms of sadistic and masochistic relationships. However, these terms and discussions seldom clarify the significance of childhood punitiveness and retaliatory drives in such sexual behavior.

The punitive parent mixes love and affection with his excessive punishment. Thus, often physical pain and abusiveness may become intertwined and enmeshed with the feeling of loving and being loved. We have all observed at some time the affectionate pinching and biting of infants, the breath-taking hugging and squeezing, the playful teasing and slapping with which some parents express their affection and adoration of their child. These activities often become an intrinsic part of the giving and receiving of love and affection. "Kiss me harder and give me a good hug," commands many a mother. "Give me a good hard kiss."

A person accustomed in this way to physical roughness, pinching or slapping in affection may feel unloved if these sensations are missing. Such persons often relate the giving or receiving of such treatment to the intensity of their emotional feelings. The punitive-retaliation cycle may, in such cases, be used to heighten sexual tension and desire. The teasing or balking "child of the past" in one partner may provoke activities bordering on cruelty in the other, who, parent-like, "punishes" with love, which is met with retaliatory acts, and so on.

As I have said earlier, one tends to bring one's "child of the past" into the bedroom. If your past background was filled with punishment mixed with love, retaliative and self-punishing feelings may easily develop in the intimate human love relationship of sexuality.

The Case of a Jealous Woman

One of the most destructive emotions commonly found in marriage is jealousy. In many instances this powerful emotion can be traced to the undischarged burning retaliatory feelings and the self-deprecation of a childhood of punitiveness. Such jealousy has little to do with events in the life of the adult. It is fed by the past.

The unhappy story of Eleanor is an example of this. An attractive young housewife, Eleanor was consumed with jealousy. She herself recognized this but claimed she couldn't help herself. If her husband looked with interest at dancers on a TV program, she flew into a blind, unreasoning and unreasonable rage, accusing, threatening, storming with fury.

She felt that she was ugly and repulsive to look at—although actually she was pretty and attractive. She believed that having two children had ruined her figure and that her husband was not interested in her, and she continuously voiced the suspicion that he was interested in other women. Filled with tension and resentment, she alternated between temper outbursts and moody "blue spells." Her behavior with her children followed these swings to extremes: she could scream at them, terrify and beat them —and then, feeling guilty, would treat them with excessive indulgence and submissiveness mixed with affection.

Her husband loved her and was not interested in other women. He tried in vain to convince her of this, constantly showing her affection and attention. Yet twice she left him and the children because she "just couldn't stand his interest in other women." When I talked with her, it became clear that while she felt she couldn't love and trust her husband because of her jealous suspicions of infidelity, she herself felt strongly attracted to her dentist, to a friendly and helpful neighbor and to the grocery delivery boy. Whatever was forbidden was attractive to her and all responsibilities were resented.

In our discussions I learned that throughout her growing-up years Eleanor, as well as her mother, sisters and a brother, lived in terror of her father. A powerful man, he drank heavily and constantly. He beat her mother and Eleanor—and anyone else who was around—on numerous occasions. When he was sober, he scorned and belittled them, sneering at them with contempt.

As an adult, Eleanor adopts toward herself the same scornful, sneering attitude her father expressed—and, in retaliation against this self-punishment, heaps anger and suspicion on her husband, lashing out at him. Deprived of loving attention in her childhood family life, she is so suspicious of it now that she cannot love anyone within her present family at this time. Yet she longs for love and attention from anyone outside her family group. Scorning herself, and anyone attached to her, she continually strikes back in retaliation for her early life, misinterpreting her husband in terms of her father's drunken rage and disgust.

After a few interviews, during which time I made no suggestions, she left her husband and their children for the third time. She went to a neighboring town where she got a job as a waitress. Her baffled husband asked his mother and father to let him and the children live with them, a request readily granted.

As a waitress, Eleanor's relations with people are more casual and adaptable to her mood. She does not have responsibilities to resent. Although her "blue spells" are now "bluer," for the moment this is a better solution for her and for her husband and children than the former situation, where she was constantly oscillating between temper outbursts and depression, between terrorizing and beating her children and then overindulging them. Until she has less need to retaliate against those close to her for the cruelties inflicted on her in childhood, she cannot manage her "child of the past" in any other way.

The Defense of Punitiveness

Many people sincerely believe that punitiveness is actually necessary to teach the child "discipline." They want the child to obey them without hesitation and do what they consider desirable—and to respect them. But punitiveness by itself is nearly a total failure as a teaching method for discipline and nearly 100 percent successful in teaching disrespect, hate and fear.

It teaches a respect for power and creates a desire for power in order to retaliate. But parents want loving respect—and when they get hateful respect, they are both hurt and more punitive. We pay a fantastic price for the end results of parental punitiveness in outlays for social services that range from child care agencies to psychiatric hospitals and elaborate police and prison systems. Financially, this amounts to millions yearly. But this doesn't begin to match the misery that punitiveness wreaks in human lives.

WHY DOESN'T PUNITIVENESS WORK? Punitiveness fails for a number of reasons. To start off with, it is based solely on power—the power of the parent. This seems natural and necessary because initially the child is incapable of acting with reason for his own safety and welfare.

But the power of the parent is generally used to meet the needs of the adult, not those of the child. What is often overlooked is that the child has feelings and, as he develops them, interests. In general, these are not respected by the punitive parent and are rather consistently ignored in favor of his own feelings; he even feels he is being a good parent in punitively "disciplining" his child. If the child protests, the parent overrules him by force and may give him a resounding slap to "teach" him not to protest against this disrespect of his feelings. The child may thus be forced to silence his protests and to obey—and at that moment he learns to hate.

As this process continues, the protests of the child become more vigorous. If he dares not express them, he may turn to deception, with the creation of guilt and self-contempt. But if he makes his retaliatory hate plain, the parent is hurt—and panicky. He fears loss of his ability to control the child. Guilt over past excessive punishment pours his panic into renewed punitiveness. "I'll teach you to respect me," he roars, but all he creates is the desire to strike back. Eventually the growth of the child's physical strength may force an end to physical punishment, but the parent's punitiveness has many forms. The child's desire to retaliate, to "get back at" the punitiveness and unnecessary restrictiveness of the parent, may then explode in rebellious behavior, in frank misbehavior, in poor schoolwork, defiance and rudeness, in promiscuity and delinquency in all its forms.

Punitiveness is a blind alley down which many American youths stagger—in the company of their parents. The adolescent rebellions and annual summer crises of delinquency, which are stimulated both by the summer school vacation and the prospect of returning to the restrictiveness of school, are often met with more punitiveness. "Back to the woodshed," cry the newspapers, demanding that the police "crack down" and that parents use harsher measures. Actually, as studies made at Harvard University and elsewhere show, between 60 percent and 90 percent of imprisoned delinquents were already being given constant physical punishment when arrested; only 30 percent of a nondelinquent group got such treatment.

Eventually, because our punishments fail to "teach," we conclude that such persons are "no good," "bad," and dangerous. By this time their retaliatory impulses are so uncontrollable that they are indeed dangerous. At this point we send them to prison. This is supposed to "teach" them once again that it is better to behave.

In the following account, written by a poorly educated young man imprisoned for retaliatory acts brought on by punitiveness, you can see the folly of such a belief:

My first institution was the truant school. At my age of 11½ years old. Society has denied me my freedom because I did not like to go to school. I was caught cussing one day. For that bad word I have said, they put a piece of soap in my mouth for one hour. For making an attempt to escape, I was put in a plain room with bars on the windows, no heat, no bed to lay on, no slippers or shus [shoes] to wear, with mice running all around me day and night. No clothes to wear but a nightshirt. This was in the month for February. So you can imagine how I felt . . .

My second place was the orphan home, at my age of 13 years old. Spent there two years. I was there about two weeks when a little lad has run out to get some apples. Another little lad has seen him. He went out and told the overseer about it. I told the little lad why has he told on him. For saying that to this lad, I get this punishment. I was taken into the assembly hall. And beat up something terrible. Which I could scarcely walk for 4 days afterwards.

My third place was ——— reformatory, at my age of 16 years. I was sent there for disorderly conduct. I have spent 9 months and 8 days there. You cannot learn anything there for your good. It was a school for teaching crime. And revenge on society. That's all you can learn from older men. Nothing good . . .

My fourth place was in ——— for one year at my age of 17 years. I went there with a bullet wound in my right hand. I have been getting it treated for two months. And my two officers in my shop took pity on me because I was a young lad thrown in among the old men. Every day they would ask me how my hand was getting along . . .

My next place was ——— prison, 2½ to 5 years, at my age of 18 years old. They doubled me up on a lad that is in the crazy house now. I have spent three nights in that cell when this lad propositioned me. I refused him. I told him never to talk to me again. So I wrote a note that night to the hall keeper asking him to single me out. It did not do any good. The fourth night I have felt sick from smoking too much when this evil-minded wretch thought he had the best of me that night. He has come up on my bed and tried to compel me to do it. I just throw him on the floor and started to fight with him . . .

. . . and treated like a beast I am going to act like a beast . . . What's left for me to do. I have lost time in —————— which I cannot get back. I have five months more for parole. If I make it I will be taken from one hell into another. I have to go to the —————— penitentiary for one year after I get through here. Can society expect me to reform. In the first place I could not reform if I did try. I was told right in my face when I came out they will send me right back. I will tell you if I get bothered when I get out it won't be well for the one that bothers me and it won't be well for me. But I don't care any more. One or the other, liberty or death. I am reddy to take what's coming. I have taken it before and can take it now . . . I have come out and gone from one institution to another. I am only a boy of 20 years of age. I went through five different places. I am going through my sixth and before I am a free man I will have gone through seven institutions.*

Thus is retaliatory crime perpetuated by punitiveness, by cruelty, shame, degradation and humiliating imprisonment. This cycle, recognized for decades now by criminologists and indeed even by prisoners, as this boy's account testifies, actually only continues the childhood desires to retaliate against excessive punishment.

Limits are necessary for retaliative people until their reactions become less vengeance-driven, more trusting and respectful. If we begin to look upon prisons as hospitals, we could begin to alter the punitiveness associated with them and to make the large-scale experiments in the treatment of such persons that are necessary.

The person who has tuberculosis is dangerous to society. We insist on limitations on his freedom and treatment until he is cured. But we do not subject such a person to recurrent hostility, degradation and humiliating punishment. We would say that he couldn't get well under such circumstances. In the same way people suffering from the excessive punishments of their parents cannot be cured in our prisons with more punishment. We could make a

* Quoted by Frank Tannenbaum, *Crime and the Community*, Ginn and Co., Boston, 1938.

significant step toward cure by raising the salaries and qualifications of the guards. At the present levels they tend to attract the person who is himself a victim of parental punitiveness and uses his job to retaliate—in the safety of society's name.

But until we tackle parental punitiveness on a broad scale and in the home, we will not be reaching the real roots of some of the greatest social problems. Few parental attitudes have such farflung implications and such disastrous results, results that are incompatible with our democratic way of life.

For example, as I write this, the Marine Corps commandant, General David M. Shoup, has ordered a halt to the "drumming out" ceremony for dishonorably discharged Marines at the Norfolk barracks. Although officially ended some years ago, the local commander revived it in the name of "discipline." In this humiliating ceremony, a disgraced Marine, who has already been condemned in a court-martial, is marched before a formation of troops while the "death march" is slowly tapped out on the drums. Then his "bad conduct" and dishonorable discharge orders are read aloud. Then an officer comments: "Escort this man from the confines of this United States Navy reservation."

The ex-Marine is then marched down the line of troops. As he reaches each unit, the commander orders "About face," and the Marine is presented with another row of backs.

This unnecessary and cruel ceremony was revived, according to Associated Press, by a local commander in 1960 and seven ex-Marines were thus "drummed out" before Marine headquarters caught up with it. Such a ceremony does not create discipline. It serves only the punitive desires of the man who ordered it.

Although at times condoned by retaliative people in power, this kind of punitiveness is no longer officially endorsed. We have made progress, as families and as a nation, in recognizing the folly of punitiveness. You can, in the treatment of yourself and others—particularly your own children—make a significant contribution to the reduction of this self-perpetuating misery.

Cultural Factors Supporting Punitiveness

Our culture, although it does provide legal means for separating children from parents who are obviously abusing them—as horrifying newspaper accounts of brutally beaten children testify—generally supports punitiveness. If you had a punitive background, this cultural support may cause considerable difficulty and confusion for you in trying to establish respectful limits to your own punishment-retaliation cycle.

Often a parent who has been severely punished as a child swears he will never punish his own child in such a fashion. But on becoming a parent, he may find himself behaving exactly as his parents did. Even though he may feel it is wrong, his exasperation in handling his child is extreme, and his desire to retaliate, treat his child as he was treated, is great. At this point our culture supports his punitiveness. Looking about him, he sees punitiveness on the part of other parents, he sees it approved and utilized in school, in the armed forces, called for by many religious and political leaders and finally carried out by our system of laws, courts and prisons.

It is at this critical point, pushed by retaliatory desires for the power to punish left over from his own childhood, that the parent becomes the "carrier" of the cultural attitude. The excessiveness of the punishment may depend, as shown earlier, on many factors. The significant thing is that punitiveness is thus perpetuated from generation to generation.

Distrust: A Special Form Of Punitiveness

There is a certain parental attitude, recognized by many psychiatrists and extensively studied, known as "distrust." While it affects relatively few persons, it is quite specific, readily identifiable, definitely incapacitating. A form of punitiveness, it is a parental attitude which anticipates a child's failure or inadequacy. Many parents are convinced their children are going to disobey them as soon as their backs are turned. Children sense this distrust and then do those things which their parents expected. You may have heard distrustful remarks like this: "He looks just

207

like his father and his father is inconsiderate. You can't expect him to be any different."

In their distrust, parents often prevent children from learning new skills because they expect failure. Comments like these stop children in their tracks: "You're too young for a bike." "You can't sing, why are you trying out for the glee club?" "You can't have a dog. You wouldn't take care of it." "A chemistry set is dangerous; you may hurt yourself. You can't have it."

Distrust by the parent creates a specific type of self-belittlement. If you distrust yourself, you anticipate your own inadequacy and failure; to use an old-fashioned phrase, "you are licked before you start." A person who distrusts himself has two marked characteristics—a gloomy, anxious foreboding of failure amounting to a feeling of being *doomed* to fail, and a tendency to gravitate into areas where he feels most distrustful and inadequate.

In its *anticipation* of failure, distrust differs markedly from most self-belittlement, which is usually abusive about past efforts. This time factor is important; often distrust becomes the reason why no effort is made. Therefore it is particularly incapacitating.

All of us have experienced at one time or another the anxious foreboding of imminent failure. Even if we fail, this feeling and continued failure seldom becomes our way of life. Yet this is what happens to the person who, continuing the parental attitude of his childhood, distrusts himself. Most of us recognize that our failure stems from certain lack of preparation or training, and that we can and will acquire the necessary knowledge and skill in time if we make the effort. If it requires muscles we do not have, we may give up the effort, without much regret. The victim of distrust, however, feels "doomed to fail"— and he does. Moreover, he renews his efforts in areas where he is almost bound to fail.

Thus, in time the person suffering from distrust characteristically shuns the making of efforts that would demonstrate his abilities and capacities are not so inadequate as he feels they are. Such a person may feel he can't get a job, can't get a date, can't behave properly, can't graduate, can't drive, can't "amount to anything." If he "makes the rounds" seeking employment, his general self-distrust expresses itself in interviews by fumbling mannerisms and lack of confidence in himself; he is a poor competitor.

And again his failure to get the job seems to confirm his own feeling that he is predestined to fail.

The second marked characteristic of the person suffering from distrust is his tendency to attempt to function in the area in which he most distrusts himself. This is no simple "attraction of opposites." Many cases have made it clear that the person who distrusts himself is often driven by his distrust itself to attempt to do whatever he distrusts his abilities to do.

THE MECHANISM OF REPEATED FAILURE: In time, the repeated "failures" of the person who distrusts himself, and the resultant feelings of despondency, contempt, dependency and misery, gradually create such profound feelings of self-contempt that he is driven to attempt the very activities in which he most distrusts his abilities. In short, he rebels against his own self-defeating and distrusting attitude toward himself. In this mood of "I'll show 'em," he attempts a brash, often grandiose feat, a "grandstand play." He hopes in this way to wipe out his past humiliation and misery and to establish not only self-esteem, but respect in others for his abilities.

However, because this effort is dictated by his powerful, long-accumulated feelings of self-contempt over past failures rather than any realistic assessment of the difficulties and preparation of the components for success, its timing is inevitably inopportune. Moreover, his past "failures" select automatically the very area in which he most distrusts his abilities instead of one in which he might feel more confident.

The result of this rebellious and compulsive effort is nearly always total failure, creating still greater despondency—and an objective failure to which to point as the cause of his unhappiness and proof of his being "doomed to fail." This failure becomes a reason for not attempting anything. "I tried and I failed," such a person may say. "There's no use in trying. I can't win."

These ill-conceived, ill-timed efforts are spasmodic, dependent on the boiling over of self-contempt, for the distrusting person often has—and knows he has—considerable ability. Often he is intelligent, sensitive and truly capable. Yet his distrust disables him. What has invariably been sacrificed between these grandiose efforts and their inevitable failure are countless opportunities for less spectacular achievements, easily within his capacities, and from which he might have gained real satisfaction. These achievements, however insignificant initially, might realistically reduce both his distrust of his abilities and his despondency and dependency. Moreover, they would help him dry up the self-punishing bog of distrust in which he can only wallow without advancing himself.

Setting Limits on Your Punitive Feelings

A sound, workable alternative to the continuation of your self-punishing and retaliatory feelings of childhood is setting respectful limits on these feelings. Sometimes when I discuss this at length with medical students, mental health and social workers and physicians, I get a response that goes like this: "Doctor, you have said a mouthful. Now just what do you mean?"

Let me explain it this way: setting respectful limits on the feelings of your "child of the past" means, first of all, that you must learn to recognize and respect your feelings, all of them and no matter what they are, whether they arise from the present or the past, whether they are anxious, hostile, guilty, self-belittling, impulsive desires, melancholy or indignant.

Most of the time we hardly recognize our feelings. We just respond to them. Recognizing them is the first step in determining clearly how you feel and "what's bothering you." Feelings tend to be cumulative—not just one incident, but a whole string or pattern of incidents or situations. Therefore, in recognizing your feelings, it may be helpful to try to discover if a whole series of events is not involved. A series of disappointments, frustrations or abuses may, for example, be involved. It isn't the "straw that broke the camel's back" that you are looking for —usually that crisis or incident will be clear enough— but the great mound that was piled on before that last straw.

You will find that simply clarifying and recognizing your feelings is helpful. What it will do is help you get a more objective picture of that "last straw" and the cumulative burden under it.

However, what can make a significant difference in developing a new way of treating yourself lies in respecting these feelings. You must not punish yourself for having these feelings. Most of the time we do not respect our feelings. We belittle and punish ourselves for having them, calling ourselves "childish," "stupid," "bad" and feeling that we are "no good" or worthless.

Recognizing and respecting these feelings, most of which arise from childhood and get their main strength from the past, does not mean giving in to them. We must limit them instead. We must not allow them to punish us, interfere with or dominate our adult lives or the pursuit of adult goals.

As a kindly but firm parent, you must say to yourself, to your "inner child of the past," "Yes, I recognize how you feel. You feel stupid and bad because that is what you were called in the past when you made an error, but I am not going to punish myself because I made a mistake. I will try to be careful and make amends for this error and get on with the job." The "child of the past" is used to self-belittling punishment. Therefore, you may feel strange and lost if you limit your self-belittlement. But gradually you will be able to be more relaxed and to enjoy your adult activities more fully because you will not be harassed so much by the feelings of the "child of the past." They will be recognized, respected but limited to the past, where they really belong.

For example, if you suffered from punitiveness as a child, you will have two main problems in acting as a parent to yourself. One results from the excessive punishment you suffered in childhood: feelings of guilt, of being "no good," bad, not worth loving, and similar self-belittling feelings. As an adult, you probably continue to punish yourself with these feelings, especially when you err or do something that was forbidden as a child, or when you meet with some disappointment or failure.

In being a kindly parent to yourself you must recognize and respect these feelings. But you must also recognize that this feeling will return if you lash out impulsively in retaliation. You must say to yourself, "That guilty feeling and self-belittling was created in my childhood and doesn't belong to my activities and life today. I am not going to beat myself up about that mistake but correct it and try to be more careful."

If you do not limit this feeling in a respectful way, your self-punishment will be carried to the point where it will force you to retaliate in some impulsive, hurtful way, usually toward someone you love. You must learn to recognize this feeling as belonging to the "child of the

211

past," respect it but learn to limit it and focus on respecting what you are now and what you have genuinely achieved as an adult—and not let these feelings of being "bad" and "no good" destroy your satisfaction in what you have achieved.

The second main problem of a person who suffered a punitive upbringing lies in the management of his retaliatory feelings. Of course, if you can reduce your tendency to punish yourself with self-belittlement, you have cut the ground out from many of your retaliatory feelings. If you can respect your feelings and yourself, you will not need to retaliate against others.

Like your self-punishing feelings of guilt and deprecation, your powerful retaliatory feelings were created by the excessive punishment and restrictions of your childhood. You must recognize and respect these feelings, your desire to hurt and smash. These feelings may lie smoldering within you and flare up furiously if someone is even a little hostile or unfair or inconsiderate of you. A petty thing like a social snub may create an inferno. The heat and fury of these retaliatory feelings comes from the excessiveness of the punishments you suffered in childhood. And almost invariably the heat and fury of these past excessive punishments pushes you into excessive retaliation; you are an adult now, you say, and you'll show 'em they can't get away with this.

You must respect these feelings—without belittling or punishing yourself for having them. But you must understand how they were created in you and limit their expression, recognizing that retaliation only brings more punishment—because when you realize the excessiveness of your outburst you punish yourself still more.

You must say, in your role as parent to yourself, "Yes, I'm really burned up, but a lot of this hate and furious resentment is simply my 'inner child of the past' raging over past punishments, punishments I didn't deserve. But part of this is self-punishment. I am not going to fly off the handle, saying and doing things that are going to result in more punishment and hostility just to satisfy these past resentments. This isn't that much of an issue. That is the way I acted before. I do not have to be a punitive parent to myself."

By acting as a kindly, respectful parent to your "child of the past" in this fashion, limiting the expression of his furious retaliative feelings, you can be more objective and express your adult feelings more forcefully, without the excessiveness that will make you sorry later, guilty and self-belittling.

Let no one think this is easy. It requires enormous patience. It requires a willingness to struggle. It will take determination. For your "child of the past" will sneer and balk, scream and make you anxious, hurl contempt on your firm limits. It will be very easy for you to give in to his fierce retaliatory demands. You can, however, control and limit these troublemaking demands respectfully.

As your ability to limit these retaliatory impulses grows, as you become a kinder parent to yourself than your own parents were able to be, you will feel yourself grow. You will not be tied in knots, wasting your energy in the punishment-retaliation cycle.

And, as a respectful parent to yourself, you will no longer need to punish yourself.

CHAPTER 16

NEGLECT—
If you feel you do not—and cannot—
"belong"

YOUR INDEX OF SUSPICION: *If you have difficulty in feeling close to others and in "belonging" to a group, drift in and out of relationships casually because people do not seem to mean much to you, if you feel you lack an identity of your own, suffer intensely from anxiety and loneliness and yet keep people at a distance, you should suspect neglect as the troublemaking pathogenic factor in your childhood. An additional clue suggesting neglect: prolonged separation from your parents, particularly your mother, by death, divorce, hospitalization or because of parental activities and interests.*

Long-term studies of deprivation, brilliantly summarized by Dr. John Bowlby in his book *Maternal Care and Mental Health*** for the World Health Organization, demonstrate that emotional neglect in childhood creates "scar tissue" in one's feelings which seriously handicaps the individual's ability to respond to others, to feel close to them and to participate with satisfaction in social activities. These studies show that the degree of neglect in childhood and its marked and specific effects in later life are directly and proportionately linked. They throw significant light on the problems of many people who might not be thought to be suffering from childhood neglect. Thus, much that has been little understood has now been clarified.

---

* John Bowlby, *Maternal Care and Mental Health,* World Health Organization, Geneva, 1951.

What Is Neglect?

Neglect is usually a parental attitude—often expressed as a preoccupation with work or "duties"—which results in the parent having little time for, interest in or awareness of the child's need for a continuing attachment with an adult to whom he can turn for help in satisfying his needs. Such an adult fails to provide interested and sympathetic support to the child's efforts to feel satisfied with himself, and so does not give the child the feeling that he has someone "in his corner."

Often a father, away during the day and when home preoccupied with adult affairs or "resting," is neglectful without being aware of it; even when it is pointed out, he may not understand the child's need for his interested attention. Similarly, the mother, who may be involved in everything from a job to PTA and hospital fund drives, may be "too busy" to give each child her individual attention in a meaningful way. Often such parents never become aware of their neglect until the child runs afoul of the neighbors or the law and the problem is brought to public attention. We have all seen the ironic news story of the prominent citizen who concerned himself with juvenile delinquency and whose son is arrested for it.

Neglect can be caused by anything that deprives a child of his full share of his parents' loving attention, whether it be social improvement, sickness, alcoholism, business, death or bowling. Often neglect is the result of elements beyond the parent's control, as it is in the case of a parent's death; this is why the word "factor" may be a more appropriate word in some cases than "attitude." But in many cases it is an attitude or preoccupation of the parent which omits or prevents adequate consideration of the child's needs.

Many of us suffered from partial or transient neglect. As will be shown later, severe deprivation in childhood has severe effects in adult life, but the effects of partial or transient neglect are milder depending on the age when this deprivation was suffered. Fortunately, most neglect has not been extreme.

Recognizing the Effects of Neglect in Your Past and Present Life

Looking back on your childhood, you may find that neglect is hard to track down. Emotional neglect is a phantom, elusive and empty thing, for the simple reason that it is the absence of something. For the same reason, it is difficult to recognize and cope with in adult life; it is again the absence of something.

Initially, what is missing is the continuing opportunity for the child to form and maintain a close, approving attachment with a parent who makes the child feel he is a "special," unique and worthy individual. Lacking this relationship, the child's feelings about himself and about others become numb, uncertain, distorted and empty. He lacks capacity to feel that he is important and to respond or be deeply concerned with others and how they feel. This makes contact with others shallow and unrewarding. If you suffered from neglect in childhood, it may cause you to go from one person to another, hoping that someone will supply whatever is missing. You may not be able to care much about yourself, and think marriage will end this, and then find yourself in the alarming situation of being married but emotionally unattached.

Because it is an absence of something intangible—never known in the first place—many people who suffered from neglect in childhood do not recognize the nature of their difficulties. In their unhappy loneliness they may believe their problems arise from some childhood traumatic experience, some fear or punitive blow for which they may search endlessly in vain. Usually it does not exist and never did. As one such person once put it: "Nothing happened." Such persons may hold enormous expectations toward others but keep them at a distance, then blame them for failing to make them "live."

Or you may feel no need to be close to others and be alarmed at their efforts to be close to you. Feeling trapped and panicky, you may try frantically to keep them at a distance. Yet if they move away in response to your cool aloofness, you may feel still more anxious or depressed. Never having been close to anyone in childhood, you may endlessly seek this warmth, yet always be frightened and withdraw at any hint of its arrival. In your loneliness, you may already have observed this pattern in your life, observed the warmth and satisfying closeness of others and come to recognize that something is missing.

Often this feeling that something is missing is the best indication of neglect in your early life. Such awareness can help you to assess the neglect you knew in childhood and help you establish your specific problem. It can also help you find ways to reduce the need for distance which is continuing the deprivation of your childhood.

Our New Understanding of Neglect

Our recognition and understanding of neglect has changed significantly since World War II. Neglect is now recognized as being a common pathogenic attitude in homes that are physically comfortable and staffed with parents who enjoy social status. In *Oliver Twist* Dickens produced a classic picture of neglected and deprived children starving for love and attention as well as for the thin gruel of the orphanage. Today it is recognized that the thin gruel of attention and affection given children in many busy middle-class homes causes the same effects of emotional neglect commonly seen among long-institutionalized children. Physical neglect, while certainly a deprivation, and often an indication of emotional neglect, is neither as common nor as incapacitating as its psychic counterpart. The essential situation can be stated simply but starkly: If you had a father who somehow wasn't a father and a mother who somehow wasn't a mother when you really needed them, you suffered from some degree of neglect.

What opened many eyes to the true character and widespread existence of neglect was the World War II experience with children in England. Those who remained with their mothers in bombed-out ruins, often on poor rations, with little water and without sanitary facilities or beds, were less disturbed emotionally, despite nightly bombings, than children moved to safer and healthier quarters but separated from their mothers.

Since then neglect has been subjected to intensive study and found to cut across all social, religious, economic and geographical bounds. Not long ago Dr. R. N. Rapoport reported on the effect of neglect on children of materially successful, "privileged" families.* Unhappy, maladjusted, often involved in delinquent behavior, these children had little or no contact with their parents. Often the parents were neglectful because they were active in socially commendable endeavors. In some instances the parents had been "drafted" to serve the entire community by developing much-needed services for children.

Yet their contact with their own children was limited and meaningless. These children could not, of course, understand the need to develop new building codes, slum clearance or the organizing work involved in creating an effective reform of the city administration. They only knew that they rarely saw their busy parents alone, that they were warned not to interrupt their parents' conversation and had been handed over to a succession of indifferently interested "sitters," nurses, maids and other adults. One of the most common types noted by Rapoport is the "poor little rich girl" who is "starved for the kinds of intimate relationships that nourish healthy emotional development." Often parents send their children off to expensive schools, telling themselves that they are getting "the best" for them, without realizing that this too can be a form of neglect.

However, neglect is not something visited only upon the well-to-do. Children are neglected in every stratum of our society by alcoholic parents, by "busy" ones, by parental absorption in all kinds of activities. And sometimes parents are overwhelmed by disastrous turns in their affairs, such as unemployment, prolonged sickness, overwork and personal unhappiness. Sometimes, the simple fact of having too many children makes it impossible for an overworked and exhausted mother not to neglect the individual child.

Episodes of Neglect

Every child needs help continuously, from early infancy through adolescence, in his efforts to become an individual. He needs to feel someone cares about him, that someone who cares is "behind me," backing him up in his effort to "be someone."

* R. N. Rapoport, *American Journal of Orthopsychiatry*, 28:656, 1958.

Most of us suffered from episodes of neglect, periods when we did not feel we had the attention and support of our parents. Generally these episodes were short-lived and due to special circumstances, but they may have been prolonged and devastating in their effect. If you suffered from such neglect, it will help you in becoming a kinder parent to yourself to have some perspective on these episodes in your childhood.

For instance, if you can recall periods when you felt that nobody really cared about you or what you did, when you felt inadequate and there was no one to whom you could turn for sympathetic understanding, you may recognize the specific kind of neglect you encountered and at what age. Sometimes what you wished for in childhood may similarly help you. You may, by recalling the specific times when you felt that nobody cared very much about you, be able to establish the duration of this episode by other circumstances. For instance, you may have felt this during a period when your mother was ill or hospitalized. Or during a period when your parents were preoccupied with unemployment or other stress.

From this you may learn that the period was long or short, and this may give you some perspective on your problem. If you find that the period was relatively short, you may be overemphasizing its effect. If it was persistent, you may underemphasize it—for this absence of attention became your way of experiencing life.

You cannot gain this perspective mechanically. Parental difficulties, for example, do not always mean neglect. A man I know suffers today from certain kinds of neglect he experienced when he was a child because his mother was always busy with the younger children. His father went off to work early in the morning and when he came home he was preoccupied with his work, and also had to be "shared" with others. As a boy, this man fell under the supervision of an aunt who, in trying to help his mother, believed he should keep himself clean, not get into rough or dirty places and not bother her. Her idea was that he "should be a little gentleman," which meant sitting straight in a chair, answering when spoken to and reading "something educational." For many years he endured a lonely existence. His own pale existence was insignificant and measly compared to the deeds of the knights he read about. He had no real feeling about himself and what he could do. His aunt constantly asked him to "help out" but then criticized whatever he did. He seldom saw his father except at the supper table and felt he did not know him.

One summer, however, his father, a much overworked man, was out of a job and remained at home. Although troubled by his economic plight, he was affectionate and interested in his son. He took over his management, allowed him to do all kinds of things previously forbidden, such as playing near the railroad tracks and the river, laughed in a kindly way at his getting dirty and at his mistakes, and encouraged him to play with anybody who felt like playing. Within the course of a few months, "My father made me feel I was somebody," the man says today.

Therefore, your identification of episodes of neglect should be carefully examined. This boy was neglected when, economically, his family was better off than when his father was unemployed. Your best guide is your memory of how you felt.

"Who Am I?"

One day an internist referred a young woman to me. Well dressed and pleasant looking, she complained she often felt wobbly and unbalanced when standing or walking. "Sometimes," she said, "I actually shake." Her obvious anxiety made her seem restless and taut. Her actual words were something like this:

"If I could only have the feeling of identity, of actually being a person. Who am I? I keep asking myself. I know my name, my address and all that sort of thing, but it doesn't mean much to me. I still feel I am not a person somehow. I never know, for example, what I want when I go in a restaurant. I just don't seem to remember what I like or want. Sometimes I have spells when I feel that I am crawling into myself.

"Other women get satisfaction from having a home and children, but they don't give me that much satisfaction. I feel restless and discontented. Anyone could do this, I think. Sometimes at parties I cannot concentrate on what people are saying to me. I just try to look as though I understand, smile and nod or frown, trying to do whatever seems to be expected of me. But I look at these people and I know I really don't know them or understand them. They are friends, people I know very well, but I don't feel connected to them. They could be strangers. In fact, I feel they are strangers—and that I am a stranger too. Sometimes at parties I've walked around feeling as though there is nothing but emptiness in me. I feel apart from everyone, even my husband."

Her husband was a rather formal person who was a conscientious, somewhat meticulous accountant. He couldn't understand his wife's restless anxiety. It made him anxious —so he just buried himself a little deeper in his work, hoping that she would eventually "snap out of it," as he put it.

This is how this woman described her home background:

"I grew up in a large city. My father did not have much education and we lived in one of the poorer sections. It was shabby and ugly. I remember being very unhappy about it in my teens. The boys around there were nasty and foul-minded, sort of sneering and mean. They looked at you like . . . well, you know, sort of aggressive and threatening.

"I couldn't communicate with my father. Not just this about the boys, but anything. It was always like that. About anything. He would go out every evening to see his friends. When I finished high school, he felt I didn't need any more education. 'What for?' he'd say. 'You'll be getting married and then what good will your education do you?' And of course I just couldn't explain about these boys, things like that, and he'd be off—accusing me of flirting with them, and the whole thing worried me.

"My mother was the same way. She didn't want to hear anything I had to say. She spent much of her time going to doctors and getting nerve remedies. She used to complain about my father; she is still complaining about him. She never sat down and discussed anything or asked me anything. She never took a really conscious interest in any of us kids.

"I did well in school, which was why I was interested in education. The teacher used to ask us who was going to college and was always surprised I didn't put my hand up. I wrote for the school paper and had the lead in some school plays. I liked that best of anything I ever did. At home I used to read in my room because there wasn't anybody I could talk to. My brother was much older and out of the house like my father. And if I stayed downstairs, I had to listen to my mother's complaints. I could never get her to listen to me."

As you can see from her story, this woman spent most of her childhood in a lonely vacuum, unable to be close to anyone. Her father, seldom around, did not take much interest in her in any active way. Her mother was too preoccupied with her anxieties about her health and her husband to form a warm, close relationship with her daughter. As she grew older, in loneliness, she became anxious and frightened in her daily activities. In adult life, her "inner child of the past" perpetuates both her inability to communicate with others and her fears about life with other people—the rough boys of the neighborhood in her childhood. She hasn't much of a relationship with herself because in childhood her parents failed to give her the feeling that she was a unique and worthy person whose feelings and interests were worth attention. What she felt and thought in childhood were never given consideration—and it makes her anxious to consider them important now.

This woman's story is typical of the kind of emotional neglect that thousands of persons suffer from. Usually, as in her situation, they escape devastating psychological damage because someone outside the home—in her case, her teachers—gives them some feeling of worth and some opportunity to express themselves. However, one of the major difficulties of persons suffering from neglect is that they have such a hazy notion of what a warm, close human relationship is like. They do not easily comprehend the value of satisfaction in such a relationship.

The childhood of persons who suffered from neglect usually reveals a father who somehow wasn't a father and a mother who somehow wasn't a mother. Thus, in adult life, the neglected "child of the past" maintains the security of this familiar emptiness and prevents the formation of any deep, close relationship. "I know a lot of people, but I have no friends. I just don't care very much for any of them when you come right down to it," such a person told me once.

In some respects the relationships of persons who suffered from neglect in childhood resemble those of an actor to his audience. In childhood such a person may have discovered that he could win the warm applause and approval of his parents, their momentary attention and love, through his achievements and good manners. Often such children are driven to accomplish many feats brilliantly in a desperate effort to win their parents' consideration. But a close relationship and mutual interest doesn't develop.

In such circumstances a child learns to expect nothing but applause. More than momentary warmth and love do not exist. As an adult, he goes on performing, winning friends and impressing them with his accomplishments, gracious manners, seeming thoughtfulness.

Yet if people try to move close to him, he will break off the relationship abruptly—even though he may really want a closer relationship desperately. Closeness threatens the security of neglect on which his "child of the past" has been nourished. To such a person, closeness is frightening, binding and entrapping.

Exploitive Tendency

Often the person whose childhood has been scarred by neglect becomes expert in exploiting others. Unable to attach himself in any deep way to anyone, he turns to using others. He knows just how to stimulate interest and sympathy in himself. And he will demand love and affection, constant attention and emotional support for his endeavors—even material support. But this is a one-way street. If such support is asked of him in return, he will abruptly break off the relationship. In many cases of severe neglect this tendency to exploit leads, in the case of a boy, into his becoming a petty thief or hoodlum. In the case of a girl, she may become promiscuous and ultimately a prostitute. Such persons tend to see life as a "racket" and they have little feeling for themselves or others except in a superficial, exploitive way.

Many investigators have pointed out that children—and adults—with neglect in their backgrounds are conscienceless. This lack of conscience tends to facilitate their drifting from one casual relationship to another, for in many cases they do not feel their connections with others in a deep way. This same lack of conscience sees exploitation of others as normal and even desirable. The rights, property and feelings of others are something to be taken and used. In his studies Bowlby emphasized the frequency of petty pilfering among children who had suffered from severe neglect and deprivation. However, most persons have not had such deprived backgrounds.

My own observations would seem to indicate that there is often a definite connection between the amount of guilt felt by an adult about doing something wrong or inconsiderate and the amount of neglect he suffered or didn't suffer as a child. If he does not feel guilty, he has good reason to suspect he suffered from neglect. If he suffers from guilt feelings he had someone close to him in his childhood. The exception is the inconsiderate person who feels guiltless because his parents, though close to him, condoned his inconsiderate actions in childhood.

IMPULSIVENESS: Because it is the absence of something never really known, many people have great difficulty in recognizing the effects of neglect in their adult lives. In many instances they fall back on impulsiveness in order to feel "alive." They rush here and there, plunge into romances, keep up a frantic schedule of activities. But usually all this activity is without any goal related to their deeper needs, and hence provides only momentary satisfactions.

Superficially, the famous movie star with her numerous conquests and marriages, the world statesman and his lonely, melancholy wisdom, and the woman whose life consists of serving others do not seem to have been particularly neglected either in childhood or adult life.

Yet often they are deeply unhappy in their continuing self-neglect. They have, regardless of the face they turn toward the world, little or no feeling about themselves as persons except those of hopelessness and despair. Rather than living, they exist as shadows. Many such people, particularly women, are drawn into theatrical and movie work because, in this work and atmosphere, they can create a fantasy identity. Their inner feelings about themselves are so despairing that they do not feel they can pay attention to these feelings. As one such woman once put it: "When you're a nobody, the only way to be anybody is to be somebody else."

Often the continuous striving for success is one of the characteristics of such persons. While in some cases this may represent an effort to compensate for some past economic deprivation, it is often an attempt to deny inner

224

feelings of emptiness by creating a reassuring display of wealth or an impressive reputation for serving others.

Establishing the Degree of Neglect in Your Life

If you suffered from neglect in your childhood, it is important to understand, as objectively as possible, its degree. Otherwise you may misinterpret the problem. You may not recognize what you have in the way of assets in meeting the difficulties, and you may not be prepared for setbacks. You may surrender yourself to sterile despair, self-pity and hopelessness without realizing that you are both magnifying the problem and capable of managing it. No matter how extreme the deprivations you knew as a child, you can help yourself today if you will accept your "child of the past" by being a kind and loving parent to yourself now—the kind of parent you did not have!

You can gain some insight into your own difficulties and assess the severity of any neglect in your childhood from studies of what are recognized to be the most severe kinds of deprivation. Such studies provide a yardstick by which you can estimate, with some objectivity, the neglect you suffered.

The most severe type of neglect, in its effects on the personality's ability to relate to others with satisfaction, is caused by the mother's death and the subsequent hospitalization or institutionalization of the child for a long period in infancy. In a way we have always known that separation of the mother and child in infancy is harmful to the child, but only recently have we had adequate scientific data to demonstrate precisely how and why.

Deprivation in the First Years of Life: Many years ago Franz Boas, the famous American anthropologist, demonstrated that children raised in orphanages did not develop physically as well as those in family homes. Yet nearly fifty years passed before pediatricians and psychiatrists were able to assemble sufficient data to demonstrate that such emotional neglect had specific harmful effects on the child's feeling about himself and his ability to concern himself with others. Independent studies by many

225

different investigators, including Drs. Harry L. Bakwin,* R. A. Spitz,† William Goldfarb‡ and others, demonstrate these essential findings.

These studies show that while in the first weeks of life the infant can be taken care of by different people without any deleterious effect, between the ages of a few months and five years the child needs the continuous attention of a single person—his mother or an adequate, loving mother-substitute—if he is to escape personality difficulties in later life.

The children studied were primarily those who had been institutionalized in infancy as a result of death or prolonged hospitalization of the mother. Dr. John Bowlby analyzed and studied the work of all investigators and supplemented it with his own work. He points out that the child thus deprived reacts in the following way:

The emotional tone of such a child is one of apprehension and sadness, there is withdrawal from the environment tantamount to rejection of it, there is no attempt to contact a stranger and no brightening if this stranger contacts him. Activities are retarded and the child often sits or lies inert in a dazed stupor. Insomnia is common and lack of appetite universal. Weight is lost and the child becomes prone to recurrent infections. The drop in Developmental Quotient [a system of measuring and grading development] is precipitous.

Yet return of the child to his mother or the appearance of a mother-substitute reverses this picture. Dr. Bakwin has described such an incident with a boy four months of age (two of which had been spent in the hospital) whose condition was critical:

His appearance was that of a pale, wrinkled old man. His breathing was so weak and superficial that

* Harry L. Bakwin, *American Journal of Diseases of Children, 63:* 30, 1942.

† R. A. Spitz, "Hospitalism," in *Psychoanalytic Study of the Child,* ed. O. Fenichel, New York: International University Press, 1945; *Ibid.,* 2:113, 2:313, 1946.

‡ William Goldfarb, "Effects of Early Institutional Care on Personality, Behavior," *Child Development, 14:*213, 1943; *American Journal of Orthopsychiatry, 13:*249, 1943; *Ibid., 14:*162, 1944; *American Journal of Psychiatry, 102:*18, 1945.

it seemed as though he might stop breathing at any moment. When seen 2-4 hours after he had been at home, he was cooing and smiling. Though no change had been made in his diet, his weight was well within the normal range. He appeared in every way a normal child.

These changes are so dramatic and beneficial that Bowlby, who studied similar cases, points out that it "is astonishing that so little attention has been given to them hitherto."

Bowlby and other investigators are agreed that introduction of a mother-substitute at the earliest possible moment does a great deal to offset the effect of separation from the mother. Most experts believe that substitute care can successfully prevent emotional damage in the first year of life. And all are agreed that continuous, interested substitute care, even if not wholly adequate, is indispensable in preventing later emotional problems.

This loss of the mother in the first five years of life is believed by most investigators to be the most serious deprivation for a child. If you were separated from your mother for a prolonged time in this period, you undoubtedly suffered greatly from the loss. Your loss was offset by someone who, while not as comforting as your own mother and perhaps even ignorant or mean, nevertheless gave you love and care during those crucial five years. Thus, your capacity to feel close to others may not be as totally impaired as you may sometimes think in "blue moods." Whatever this capacity, you can, in being a kind parent to yourself, enlarge it through your understanding.

The loss of a parent through death, which is irretrievable, is, of course, a serious deprivation for a child of any age. However, this loss becomes progressively less severe in its results as the child attains his sixth year and grows older, although often it is felt severely even in adolescence.

By understanding this most severe loss, you can begin to put your own deprivations into an objective perspective. This will help you in being a parent to your "child of the past." You can begin to recognize the old feelings of your "inner child of the past," feelings of desolation, rage, withdrawal and detachment. These feelings have caused you to deny yourself the warmth and closeness you never knew as a child in sufficient quantity to feel "at home" with them. You can set aside these feelings now as belonging

227

to the past and gradually permit yourself to enjoy the friendship and intimacy of others bit by bit until you feel "at home" with these feelings. If you give yourself times and places when you can retreat into distances that feel secure, you can, with patience and understanding, gradually diminish this past need for distance.

Grief: Protest, Despair, Detachment

What is profoundly involved in this early deprivation separating the child from the parent are the grief and mourning processes within the child over his loss. This takes place even if the loss is temporary, as it sometimes is when the child must be hospitalized for several months. It is the loss—not the cause of the loss—that sets off these processes.

According to Dr. Bowlby, who has made intensive studies of grief and mourning in children, the child goes through three significant phases in his mourning: protest, despair and detachment.

At first, with tears and anger, he loudly demands his parent's return and he may seem hopeful that he will succeed. This may last for several days. But eventually, while still preoccupied with his absent parent and yearning for her return, his hopes dwindle and fade—and this signals the beginning of the despairing phase. He whimpers softly and despairingly for his parent. For a while the child may alternate between protest and despair.

But then a still greater change occurs. He seems to forget his parent altogether. If at last she comes for him, he may remain curiously uninterested in her and may not seem to recognize her. This is the detachment phase.

"In each of these phases," Dr. Bowlby points out, "the child is prone to tantrums and episodes of destructive behavior, often of the disquietingly violent kind. Depending on how long the separation has been, this unresponsiveness may last from a few hours to weeks. Then he may cling to his mother and become enraged or acutely anxious at her absence even for a moment. If the child has been separated from his parents for a long period, the child may reach an advanced stage of detachment and remain detached, never recovering his affection for his parents."

What is the effect of this loss of the parent on the adult?

One such patient has been described by Dr. Helene Deutsch in this way: "He showed a complete blocking of affect [his feelings] without the slightest insight . . . He has no love relationships, no friendships, no real interests of any sort. To all kinds of experience he showed the same dull and apathetic reaction. There was no endeavor and no disappointment . . . There were no reactions of grief at the loss of individuals near to him, no unfriendly feelings and no aggressive impulses."*

In commenting on this case, Dr. Bowlby observes that this man's mother had died when he was five years old. He had no memories of events prior to her death but afterward he left his bedroom door open in the hope that "a large dog would come to him, be very kind to him and fulfill all his wishes."

Dr. Bowlby points out that this man, presumably unable to express his protest, anger and yearning for his mother over her seeming desertion, had moved swiftly into a stage of detachment from which he was not able to free himself and all his feelings: ". . . the yearning and the anger had become locked inside him, potentially active but shut off from the world . . . and only the remainder of his personality had been left for further development. As a result he grew up gravely impoverished."

Often if the feelings of anger, rage and despair and yearning involved in the mourning process, and pent up since childhood, can be fully expressed to someone who is liked and trusted, the entire personality may gain a new state of balance and become able to function in areas previously shut off.

If you lost a parent in childhood, you may vividly recall some of your feelings of protest, of anger and rage, of helpless despair and yearning—or you may, over the years, have tried to deny them. If this loss occurred when you were old enough to know, for example, that your parent did not die deliberately to hurt you, you may have been ashamed of these angry feelings and felt guilty about them. You may still feel that way about them. But actually these are very natural feelings and in being a kind parent to your deprived "child of the past" you should recognize this and not be ashamed or suffer guilt over these feelings.

Often the loss hurts so much that in his anger and rage against the parent who has seemingly abandoned him, the

* Helene Deutsch, *Psychoanalytic Quarterly*, 6:12, 1937.

child is filled with retaliatory feelings. He wants to strike back against this unfair blow—and, particularly if the loss causes other severe problems and deprivations, he may accumulate so much resentment and retaliatory hatred that he forgets his parent is a human being. For example, a timid and quiet man married to an intelligent but dominating woman was pushed this way and that by her. She gloried in her role as mother of their growing brood of children, demanding and bossing him in their name. Her husband finally rebelled—and deserted the family. His loss was felt keenly by the children and bitterly by his wife. "He was," she reminded the children as they struggled along on relief allocations, inadequate clothing allowances and many deprivations, "a no-good bum." His oldest son, who had particularly enjoyed his father's quiet affection, now had thrust on him many of the responsibilities and chores his father had performed. With intense bitterness, he now blamed the family's economic problems and often desperate plight on his father. He would grind his teeth with rage and promise himself that "someday I'm going to catch up with him and tell him what a rat, what a louse he is, what he did to us—and what the hell did we ever do to him?"

Years passed, but his childhood goal—the retaliatory demolition of his father—was not forgotten. One day more than twenty years later he learned that his father was living in a nearby city. He lost little time in getting there. He went directly to the neighborhood where his father lived—and then realized he probably wouldn't know his father, his father wouldn't recognize him, and his hot and angry questions might be ridiculous instead of wounding. So he then telephoned his father and told him he was coming up to see him.

His father opened the door and greeted him quietly, somewhat guiltily. As he tells it: "I saw him as though for the first time in my life. I saw he was a quiet, timid little man and the minute I saw him I knew why he had run away. He just couldn't stand my mother's demands, her bossy ways, her noise, the kids. He just wasn't built for it. I knew it because I had had to take it—and I couldn't take it, and this little man couldn't take it half as well as I could. And suddenly it seemed pointless, my dreams of making him pay for all the trouble we had seen. He had had his troubles. He had been hurt too. I know he loved us when we were kids.

"So I just said I had wanted to see him for a long time and we stood there, sorta stupid and dumb for a few minutes. Finally, he asked, 'How is everybody? How is your mother?' I said, 'They're all okay, they're all okay,' and for a moment I almost said, 'And no thanks to you, old man.' But I didn't. He said, 'I am sorry about everything, but that, I guess, is the way it had to be.' I said, 'I know, I know.' Then I realized he was going to tell me he was sorry and I didn't want to hear it, but I let him say it and then I felt like a damn fool. I just kept saying, 'I know, I know.' So I grabbed my hat and said, 'Well, okay, I just wanted to see you,' and then I left. I walked out and I hadn't said a single one of those bitter nasty things I had been saving up for years. I saw that I was a man now and he was a man, and I understood he couldn't have stayed with my mother and stayed alive. He just had to get out to save himself, and I don't blame him any more, but I had to see him to get it out of my system."

The long-stored-up retaliatory feelings of this man's "inner child of the past"—mixed with some of his past yearning for his father's return—drove this man to seek out his father after twenty years. *But when he actually saw him, the adult this man had become—and not the "child of the past"—took over and saw his father as a human being.* He recognized this quiet, timid man—who had appeared as an affectionate and powerful giant to him in childhood—had never really been capable of living happily with his bossy, dominating mother. Thus, he both discharged his retaliatory feelings and came to a new understanding of his father as a person, with weaknesses and failings as well as qualities that made him even lovable.

In many cases, however, people who have suffered from neglect never get the retaliatory feelings of the "child of the past" out of their systems as this man did. The feelings of retaliation come not so much from parental neglect, but from the punishment which the child has to endure as a result of the neglect. This man had to endure excessive responsibility, physical deprivation and a bossy mother, all having a punitive quality to them. Often neglect is combined with punitiveness, and retaliatory feelings develop which may go unresolved for years.

If you can recognize that such retaliatory feelings really belong to the child you once were and not to the adult you have become, you can make a significant step forward in managing your life. When you are able to accept your parents as human beings, you will not continue to waste your energy in nursing bruised feelings of the past and you will be able to ease the misery of your neglected childhood by acting as a comforting parent to yourself.

This is a particular problem for the children of divorced parents, who initially feel the loss keenly and may even blame themselves for having caused their parents to separate. They also have the feelings of protest, anger, retaliation and despair which are common to all kinds of separation from a parent, but because the loss is not permanent and always offers hope of eventual restoration of a warm, close relationship, the despair is not as deep and the detachment may not be so pronounced.

IDEALIZATION OF THE ABSENT PARENT: It is not at all unusual for the individual who has suffered the loss of a parent for any reason—death, divorce, hospitalization, imprisonment—to create in his childhood fantasies of a highly idealized parent. In his imagination this idealized and loving parent would correct all the difficulties he encounters, would appreciate his efforts, indulge him endlessly without ever setting limits or punishing him. In childhood this idealized parent may represent many things: a yearning for love, a form of grief and mourning, a dislike or rejection of a step-parent or a defense against liking a step-parent when such liking engenders feelings of disloyalty in the child.

In childhood this idealization of the absent parent also causes problems in the adjustment with the step-parent or foster parent. Such an idealization may prevent the child from cooperating with the step-parent. The child may also use this idealized image as a weapon to force submission to his demands and wishes: "If my real mother were here . . ." Often it prevents the most sincere and loving step-parent from forming a close relationship with the child, although generally if the step-parent is patient and waits for the child to come to her voluntarily, the idealized parent will gradually be abandoned.

However, if continued into adolescence and adult life, the idealized fantasy parent may prevent formation of close relationships with members of the opposite sex. The idealized, saintly and angelic mother, for example, makes all other females seem trivial and shallow, often even sinful. Saints do not engage in sexual activities.

Thus, absence of the parent deprives the child of the

232

opportunity of seeing his parent as he really is—a human being. Children naturally tend to idealize their parents and see them as all-powerful. Without the chance to reduce the parent from this inflated status to human size through daily involvement with his parent's human strengths and weaknesses, the child is equipped with inadequate and inhuman standards by which to judge himself and others. For example, a boy whose father was killed in the war may create a fantasy father whose bravery far exceeds anything known to man; such a child may then drive himself into all kinds of misguided reckless feats because he feels himself lacking in courage, "chicken," not as good as his father. Of if his father was a self-employed business-man, he may, regardless of whether his father was actually successful, feel himself to be inadequate if he works as someone's employee.

If he was deprived of knowing his mother, he may find it difficult to form a free, intimate relationship with a woman. His idealized mother image creates an unrealistic standard for all womanhood. He may be so attached romantically to this ideal that no girl can possibly measure up to it, and he may be disappointed and uninterested in those he meets. Similarly, a girl who has lost her father may idealize him and reject men who might make excellent marriage partners because she feels they are lacking in the finer qualities of a gentleman and a scholar.

If you lost a parent in one way or another, you may already realize how you idealized or invented memories of that parent. You may already understand how that image interfered with your relations with others, par-ticularly a step-parent. However, such idealizations met a genuine need at the time and you should not belittle yourself for having created a fantasy parent to hold your hand. The significant question in your adult life is whether this past idealization is interfering with your capacity to enjoy life as an adult by setting impossible standards by which you measure yourself and other people who might enrich your life. Do you want women on a pedestal? Do you expect a man to be a selfless knight in armor? Did you ever realize that your own parents were human beings who were happy at times, sad at other times, made love and scolded each other, ate too much and worried?

Until a person achieves adulthood and has had some experience with life itself, he may not be able to recognize and accept his parents as human beings. When he does, he

233

grows because in that recognition he fully assumes responsibility for himself and can undertake the job of being a better parent to himself than his parents were able to be.

The Causes of Neglect

Neglect can be caused by anything which prevents the parent from giving adequate attention to the child. In many cases these causes lie beyond the control of the parent, the most conspicuous example being death. But regardless of their specific character, the causes are not important in themselves. Far more important—and something you can do something about—is the fact that neglect, like other pathogenic attitudes, tends to be passed along from one generation to another. The neglecting parent usually was neglected himself. You are in a unique position to end this long chain of drifting unhappiness by becoming an attentive and considerate parent, first to yourself—and then to your children.

Many people who suffered from neglect as children worry and wish about the past. They worry that their childhood contained something so terrible that they are badly hurt and cannot find the causes. If they recognize they were neglected, they believe something inside of them caused their parents to neglect them. Or they may imagine they are really only waiting for recognition by the prince or princess who will change their life. "Cinderella," for example, is a story of punitiveness and neglect.

This worry and wishing does not help you in meeting your adult problems; it wastes your energies and directs them into a dead-end street.

What caused your parents to neglect you, for example, is of little importance today. Even if you knew the precise answer, it could not alleviate your present emotional difficulties. Such knowledge can, however, give you some insight into your parents' problems as ordinary human beings. Blaming them is another dead end and will not help you feel better.

If you can discover the mechanism which causes you to withdraw from others and move away from them, you can help yourself significantly. You will find that certain circumstances cause you to do this more than others. You will also find that at other times, in other circumstances, you will not have this need to put up the barriers of distances in your feelings. By carefully observing your own feelings and reactions you will be able to do two things:

1. Extend those periods when you do not need to separate yourself from others.

2. Resist the need of your "child of the past" to set up these distance barriers in order to feel comfortable. This will make your "child of the past" feel anxious and uncomfortable. But because you can recognize these feelings as belonging to the past, you can patiently try to reduce them gradually. In time you will begin to feel more comfortable and relaxed in your capacity to be close to others.

These immediate "triggering" causes of your withdrawal and detachment are more important in your management of your "inner child of the past" than the original cause of your being neglected years ago. About those causes you can do nothing. But you do not need to continue to live in this past atmosphere of neglect and loneliness.

Cultural Factors Supporting Neglect

Our culture does not directly support a neglectful attitude toward children. But confusion, ignorance and emphasis on economic, social and material "success" have frequently contributed to the parental preoccupations that mean children are neglected. Striving for economic and social status has often weakened appreciably family closeness. Many children grow up today without really knowing what their fathers or mothers do all day or where to find them. And each year we are producing a significantly larger group of persons who are particularly vulnerable to neglect: illegitimate children, whose recorded births now total some 200,000 a year and whose mothers, often neglected teenagers, are generally forced into giving up their child or working, which separates them from the child during the important first five years.

Until recently we did not, as a society, begin to understand that neglect is not wholly physical. Yet the continued stress put on financial and social "success" seldom takes into account the unhappiness and emotional emptiness of the man and woman who "have everything."

One of the difficult problems facing the person who has suffered from neglect is the establishment of his own goals and making persistent progress toward them. His difficulty in feeling close to others tends to cause him to drift without much feeling about what he wants out of life, governed chiefly by his impulsiveness and need for distance.

To help yourself, try to set down in simple one-two-three fashion what you consider worthwhile goals for yourself in human emotional satisfactions. By taking time each day to consider briefly whether you are making progress toward these goals you will begin to make progress. If you push this question of definite goals off as something to be done "someday," you will make no progress. You are, instead, willing to wait for a prince or princess to bring warmth and closeness to you.

How Neglect Affects Sex and Marriage

In the emotional intimacy of love, sex and marriage, the person who has suffered from neglect in childhood often has his greatest difficulties. In fact, one strong indication in the adult of childhood neglect is often his marked difficulty in sexual and marital relations. To be satisfying, these relations demand closeness and warmth, meaningful affection and identification with the partner—the very emotional qualities he has never known.

The person who suffered from emotional neglect in childhood constantly feels dissatisfied with his relationships with others. He learns to maintain superficial social relations, but he constantly yearns to meet people on a deeper, closer, more intimate level. This frightens, indeed, panics him, for he realizes his longings for intimacy are so deep that he wants to be mothered as a child is. This would upset his own adult adjustment—and he flees from the prospect of closeness. Because his need for closeness is never met, he constantly feels he is on the outside. He envies those who enter relationships easily for he feels awkward and gauche. He says to himself, in effect, if people really knew me they'd find me completely unacceptable because I really long to be a little child and be taken care of—and I can't accept this in myself for if I gave it free rein it would wreck my own attempts to be an adult.

Thus the person suffering from neglect flees and struggles to escape from opportunities for closeness, frankly shunning them in his response to the powerful demands of his "child of the past" for mothering. This aloofness and coldness inevitably reduces the warmth, interest and affection of his partner, often to the point where the relationship is never really developed.

Yet such persons often suffer agonies in trying to make contact and communicate emotionally with others. What is a major effort for them in this respect is often not recognized as such by persons to whom emotional interchange is easy. As one patient put it, "My trouble seems to come from within me. It takes a great effort for me to express myself in an emotional sense—and I get into a panic when I feel close to her and feel her close to me. I just want to run."

Certain reactions, initially developed in childhood and often later supplemented with fears and inhibitions, maintain the wall which keeps the "neglected" person from enjoying closeness with others. One of the most common of these reactions is an attempt to deny the need for closeness—and thus escape the discomfort it creates. This denial may lead to tremendous striving for self-sufficiency or independence. On a superficial and casual level, such persons get along well with others, enjoy their respect and esteem. But no one is really able to get close to them. They withdraw in panic from any relationship offering more than casual friendship. Often such persons are attractive and talented, have poured their lives into work and even won notable success. But they suffer intensely from loneliness and often withdraw from social activities or try to eliminate them from their lives. Seeing others enjoy one another's warmth and affection heightens their own feelings of desolate loneliness and inadequacy, their painful feeling that something is missing.

Often such persons realize that it is their own precipitous flight from the welcoming warmth of others that triggers their difficulties. They struggle against the defensive reactions of their neglected past, and may make advances in this respect. But often before this can happen the opportunities which they should have seized have slipped by. This is the story of many people who have never married, who are not only lonely but melancholy.

"LIVING WITH MUSIC": George is a slender and sensitive looking young musician. In childhood he was neglected by his busy, overworked mother; he rarely saw his father, who was constantly traveling in the course of his work. As the oldest child, he suffered the kind of painful hurt that results from the mother's attention being given to the newest baby. However, when he was quite young a musician in the neighborhood discovered George had musical talent, gave him lessons and encouraged him. From the musician he got attention, friendship and praise, but no real closeness. However, the excitement which George created in the family with his music did win for him some momentary attention from his parents.

All this caused him, even as a child, to turn to music as his way of conquering the world. He studied and strove, playing music far beyond his years. He had no friends. In order to earn money to continue his studies, during his adolescent years he played at weddings and parties where there was often much warmth and friendly, stimulating interchange. But in his capacity as a professional musician he was not included in it—and he has a kind of bitter contempt for social activities today. He lives a lonely, withdrawn life, dedicated to his practice and study, trying to avoid contacts with others.

Women who have been attracted to him have been hurt by his indifference. He likes their attention but doesn't want "to be involved in all this baggage. After all, I am living with music. What do I need her for?"

He has perfected his musical technique and while he has reached the concert level, critics have pointed out that his playing is often lacking in depth of tone and color, is often merely brilliant technique. This has hurt him deeply. He rages and despairs about the critics' "stupid comments." Recently his old friend and first music teacher, who is closer to him than anybody else, said to him: "George, you know all there is to know in the area of technique. But music is essentially feeling—and feeling comes from life, from experience.

"To advance you must live—not as a mole, but as a man, a human being—not as a rehearsal machine, not as a saint. You can't go on rehearsing for perfection. You need to live a little."

This has brought about a crisis in George's life. He alternates between moods of melancholy and rage. He allowed himself to be drawn into a love affair with an attractive woman. But he cannot stand her closeness—or her presumption in feeling that she has something to say and that some consideration is due her. He has turned against her, his desire to retaliate against anyone close to him coming to the fore, and he sees her as the cause of his lack of emotional tone in his music. In this fashion he has driven her away. What the outcome for George will ultimately be, no one can say at this point.

THE STORY OF GRETCHEN: Gretchen is a dignified and thoughtful woman. The daughter of pious farmers, she grew up on a lonely midwestern farm where she had little opportunity for contact with others. Her parents were sincere, strict and hard-working from dawn to dusk. They had little time for their daughter as they worked their poor soil. She was carried into the fields with them in a basket. Once she had learned to walk, she toddled after them in the fields and, initially in imitation, worked beside them. When they were not busy on their farm, they worked to build their church.

But Gretchen never got much loving affection, playful intimacy or mutual interchange. When she was older, they worried her with ideas about sin, about strangers, about God. She doesn't recall a single conversation with either parent about how any of them felt about one another. "If I were to use my mother's words," she says, "we just 'did our duty by one another.' "

Because she had known how to work hard all her life, Gretchen put herself through college. Since then she has won a place for herself in a large corporation. Her conscientious work, intelligence and restricted life have made her almost the "perfect employee."

But she suffers from loneliness and the emptiness of her life, the fact that she goes home to an empty apartment. "It is when I go home, on the way home in the evening," she says, "that I feel the worst. It is knowing that no one is there, that there is no need to rush while everyone else is hurrying. That hurts. But once I am home, I don't mind it so much."

Gretchen has never been able to feel close to anyone although she noticed she immediately feels warmer and more relaxed with anyone she meets who has the same midwestern drawl she knew as a child. She has devoted most of her free time to her church and served on its committees like a tireless servant. In fact, during most of her adult life Gretchen has squelched her own feelings of loneliness as being unworthy of a Christian and tried to comfort herself with church work.

When she first got out of college, she attracted the attention of several young men, but the idea of going on a date panicked her and she abruptly terminated these relationships. Her preoccupation with her job and her tireless church work have, to some extent, restricted her potential marriage opportunities. She herself sometimes says she is resigned to being "an old maid." She recognizes now that she has always shunned or subtly discouraged any man who took any personal interest in her. "But I have noticed," she says, "that if I can work with somebody, well, I don't need to put this distance between us and I can feel close to such a person then and really enjoy it and feel good about it. It means a great deal to me and if I am ever to get settled down and get married, I believe it will be to someone who has worked with me. I would think nothing of going to dinner with ————," naming a man with whom she works, "but if he did not work with me, and worked in another part of the office, I would be petrified, just frozen, if he asked me."

Because she recognized the problem more clearly than most people who have suffered from neglect do, Gretchen had already found some significant aspects of her inability to feel close to people. Her "child of the past" could tolerate closeness in a "work atmosphere," which was the only atmosphere in which Gretchen really felt close to her parents as a child. This has provided a "bridge," permitting her to become close to a man whom she now hopes to marry—and helping her to understand why she still has trouble feeling close to others in other areas. However, in time she will be able to reduce this continuing need for distance.

Meaningless Love

While some persons, like George and Gretchen, attempt to deny their need for affection, warmth and closeness, most individuals who suffered from neglect in childhood do not follow this path. Instead many actively seek social participation, sexual love and affection—"can't get enough of it," as one such girl declared. Once they have overcome an initial timidity, they may plunge into any relationship that seems to promise companionship, affection, closeness or excitement.

The lack of mothering in childhood tends to dominate the sexual activities of such a person. Such a person is interested in and wants tender, mothering love—not sexuality—and tends to convert the partner into a mothering

240

figure who takes care of him. A woman whose parents left her with a relative when she was an infant alarmed her husband after their marriage. She did not really respond sexually to his love-making and she insisted on having a large special bed made for herself which actually resembled a baby's crib, complete with ribbons and even a rocking mechanism. What she wanted was for her husband to pet and caress her in a mothering way.

However, in most instances persons who have suffered from neglect in childhood tend to overvalue sexual satisfaction. They have eroticized their dependent longings and emphasize these needs above all others. Not having had these dependent needs met in childhood, they cannot be satisfied, and cannot discriminate because their need is so great. However, this emphasis on the physical satisfactions of sex tends to exclude the emotional interchange which is necessary if sexual love is to be meaningful. Often the result is meaningless love.

If such persons become too self-critical, this destroys their ability to function sexually. They are also subject to depression because their unfulfilled longings for mothering worry them. "I have these feelings, these desires and wishes to be taken care of and loved, mothered and caressed like a baby. In fact, I want to be babied," said one woman. "There must be something wrong with me." This is a common reaction for many people, not understanding how the neglected "inner child of the past" expresses his feelings, and they are ashamed and guilty about these feelings. In becoming a kind of parent to your "child of the past," one of the basic requirements is that you recognize you need not be ashamed or guilty about these feelings of childhood. However, you do not need to indulge them, but can respectfully set firm limits to their expression.

The inability of the person who has suffered from neglect in childhood to contribute much emotionally to a relationship often causes its disintegration. Its maintenance is left to the other partner—and he tends to move off because he is tired of the burden. Moreover, the person who has neglect in his background is always restless and anxious because he cannot obtain emotional satisfaction in his relationships. He wants to keep moving, drifting from one relationship to another, in the hope that the next one will really provide the "something that is missing." These restless, impulsive moves help to create the illusion of living

241

emotionally. But usually there is little lasting satisfaction. Such persons may, as in the case cited earlier in this chapter, be married and not feel at all close to their spouse and children. They are sometimes frightened and shocked by their own lack of conscience and disloyalty. Such a person may, for example, be engaged to be married to one person and simultaneously be maintaining sexual relationships with two or three others. Anyone who offers admiration and affection has appeal to them—and because their need for affection is so great, their ability to discriminate is severely impaired. Much meaningless promiscuity is the result. Ironically, the meaningless character of this sexual activity and its lack of emotional satisfaction often is not recognized for some time because it creates an illusion of being capable of loving intimacy which prevents this recognition.

The Hidden Mechanism Involved in Neglect

One of the noticeable characteristics of persons who have suffered from neglect and deprivation in childhood is that they maintain certain reserved aloofness in their contact with others. Often this aloof detachment is referred to by them—and others—as a "kind of wall." Understanding this "wall," how and why it is necessary, may help you reduce the need for it.

The person who has suffered from serious deprivation in childhood is filled with tremendous longings for someone to care for him—longings unfulfilled since childhood. On becoming aware of these intense desires, he may try to stifle them but generally this is only possible by quickly shifting the scene. Moreover, the desires return. Often the neglected person is both frightened and ashamed of these longings. He recognizes that they are so deep and intense that if permitted expression he would demand the right to be an infant and to be taken care of as a baby is. He may realize, for example, that he wants his wife to be a mother, not a wife.

Therefore, such a person tries to hide and restrict these tremendous longings. He withdraws from or breaks off any relationship which threatens to have a deep emotional character. For example, encountering a really mothering person may threaten the entire adult adjustment of such a person. He feels that he will be permitted, even encouraged, to be infantile—and this is frightening. To maintain his self-respect, he must ward off such encouragement. Moreover, in many cases, the aloof, detached person recognizes that his tremendous dependent longings make him vulnerable—and thus he seeks protection against exploitive types with his reserve.

While the "wall" often successfully hides these childhood longings for affection and tender care, it also prevents participation in a mutually satisfying way in the emotional interchange which is natural in adult marital and sexual life.

The Attraction of Opposites

Frequently, in what would appear to be the attraction of opposites, the person suffering from childhood neglect is drawn to the impulsive person whose parents were overly submissive to his wishes and who continues to seek this permissiveness in adult life. Superficially, there is a kind of dovetailing of the needs of these two types. The impulsive person moves quickly and easily to the emotional warmth and closeness which the person suffering from neglect cannot do—and the latter welcomes the impulsive person with tears of relief and desperation. The impulsive person can express the feelings of the neglected individual who thinks that at last someone has crashed through the "wall" behind which he has had to hide these feelings.

However, there is often much unhappiness in this combination. For example, the relationship is immediately thrown out of balance because it inevitably means a great deal more to the person suffering from childhood neglect than it does to the impulsive person. The person suffering from neglect cannot form a relationship easily. On the other hand, the impulsive person forms such a relationship easily and quickly. This difference in capacity often creates an unhappy and exploitive situation. The person suffering from neglect will often tolerate almost any amount of exploitation to maintain the warmth and closeness given by the impulsive person. However, the impulsive person is used to and wants response from others, something which the neglected person cannot easily give. The impulsive person, tending always to move impulsively and to seek situations and people to whom he can respond impulsively, generally moves on. Thus, such a relationship, unstable and fragile, seldom lasts for very long—and yet neither person recognizes and understands the role of his "child of the past" in creating this unhappy situation.

Sometimes two persons, each of whom suffered from neglect in his childhood and has little capacity for forming a lasting relationship, may find their needs for distance approximately the same, and may marry. However, what generally happens in this situation is that each person expects the other to overcome his own "wall" of detachment, to fulfill his life and provide happiness. When this does not happen—and it may take years for this to be recognized— each blames the other, and the warfare, nagging, subtle undermining and contempt are often very bitter. Each sees the other as the person who "ruined my life."

For instance, Ginger and Ken both suffered from obvious neglect and deprivation in their early childhoods. Both lost their families at very early ages and were raised in orphanages. When they met in their early twenties, Ginger was an attractive clerk in a fashionable suburban store and Ken was just starting in business with a small machine shop. What they had in common, aside from being healthy and attractive physically, was their unhappy backgrounds. Their memories of the orphanages, of their wishes for a family, for someone who would care for them were so strong that they married. For a long time this seemed to be the solution each had always dreamed of, and both were happy although restless and anxious at times.

Although they prospered economically, they gradually found they had little in common. Subtle differences became enlarged. They built first one and then another house, trying to decide "what they wanted." One day Ken came home and found Ginger had been drinking alone and had passed out on the living-room floor. When he brought her around with cold cloths and black coffee, he gradually learned she had been drinking alone for a long time because she was very depressed and unhappy. Only drinking seemed to alleviate her misery and inability to feel close to anyone, even Ken and their children. Although he had some insight into the cause of their difficulties, Ginger's plight overwhelmed Ken. He himself had been unable to be close to anyone and had been secretly despairing about it. He became so nervous and depressed that he could barely work.

Each tended to blame the other initially. By long patient examination of the role of the "child of the past" they

each came to recognize that no one could fulfill the longings of their deprived and neglected childhoods, and
ceased to expect such fulfillment from one another. Today
they also recognize that having both been orphans does
not necessarily give them something in common. They
recognize that they are different people, with different
tastes, different interests—and that their great difficulty is
in feeling close to one another. Fortunately, because they
understand the loneliness and deprivations of their childhoods they are able to help one another. One of the things
they have found they must accept is that there are periods
when they do not feel close.

Managing a Neglected Child of the Past

The neglected "inner child of the past" longs for the
ultimate loving and complete acceptance which a mother
gives her child. Because he is unable to express these
longings, such a person feels he is on the outside even
when he is ostensibly participating in activities with others.

In some respects the person with such a neglected "child
of the past" has certain special problems in acting as
parent to this child. The "child of the past" did not get
sufficient mothering in childhood—and such needs cannot now be fulfilled. He must learn to live with this ache.
This scar of early deprivation must be accepted, with tender consideration, respect and love, in the same way that
you might love a child who has been badly hurt. It is
important not to ridicule yourself as "childish" for having
these wishes for mothering or to turn against yourself
in a self-critical, demanding way. You cannot escape these
feelings. In acting as a parent to your neglected "inner
child of the past" you can respect these deep feelings—but
you cannot fulfill these past longings and you must establish firm limits on efforts of the "child of the past" to get
someone else to take over this mothering role. This "someone" in the present cannot step back through the calendar
and satisfy your needs from the past, even if he or she
wanted to. Your sweetheart cannot be your mother without destroying your adult relationship.

If you can learn to accept these longings from childhood
as a scar, without giving in to them and allowing them to
dominate your life, you can then begin to get satisfactions
from your daily life in the present. To your "child of the

past" these things do not hold the promise of "all-giving mother," but when you stop chasing the will-o'-the-wisp of an "all-giving mother" you can begin to get satisfactions that are actually obtainable.

And if you will give yourself times and places when you can retreat from the closeness that your "child of the past" both demands and feels uncomfortable with, you can participate with greater satisfaction in all activities.

All of this requires great patience, firm limits and profound acceptance of the child you once were.

CHAPTER 17

REJECTION—
If you are painfully self-isolating

YOUR INDEX OF SUSPICION: *If you do not feel accepted by anybody, including yourself, consider yourself a kind of lone wolf or outlaw, are at times accused by friends of being self-centered, often distort the attitudes of those close to you and flare into hostility against them, suffer from anxiety, bitter self-deprecation and low spirits, you should suspect that your "inner child of the past" is still suffering from parental rejection.* However, this is a relatively rare parental attitude; do not jump to the conclusion that this is what troubles your "child of the past."

Because rejection was one of the first pathogenic parental attitudes to be studied intensively, it was popular years ago to attribute nearly every person's emotional difficulties and unhappiness to his having been "rejected" as a child. In time greater precision in psychiatric studies has revealed that rejection is really rare and that the word "rejection" is frequently misused.

Rejection is a parental attitude that denies the child any niche of acceptance; he is considered and treated as an unacceptable individual and an unwanted burden, a nuisance and source of trouble. While parents may hold troublemaking attitudes, may even be abusive and extremely punitive, they generally do their best to accept and make a place for their child in their affection and esteem. True rejection seldom happens. The mere fact that a parent forbids or objects to certain behavior, denies the child's impulsive demands or punishes him, does not necessarily mean that he is "rejecting" the child, as was once popularly believed. Indeed, all children need limits established by their parents in order to feel protected and secure.

Recognizing Rejection in Your Background

If you were rejected as a child, you probably already know it. As in the case of the woman patient described in the earlier pages of this book who was called a pig and told to walk out into the ocean and keep walking by her mother, the parent's hostile rejection is both unmistakable and unforgettable.

There is nothing subtle or sly about rejection. You are made to feel unwanted. Eartha Kitt, the internationally famous singer and entertainer, has told a classic story of rejection in her autobiography, *Thursday's Child*. Unwanted and rejected, she was cast aside as a small child when her mother, who had been deserted by Eartha's father, got a chance to marry a man who made Eartha's abandonment a condition of the marriage.

Turned over to a relative who did not want her either and who viewed her as a troublesome burden, Eartha existed in a desolate and forlorn loneliness, marked by abuse and scorn. Finally she discovered that she could win a small niche of acceptance and even approval from her relative by singing in church. This turned her at an early age toward singing and performing as a way of gaining acceptance and approval. Yet even after she was a famous star the deep scar of rejection suffered in childhood made her unhappy and miserable, easy prey for exploitive "friends" because she still needed affectionate approval so desperately. Only after a prolonged and determined struggle was she able to understand her "inner child of the past" and to accept herself as a worthy individual.

People who have been rejected in childhood tend to be easily hurt and then bitter and hostile. They are so certain they are not wanted that they see a rebuff or slight in what others may consider ordinary conversation. Some such persons are actually suspicious of any friendly overtures made to them, being unable to overcome the deeply imbedded feeling of the "inner child of the past" that he is unwanted; to these persons, a friendly overture is a trick leading up to another hurtful rejection. Often, in "testing" the sincerity of friends who find them attractive or interesting and desirable companions, such persons behave in a hostile or obnoxious way which tends to force people to reject them or abandon efforts to be friendly with them. Thus, they bring about the experience of rejection to satisfy the anxious, embittered "child of the past" who feels insecure and nervous on the threshold of acceptance, affection and approval.

If you find that you tend to get into situations where you are, in effect, demanding rejection by others, you should look for other evidence which may help to confirm or rule out rejection in your early home life. Sometimes children are rejected because they are illegitimate or because of the color of their skin, or because they are afflicted with some disorder like cross-eyes or a harelip, or happen to be the opposite sex from that desired by one or both parents. However, merely being so afflicted is not in itself a sign of persistent rejection; many such children are loved from the start. Others, while initially rejected to some degree, have come to be deeply loved and accepted by their parents. Thus, the more significant signs of rejection in adult life are emotional in character: the misinterpretation of friends' comments, the hostile "demand" for rejection, the anxious disbelief in one's acceptability as someone worth loving, the easily hurt feelings and self-critical isolation of the rejected "child of the past."

Alcoholism sometimes may be a sign of rejection in childhood. Under the influence of alcohol, such a person may be able to ease up on his self-critical rejection of himself. In the jovial company of other drinkers, he may momentarily feel that he is an interesting, desirable person. Yet his rejected "child of the past" feels deeply uncomfortable, anxious and distrusting in the midst of friendliness and warmth—and may become obnoxious or belligerent in testing the reality of his acceptance.

Such misbehavior then results in his being rejected, often physically ejected from the circle of friends. The "child of the past," having once again proved he is unwanted, becomes both depressed and filled with hostility. Added to these feelings of rejection is the extra burden of guilt which accompanies excessive alcoholism. His abusive, isolating and immobilizing self-criticism frequently creates such abysmal feelings of contempt and self-hatred that only more drinking can anesthetize the deep childhood feelings of rejection.

The Origins of Rejection

If you suffered from rejection as a child, your need to continue this hurtful attitude toward yourself may be effectively diminished if you understand how this attitude arose. Such an attitude existed because of personal problems in the lives of your parents—and had little to do with you. The most common problem involved is the mother's unhappy adjustment to marriage. One study of a group of rejecting mothers revealed that 95 percent were disappointed in their husbands. Often the mothers were rejected themselves in childhood. Some were immature and poorly prepared to become mothers. For example, in some cases the rejection was revenge on the child because the mother had had to give up her social activities for the child. Others feared, without basis, and without even trying to find out the facts, the inheritance of "bad blood." Others felt that pregnancy had forced them to marry men they did not love. Some were disgusted with both sex and pregnancy. Others attributed their rejecting attitude to their husbands' being poor providers or quarrelsome. According to Dr. W. H. Newell,* who made intensive studies in this area, in some instances a mother or father who had a hostile attitude toward his own parent assumes a hostile attitude toward a child of the same sex: a woman who hated her mother may hate her daughter; a man who hated his father may hate his son.

You can realize from all of this the fundamental fact: none of this had much to do with you as a person. If the person you most admire had been born to your parents, he would have been treated in the same way.

One study in the field, made by Dr. A. J. Simon, concluded that many rejecting parents "were children emotionally, and manifested this in their disinterest in and hostility toward their own offspring as children who needed to be reared."†

This is an important and significant point. You can, by being a kindly parent to yourself, put aside the hostility and rejection with which you were viewed in childhood. Not only do you not deserve it—but these attitudes are

* W. H. Newell, *American Journal of Orthopsychiatry*, 4:387, 1934; *Ibid.*, 6:576, 1936.

† A. J. Simon, *The Nervous Child*, 3:119, 1944.

really not yours and you do not have to continue to apply them toward yourself. If you will realize that your rejection in childhood was caused by the deep unhappiness, misery and poor marital adjustment of your parents, you can begin to accept your own feelings and your achievements as worthwhile. They entitle you to consideration and acceptance—from yourself.

Your problem is to overcome the rejection you suffered in the past by accepting yourself today, first in little ways. What do you do today that is worthwhile? Make a list of these things, especially those which give you particular satisfaction. Each of them is a weapon you can use in combating your own continued rejection of yourself.

Cultural Factors Supporting Rejection

While many positive factors in our culture, particularly our schools, call for acceptance and recognition of every child on the basis of his own achievements, other elements contradict this. Moreover, they tend to affect the child before he reaches school age. For example, the entire situation of the unwed mother is one that has rejection built into it, both for the mother and her child. The label of illegitimacy harasses her, increasing her feelings of guilt and complicating her problems in raising her child. Often the illegitimacy itself has resulted from the young mother's rejection by her own parents. The person who has been rejected has so great and desperate a need for love and affection that he is often not capable of making discriminating choices in the area of sex and marriage.

Our cultural attitudes toward money, success and material possessions also contribute to the rejection of children in some instances. A child born when the financial straits of the family are dire may be rejected. Similarly, if the parents cannot get along together, they tend to see children as a chain binding them—and adopt a rejecting attitude. Our society generally considers children to be an economic burden. Often the economic problems of the family and the loss of income involved in the mother's attention to children contributes to her irritation and annoyance with her children. While this cannot be said to be the cause of rejection, it frequently aggravates attitudes of rejection.

In some cases the physical appearance of the child may

251

cause rejection. The mother, unable to bear her disappointed desire for an unusually beautiful child, rejects the child. Our cultural ideas, in their stress upon physical beauty, overemphasize this aspect and fail to give adequate expression to the emotional and spiritual qualities which provide deeper satisfactions.

How Rejection Affects Sex and Marriage

Because the person who has suffered from rejection in childhood has a desperate need for affection and approval —and an almost complete inability to accept any offer of love as sincere—he frequently has great difficulty in maintaining a satisfying sexual and marital life. Often the person who has suffered from rejection brings himself to the point where he accepts the fact that a particular individual loves and wants him. Having been starved for love all his life such a person then seems insatiable in his demands for affection. He becomes so intensely absorbed in his own feelings of happiness and in the partner's expression of it that the experience may become burdensome to the partner who does not have the same intense need as the rejected person. Any slackening of intensity is misinterpreted by the rejected person as a renewal of the old rejection, and he is hurt, then hostile.

The rejected person has, in effect, a built-in short-circuiting mechanism which destroys most of his opportunities for a stable and continuing relationship. On being accepted as a partner in such a relationship, the person who has been rejected in childhood says, in effect: "All right, you say I am lovable and that you really want me. I'll go along with this because I want you—but I don't believe you." He then continually tests this love and loyalty searching for oversights, slights, indifference, disloyalty. And as long as he finds no grounds for complaint, he grows somewhat more relaxed and happier. But his uneasy expectation of rejection grows. He keeps up such pressure in his "testing" of the partner that eventually the partner snaps back with irritation. At this point the rejected person reacts with deeply hurt feelings and says: "At last the truth is out . . . you don't love me and you never did." And moves off into an isolation cell where his self-criticism finally causes him to lash out at others in hostility. This, of course, further isolates him.

A man married to a woman who had suffered from rejection as a child once complained: "Being married to Vivian is like being a yo-yo. Either she is very affectionate —and I am going up—or I am going down because she has taken offense at something and imagined I intended it as a dirty dig. If I tell her that her stocking seam is crooked or that the soup could use a little salt or that Jim Baum's wife cooks rice with onions, her feelings are hurt. She takes all this as criticism. First, she rears up in a hurt, silent way, then leaves the room and then comes back with all guns firing. I never saw anyone whose feelings are so easily hurt. I can't live with her because I can't live with anybody to whom I can safely say only one thing: 'Honey, you are sent from Heaven and a dream.' Maybe somebody can do that, but I can't.

"If I say anything that is not one hundred percent hurrah—both in words and tone—she is off. One word is a flood, the way she sees it. And the first thing that gets cut off is a kiss at the door, and sex, and if I am not running around wringing my hands with apologies, trying to smooth everything over, I can count on a delayed uproar. The worst of it is, I never really know what has hurt her feelings. And then she herself becomes very self-critical. She says she knows she is no good and stupid and ugly and goes to her room and won't even talk to me."

The tremendous swings in mood described by this man are common in the close relationships of people who have been rejected. Such persons, who seem to seek something to feel hurt about, then feel deeply hurt, shriveling up inside and isolating themselves. This isolation is always marked by a reopening of the old childhood wounds of rejection characterized by abusive self-criticism and culminating in hostile, distrustful and antagonistic attitudes toward others, particularly those close to them.

Persons who have suffered from rejection in childhood tend to be deeply attracted to persons who are not kind to them, who treat them with contempt, may slap them around physically and continually sneer and belittle them. Often these characteristics are plain to objective observers, but the rejected person is almost totally blind to such attitudes.

The rejected person is deeply hurt by this continued treatment, yet cannot easily withdraw from it. One word of affection from the unkind, often cruel and abusive partner means everything to him. In effect, what is often recreated in the close relationships of such persons is the entire atmosphere of childhood in which the child was rejected in a cruel and punitive way. As a child, he suffered deeply from this treatment but was, understandably, unable to turn to any other source for affection, attention and approval.

However, in adult life, withdrawal and search for a new partner is possible. But often the atmosphere of rejection seems almost necessary for such persons. *The rejected person becomes closely attached to the partner who is forced to reject him. No one else has the same significance. What would appear to be important is the maintenance of the atmosphere of rejection.* Few more miserable and unhappy situations can be imagined.

The Story of Mrs. George

One of the major themes of this book is that parental attitudes pass from generation to generation. In adults these attitudes "live" by becoming the attitudes which the adult employs in acting as a parent to himself. This is particularly clear in the case of rejection, which is nearly always marked by severely deprecating self-criticism.

Mrs. George, for instance, is an attractive young housewife of twenty-five years. Although well groomed, her facial expression is flat. This is the way she talked about herself: "I've been depressed for a long time. I am also anxious, irritable. I get low in my spirits and can't drag myself out of it. My husband tries to kid me out of it but he can't. I have a child who is four. I get angry very easily, sometimes at things my husband says. I keep thinking I'm a vain, shallow, selfish and stupid person. I can't stop feeling low. It's stupid—but that's me.

"I think I would be all right now if I hadn't been out of line before I got married. Now I can't hold my head up. I've been a faithful wife, but that doesn't help what I've done in the past. I look at my child and think this kid's mother is nothing but a tramp."

Such self-criticism only isolates her and neither changes the past nor alleviates her present mood and problem. Mrs. George went on to tell the story of her childhood and how she happened to be in her present situation:

"My mother left my father when I was five years old. I lived with her for two years after that, but I never saw my father again and I really don't know much about him that I can remember. All she ever told me was that he was no good. When I was a kid, I was a little brat, I'd say, but my mother never disciplined me. Oh, sometimes she'd just blow up for no reason at all and slap me. Just give me holy hell. I never knew what for most of the time. She wasn't affectionate or close—she just didn't care or wasn't much interested, I guess. When I was seven, she went off to another town to look for a job and left me with an aunt. She said she'd send for me. I looked forward to this because I thought it would really change things. But I never did live with her after that.

"Instead I was with my aunt, the one she left me with, for only a few months. She sent me off to a convent school for a year. After that I was in some foster homes. Finally, when I was ten years old, I went to live with another aunt. I stayed with her for seven years.

"My aunt and uncle were old—and old-fashioned. My aunt was sick and she wanted me to wait on her hand and foot. I was just the errand girl. I wasn't allowed to look in a mirror or I'd be called 'vain and selfish like your mother.' That's what my aunt would say. If . . . well, if I wanted to go out on a date when I got older, my aunt would say, 'Absolutely no, you just want to act sexy like your father, and you know he was no good! What did he ever do for you?' Honest, the first times she said that I didn't even know what she was talking about.

"She was always criticizing and picking on me. Nothing I ever did could please her. She got so sick it affected her mind. She became more and more irritable and complaining, distrustful and suspicious. She'd accuse everybody of all kinds of things. Finally, in my last year of high school, another relative took me into her house until I finished school. Then I had to get a job and be self-supporting.

"And let me tell you, all this isn't over. I still feel exactly as I did in those days. I feel I had parents who didn't care a hoot about me at all, who didn't want me—and who got rid of me. My mother never really cared for me. If she had, she'd have sent for me. She has never cared about anyone except herself—and that's what finished off my father with her. I worshiped her as a child. I kept hoping she'd have time for me, or something for me, I don't know what. But she never did. I can't understand how she could have gone off and left me the way she did. Now I resent her. Sometimes when I get to feeling low, I think that I will do the same thing to my child, just go off to some other town and forget about all this mess and all these people.

"I really fear older people. I don't like them and never did. They have nothing kind to say, just what's wrong, how you could do it better, how you could do it cheaper. They know it all. I sometimes think of suicide.

"My husband is a cop. He is strong and self-reliant. But I wasn't in love with him when I married him. I wanted security. I just wanted to get in out of the rain, if you know what I mean. I try to be a good wife to him. He is faithful, but he is so bossy, criticizing and overbearing —just like my aunt, I think. I get nasty and sarcastic when he talks like that. He orders me around and I obey and try to do what he says. It's the least I can do, I think. I feel sick and I feel scared lots of times. I feel I better be extra nice to people to make up for the bitter way I feel inside. Lots of times I just sit in my bedroom boiling with hate."

In becoming a kindly, accepting parent to herself—the kind neither her mother nor aunt was—Mrs. George had a difficult time. Accepting and not continuing to reject herself was trying. Long after she recognized that she was reacting to her husband's comments the way she had to her aunt's nagging criticism, she was still deeply hurt by them and sarcastic and nasty in her rejoinders. But by reminding herself that her husband was not her heartless aunt, she learned to control this aspect of the feelings of her "child of the past" even though it increased her anxiety. She has begun to enjoy life with her husband more, accepting his "bossiness" as his kind of affectionate attention; this has made it seem less critical. From watching her own child develop, she has been able to recall how unhappy and lonely she felt in childhood—and been moved to help her youngster. But at times, when a series of setbacks and disappointments converge in a brief period of time, she finds her depressed feelings returning—and then she again calls herself a "no good, stupid, lowdown, tramp."

The Road Away from Rejection

In acting as a kind but firm parent to himself, the person who suffered from rejection has a particularly difficult task. If he suffered from rejection early in life, his own isolation and hurt feelings are especially difficult to overcome. In acting as a parent to himself, he must bear in mind that he has known only harshness and that he may swing from depressing self-criticism to overindulgence, which represents all the things he wished for in childhood. He must establish limits to both overindulgence and self-belittling criticism as well as to his self-isolation.

In acting as a parent to yourself it helps to understand that the child—any child—thrives on parental encouragement, approval and stimulation, all of which are based on acceptance of the child for his own sake. This stimulates the development of a balanced personality.

But the rejected child—your "inner child of the past" if you suffered from this attitude—has known none of this, only harsh rejection, indifference, contempt. His thwarted needs for acceptance and stimulation have made him feel helpless. The hostility with which he is viewed, as an unwanted burden, convinces him the world is hostile. Parental rejection is interpreted by the child to mean that he is not worth loving and "no good," the cause of trouble for others. This obstructs and prevents the development of sound self-esteem and usually sets up the self-defeating pattern of rejection described in this chapter.

Acceptance and Achievement

There is a road away from rejection but at first it must be traveled in a slow, two-step motion. If you have seen a child learning to go up stairs, or remember learning it yourself, you will recognize the kind of process that must be utilized. Such a child puts one foot up on the step, then lifts himself up on it until his second leg also rests on that step—instead of swinging easily to the next step. At each step he repeats the process. In time he gains confidence and can move rapidly with one leg taking one step and the other the next.

In dealing with your rejected "child of the past," the first step is to provide acceptance—and the assurance which flows from acceptance. As an accepting parent to yourself, you have to stop belittling, berating and rejecting yourself. You have to put your arms around yourself and tell yourself you are all right, lovable, worthwhile, capable and endowed with something to contribute to others.

You must also recognize and accept as part of the feelings of your rejected "child of the past" your wish to hurt and reject others—but limit its expression. It will be possible for you to do this if, in accepting yourself as worthy, you can limit your own self-belittlement and self-criticism. Until you make this first step and—getting one leg up on the step—begin to accept yourself, you cannot free yourself from the self-defeating pattern of rejection. Learning to accept your hurt, rejected "child of the past" as part of yourself—without criticism or self-belittlement—is something you will have to do day after day, even hour after hour. You will need this kind of reassuring even after you have begun to take the second step—just as the child going up the stairs moves first one leg, then the other.

The second step is the one that can ultimately lift you out of the depressed feelings of rejection. It will also help you to accept yourself and find yourself an interesting and worthy person. The second step is to establish—no matter how difficult your problems may be—some area in which you are able to perform with more skill than others. Most people suffering from rejection look at a list of what they feel they can do—and then use the list as a further reason for self-criticism; their abilities do not seem important. Such self-criticism is limiting; it continues the rejection felt in childhood. To end it, you need to accept the idea that you must first work in a limited way to achieve something.

Building Self-Esteem

By carefully selecting an area in which to work, and by working to achieve that goal, you can achieve something on which you can begin to build genuine self-esteem. The goal itself is not as important as the very deliberateness and persistence with which you set the goal and carry out the work. Do not be ashamed or self-critical about taking small steps at first. You are consciously setting out to build an area of competence and achievement—an area that will provide you with the satisfactions of achievement and self-esteem. By accepting what you can do right now, however limited, and striving to accomplish a little more in a persistent program of self-development, you can reduce your own need to self-critically reject yourself and recreate the hostile atmosphere of your childhood.

In finding this area, in accepting what you can do now, you will find real enjoyment and satisfaction. This does not mean that this is the only effort of which you are capable. You may also have a flair for wearing clothes attractively or listening to others who are troubled. Eartha Kitt found such an area in gospel-singing—and moved down that road toward self-acceptance and achievement.

This is not an easy task. One can follow a road map easily, but the journey itself is often difficult.

If you suffered from rejection in childhood, you will feel anxious and alone when you first try to accept your rejected "child of the past" and to achieve your potential. Such a self-acceptance begins with the things you have achieved—even if they are no more than having stayed alive to reach physical adulthood. You need to reassure your "child of the past" that you understand him and his tirades and recognize these irritations as efforts to establish the security of the familiar—the hostile, rejecting atmosphere of the past family life. You also need to use whatever gifts or talents you may have to develop a genuine self-esteem which will counter and deny the rejection of childhood. Such self-esteem may be built by being a kind and encouraging parent to yourself, the kind of parent you did not have.

But no one who has endured the pain of rejection as a child should underestimate the size of his problem. The old hurt will throb. Discuss your efforts with a sympathetic friend, your physician, your minister. You may meet many setbacks because self-acceptance and the acceptance of affection are difficult for you to believe in, and you may become easily discouraged. In such instances an understanding friend or physician can help you in the role of parent to yourself, stimulating and encourageing your efforts to find yourself worthy of approval and affection.

CHAPTER 18

SEXUAL STIMULATION—
If you seem to misjudge the role of sex

YOUR INDEX OF SUSPICION: *If you tend to emphasize the physical aspects of sexual activities, cannot form or maintain a loving sexual relationship, are often preoccupied with sexual fantasies, and generally feel your intimacies are unrewarding, unsatisfying and tending toward the impersonal, you should examine the role your parents' attitudes played in the stimulation and development of the sexual feelings of your "inner child of the past." Such stimulation may have taken the form of complete prohibition, which results in excessive sexual fantasies, or it may have been frankly or unwittingly seductive.*

In general, parental attitudes about sex reflect our current cultural viewpoint. These broad cultural attitudes, which have swung from the strict prohibitions of Puritanism to the present approval of mass sexual stimulation— without permitting sexual satisfactions for young people at the peak of their physical powers—are creating an explosive situation. More than that, through the approval of the constant mass sexual stimulation, they are forcing the continuation of childhood's sexual fantasies—unrealistic, impersonal and immature. The "child of the past" is kept in a psychosexual kindergarten of fantasy.

The much-applauded diminution of Puritanism can hardly be said to have reduced our sexual problems. It has removed some unnecessary and cruel taboos, but the whole question of sex and its place in life is probably the most confused and abused subject in American life today. With the story of the seduction of a child, *Lolita*, a best-seller, and *Playboy* and its publishers held up as successes in the one-time family magazine *The Saturday Evening Post*, it can safely be said that we hardly know where we are going.

We are all now subjected to more direct visual sexual stimulation than any people has ever known. How this affects those of us who are adults will depend on many factors, and particularly our respective and individual "child of the past." But probably the most significant fact about it is that our children are being raised in this hothouse of eroticism; as we will show later, there are already signs of trouble on the horizon.

Recognizing Sexual Stimulation in Your Background

While this chapter obviously cannot be a complete discussion of all the sexual problems afflicting adults and children, the parental attitudes toward sexual activities often form a significant and revealing pattern. For example, each of the pathogenic parental attitudes previously discussed has its characteristic expression in the sexual area. Thus, the perfectionistic person tends to emphasize performance in sex, the overly-submitted-to person is impulsive and inconsiderate of the rights of others, the hypochondriacal cannot tolerate sex because he feels ill, the overly coerced resists "doing one's duty" and the neglected find it difficult to feel close to anyone in their intimate sexual lives, and so on. However, an isolated or separate pathogenic attitude toward sex does not usually exist by itself. Instead, the sexual stimulation of children, including seduction, is generally the result of other pathogenic parental attitudes and the dissatisfaction that ensues from these attitudes.

Any child develops his sexuality against this background of his parents' attitudes. When properly guided, sexual drives can contribute to the individual's feelings of worth and effectiveness, his happiness and social adjustment. Misdirected or distorted, these same drives produce unhappiness, social disapproval and wasteful emotional conflict and anxiety.

Sex becomes the area in which the various pathogenic parental attitudes are released. In fact, these pathogenic attitudes are usually expressed in bold terms in sexual activities. For instance, the impulsive person whose "child of the past" has known only oversubmission demands his sexual wishes be submitted to, and the perfectionistic person forever seeks a sexual performance that ourshines his last performance.

Dissatisfaction in their adult lives as a result of these pathogenic attitudes may cause parents to seek satisfactions with erotic undertones in their relations with their children. Two authorities, Dr. Adelaide M. Johnson and Dr. David B. Robinson, of the Mayo Clinic, have made intensive studies of this problem. They point out that seduction, which they define as a sensual tempting and stimulation of the sexual feelings of the child by the parent, "occurs more commonly than it is comfortable to contemplate, regardless of the socioeconomic status of the family. The seduction may be as subtle as a caress or as blatant as actual incest." Such parents are "emotionally very confused, badly maladjusted, and definitely sick, belying every outward appearance of their stability in the community. All such parents reveal an unsatisfactory marital sexual relationship."*

In short, sexual maladjustment is a part of the total picture of pathogenic attitudes combining in an individual. It almost never exists by itself. The sexual experiences of your "inner child of the past" are inevitably colored and influenced by the specific attitudes of your parents—and should be understood in relation to them. Perfectionism may, for example, lead to much striving anxiety in a child. In masturbation he finds a pleasurable relief from tension. But this is forbidden, creating guilt and renewed anxiety. Unable to find a "perfect" partner in adult life, he may resume masturbation. Thus the "child of the past" continues to offer security and relief from certain kinds of anxiety. But it thwarts his development as an adult. Yet his problem is not sexual; it is the perfectionism which dominates his life.

STARTING POINT: Sex is a natural drive which, in the human being, is intimately bound into his emotional associations and attachments. By the time adulthood is reached, sex is interpreted by the individual in terms of his parents' attitudes or the emotional atmosphere in which

---

* Adelaide M. Johnson and David B. Robinson, *Journal of the American Medical Association*, *164*:1559, August 3, 1957.

they raised him; and these attitudes were, in turn, handed down by their parents and largely molded by broad cultural views about sex, its desirability and acceptability at certain times and places. As a result of these factors, distortions and even complete misconceptions have often become part of what should be accepted as a natural and life-giving force in human lives.

To clarify some of the problems involved, it is necessary to realize that excessive sexual stimulation in childhood may arise from either a parental prohibition of sexual interests and activities—or the sly, sensual tempting and excessive stimulation of the child's sexual feelings by the parent.

NATURAL DEVELOPMENT: In our culture more restrictions are placed upon sexuality in childhood than on any other human drive. While aggressive, moving-forward behavior is encouraged in other areas (how we applaud that first step!) any overt sexual interest or activity is met with frowns and worry. Prompt efforts to restrain, distract, prohibit are initiated. What would be ignored in Polynesian or even some European cultures frequently arouses great parental anxiety in ours. Often this anxiety results in an attempt to deny and suppress sexuality in the child—and later in the adult.

When, just before World War I, Freud pointed out that sexuality was an actual fact in early childhood, he exploded a myth of Victorian propriety and set off a storm that provoked many discussions and investigations of child-rearing. It has now been thoroughly and scientifically established by pediatric, psychiatric and psychologic studies that the forerunners of sexual feelings develop in an individual at a very early age. They are natural and do not result in any harm to the child. The infant finds pleasure in touching and rubbing his genitals and as he grows older he develops curiosity about his own body and that of other children. Bosoms and bottoms interest children. It is not at all unusual for curious children at the age of three or four years, playing "doctor" or "house," to peek under clothes and inspect, perhaps touch each other's genitals.

Masturbation is often openly performed and it is, Dr. Hale Shirley* has pointed out, no more an indication of emotional upheaval or of a need for drastic measures than

---

* Hale Shirley, *Psychiatry for the Pediatrician,* Ch. 6, Commonwealth Fund, New York, 1948.

other common habital manipulations, such as those of the mouth, nose, ears or hair. Around puberty a marked increase in sexual drive results in almost universal masturbation in both girls and boys. In adolescence this increase in sex drive is accompanied by increasing interest in the opposite sex. From this come the first efforts at dating, the prologue to mating and the eventual formation of a permanent marriage relationship.

Basically, the child acquires his own idea of how to be a good husband or wife, a good father or mother, through identification with his parents. His early family experiences teach him the rudiments of living with others. What he observes of his parents' marital behavior is the basic pattern he seeks as appropriate for himself. In this process he needs to experience the love of the parent of the opposite sex to provide the foundation for his feelings toward his future mate. At the same time identification with the parent of the same sex establishes the basis for his own adult sex role. This acceptance of sexuality as natural and its intertwining with the emotional development of both sexes creates a sound, realistic basis for future happiness and well-being.

This years-long process has been summarized here because at almost any point parental attitudes may interfere with this natural development. There is nothing inherently evil, disgusting, dirty or frightening in sex, but some parents implant such emotions in their child's sexual feelings from infancy onward. Shame, guilt, embarrassment, fear —even feelings of helplessness—may result from these anxious and stern efforts to deny or prohibit sexuality.

PROHIBITION AND RESTRAINT: Few such parents realize that they are creating, with such restrictions and attitudes, profoundly pathogenic and troublemaking attitudes with their cries of "Shame . . . bad . . . never let me catch you again . . . God is watching you . . ." Even when some parents realize that much of their own unhappiness comes from such parental attitudes in their past home lives, they are unable to control such reactions, surrendering to the "child of the past."

In their prudish anxiety, which is always woven into their other pathogenic attitudes, they are simply responding—as in childhood—to their own parents' attitude that sex was sinful, shameful, dirty, bestial and so on. Few recognize any connection between this and the results of other pathogenic attitudes toward themselves: their ineffectual work, their dissatisfied and unhappy marital lives and their self-belittling.

Children need limits when the dignity and privacy of others are invaded. But making a child feel guilty about his sexual feelings and his interested, natural curiosity connects guilt, anxiety and sexuality within him, often in an extremely painful and persistent way. To state it in its simplest form, he is made to feel guilty over what he enjoys. The guilty emotion may become an important component of his sexual life, with the result that he may be more "at home" in the illicit love affair with its attached guilt than he is in married love. Moreover, since sexuality cannot be removed from human life, parental condemnation merely forces its expression into secrecy, causing an ever-increasing feeling of guilt.

Prohibition also creates hostility, particularly toward a forbidding parent of the opposite sex. The child realizes —and later comes to know—that he actually has only the innocence of a child and is not bad, evil, sinful, dirty. He eventually resents being made to feel so evil.

But most of all, such prohibitions and suppressions stimulate curiosity and sexual fantasies. What is denied or punished if expressed may be safely tried out in fantasy. Often, "because God is watching," such fantasies are indulged in, then condemned by the child who has been made to feel guilty about his sexual feelings. As he condemns himself, becoming anxious and fearful, he hungers for more fantasies. As has been pointed out by many writers, particularly by Somerset Maugham in "Rain" and Sherwood Anderson in *Winesburg, Ohio,* the puritanical are often preoccupied with sex. Ostensibly, they are denouncing it, but actually they are deriving significant satisfaction from it in fantasy, which makes them feel guilty and contaminated—and more zealous in trying to stamp it out.

These fantasies, created by suppression, overstimulate the child's sexual feelings. They tend to become his way of expressing his sexuality. They provide, in adult life, the familiar "at home" feeling in sexual activities which the "inner child of the past" always seeks. What is wrong with prohibition is that it leads to curiosity, to excessive preoccupation with sexual fantasies—which are divorced from human interchange and reality—and tends to depersonalize sex. Sexual satisfaction in fantasy prevents the development of a normal "give-and-take" sexual relationship. Usually even the secrecy and forbidding atmosphere of the parental home are continued as part of the fantasy setting; they were an integral and exciting part of the sexual activity of the "child of the past."

In adult life, the "child of the past" tends to seek this fantasy sexual activity if in childhood sexuality was forbidden and considered "bad." Sexual curiosity, suppressed in childhood, may be expressed in adult life in "girlie" magazines. It may be the only kind of sexuality that can be enjoyed with a feeling of security. An actual sexual situation with a member of the opposite sex whom one knows and respects may produce anxiety or even panic. Thus, such visual stimulation tends to become meaningless. The person fantasied about is unknown—and unknowable. Such sexual activity becomes completely depersonalized. Masturbation, another forbidden and depersonalized sexual activity of the "child of the past," may be similarly continued. All such immature activities tend to prevent the development of the adult who can fully participate in a sexual relationship with deep satisfaction.

One cannot begin to catalogue the sexual dissatisfaction and ensuing feelings of depression and self-belittlement that result from the preoccupation with sexual fantasies with no reality to support them. Few of us have altogether escaped this plight, for suppression of sexuality in childhood is one of the common experiences of our society. Yet we live in a cultural atmosphere that is in itself preoccupied with sexuality. Our mass media focus on the erotic physical aspects of sex, deepening the separation of the interpersonal and physical created in childhood by guilt. Thus, in our society, the goal tends to become glandular rather than affectionate interchange. When sex is glandular, it tends to be impersonal—another note reinforced by the mass media's emphasis on physical allure.

Such depersonalization, one of the main trends in our sexual activities, is one of the major roots of our pervasive loneliness. It, too, tends to reinforce the need to live in fantasy. We are too depersonalized in this area to be able to speak to someone, to share out feelings and desires.

You will have to judge for yourself the degree to which these guilt-arousing admonitions of the past, and the denial and suppression on which they are based, have affected your sexual development. Have they caused you to drift into excessive preoccupation with sexual fantasies rather than seek satisfactions in reality? Have they caused you to try to deny, as your parents may have, the existence of your own sexual feelings? Have they caused you to separate sex, as something physical, from love? Have they caused you to emphasize the physical satisfactions rather than the emotional ones of mutual interchange and fulfillment?

You can, by accepting sexuality as a natural part of yourself and nothing of which you need to be ashamed, gradually reduce the interfering, fantasy-seeking, guilty "child of the past" in your sex life. This pushing aside of guilt and asserting your right to full adult sexual satisfaction may make you feel anxious at first. But gradually you can release yourself from a bondage to childhood which frustrates your ability to feel satisfied with yourself and prevents satisfaction for your partner.

The Story of Beth

Our parental attitudes about sex, interwoven with the other attitudes of the family, are transmitted from generation to generation, but they are significantly affected by the prevailing cultural attitude.

However, punitiveness and distrust—which anticipates "badness" and punishes in advance by stricter prohibitions —often become involved in our efforts to manage sexual feelings if we have puritanical backgrounds. Many persons with such backgrounds, for example, become involved in casual and indiscriminate sexual affairs—and then punish themselves for becoming involved. They blame their "terrible" sexual feelings and longings, their preoccupation with sexual fantasies.

Rebellion against parental overcoercion may also be propelling them into these meaningless sexual episodes. Or they may be excessively submissive to their impulsiveness, just as their parents were.

For example, let me tell you the story of Beth, a high school senior, who came to see me at the frantic request of her mother. Although attractive and only seventeen years old, Beth was quite intent on portraying herself to me initially as a fully grown-up, bad, beautiful woman, a problem to herself and irresistible to men. She talked rapidly:

"One minute I can be sweet. The next minute I can be horrible and nasty, swear like a sailor. I never know what terrible thing I'm going to say or do next. May I smoke? I'm in the twelfth grade. I get fairly good grades in school and I get along okay with the teachers. But I don't like the principal—he's two-faced. I don't get along with some of the kids in my class too well. The minister I talked to said my trouble is rebellion against my mother. She's not actually very strict, but she is always picking on me about little things. She gives me long lectures about not smoking and about being a good girl. She has never trusted me. Boy, she should know the joints I've been in!

"She listens on the downstairs phone if I talk to boys—and I'm always talking to them, lots of them. They even call me up long distance. She invades my privacy, opens my letters and reads them, studies my underwear, goes through clothes, pockets, pocketbooks, compacts, even my schoolbooks. Honestly, I really can't stand to be around that woman very long. When I come home from a date, she grills me for an hour. Where have I been? What did I do? Did we hold hands? Did he kiss me? On the cheek or on the mouth?

"Honestly, she really asks me those things. I want to explode. Usually when I come home, I just slam right past her, go upstairs and hibernate. Then she stands outside my door, complaining, crying. I'm ruining her life, she says. What does she think she's doing to me? I say to her, You ruined your own life. It wasn't me. And lay off me, I say.

"Sometimes I've been drinking—and if she smells it, she has a fit. So what, I say. It's not her business. She is also always warning me: You're going to get pregnant. So what? That's my worry. It's true I've been sleeping with different boys. If I feel like it, what's wrong with that? I mean, if I like the boy . . . Well, what's wrong with it is this: I don't want things to go on the way they have been. I get low and depressed, real blue, even though I always act gay. Fellows don't like a girl who sits and mopes. I call myself, 'You bitch, you whore.' Often I think I ought to feel worse and guiltier than I do.

"There is one boy I've gone out with over the last two years. He's really sweet and he loves me. But he scares me. I mean, he is everything I am not. He's reliable, steady and hard-working—not fooling around. I am afraid he might . . . well, you know, find out about me. But still

I can't sit home and listen to my mother yap all day. Honestly, she just picks at me all the time—or she's trying to head me off, finding things for me to do so I can't go out. When I get out of that place I can't wait to have some fun."

Beth's major problem is not her sexual promiscuity, although it is an important symptom of her difficulties. This was clear in talking to her mother, a stern-faced stout matron who was obviously upset. She talked about Beth in this way: "My daughter—only a girl, she is—has been having sex relations with various men. I found a letter in her drawer the other day from a boy. In it he referred to a sexual affair. I confronted Beth with this letter and she was defiant—saying vile things to me, horrible things.

"She has never had much discipline. She's always been very determined about what she wants, likes to have her own way, and she is fairly smart—at least she gets pretty good school marks. But she has always been involved in this sex sort of thing. Well, I shouldn't say always, perhaps . . . But when she was only ten years old, the neighbor lady told me that Beth and some of the other girls had started a sex club in the garage. It really didn't amount to much. Some of these older girls were developing breasts —not Beth so much as the older ones—and they showed their breasts to one another. I stopped it. I just told Beth she wasn't to do that sort of thing any more. But some of the kids in the neighborhood talked about it and it gave her a bad name. I told Beth she would have to be extra good to change everybody's mind about her. . . .

"But this sex thing has always been on my mind. It has been worrying me for years, even before I was married. I'm embarrassed to tell you . . . but I often thought about sex. Some days it seemed that I just couldn't think about anything else. Of course, I never did anything. But still it was wrong to think about it . . . and I've always been scared to death about it. And then when Beth was born, well . . . I knew somehow this sex thing would turn up. I would try to prevent it, but it would still happen. And when that business about the sex club happened, I have not been able to think of anything else. I just hope some boy marries her.

"I don't know what will ever happen to her. She's no good. No decent girl would talk the way she does. Over the last two years she has been going out with older men. She puts on more make-up to make herself look older.

She sneaks cigarettes. She drinks. I say to her, 'Beth, please don't. It hurts me so to have you do it.' I'm sure she will get in trouble with one of these men. I've tried to warn her, to tell her about sex and these dangers. Why, she might even get a disease. But she won't listen to me. I'm nothing."

Beth's mother is obviously continuing the guilty parental attitude of her own childhood. The anxiety and guilt of her "child of the past" over her own sexual feelings has been turned into a form of punitive distrust against Beth. She has nagged and lectured Beth, opened her letters, listened to her phone calls and otherwise invaded her privacy—all of which is destructive to Beth's sense of being a capable and competent individual. And while she has not trusted Beth, she has also not firmly limited her. When Beth's mother says, "You hurt me so," it makes Beth feel guilty—and hostile—but this is a far cry from a firm "no." Moreover, in her nagging, overly coercive direction and redirection, she constantly stokes the furnace of rebellion which drives Beth to defy and to seek "fun" and affection wherever she can find it.

In listening to Beth's story, one tends to judge her and warn her of the consequences of her behavior. She invites "straightening out"—but such a lecture would merely renew the same criticizing, nagging atmosphere of her home and prompt her to rebel.

Left on her own, Beth treated herself exactly as her mother treated her. This was pointed out to her. She was told she could treat herself in her own way—but not her mother's way. This meant that she had to say "no" firmly to her impulsiveness, without criticizing herself, and to provide her own directions—without rebelling against them. When she wasn't basing her life on defying her mother's nagging, she was basing it on defying her own critical "blue" lectures.

When Beth did not have to submit to her own impulsive defiance and did not have to belittle herself, she did not have to rebel—and this helped her be less impulsive.

All these factors were much exaggerated by her mother's preoccupation with sex—and, in effect, she directed Beth into these sexual activities with her excessive stimulation by prohibition, guilt and suppression. When Beth became her own uncritical parent to herself, she settled down. She did not get pregnant. She now has a good job and goes with the young man she mentioned so favorably.

The main point, however, is that while originally presented as a sexual problem by her mother, Beth's real problem was in becoming a kindly, trusting and firm parent to herself. Her mother's alternating moods of overcoercion, oversubmission and punitive distrust were pathogenic—and focused in characteristic ways in the area of sexuality with her own distrust, prohibition and guilt predominating. The result was the excessive stimulation of sexual activities in Beth.

This is not at all unusual. It is literally the story of thousands of people in whom excessive sexual stimulation results from the prohibitions established by their parents.

Seduction

In some instances, as a result of the dissatisfactions arising from the pathogenic attitudes with which they treat themselves, parents may directly stimulate the sexual feelings of their children excessively. This may occur with or without awareness. As Drs. Johnson and Robinson have pointed out in the paper referred to in the section on recognizing sexual stimulation, this occurs more often than it is suspected. In contrast to the parent who tries to prohibit sexuality—and causes excessive stimulation—the parent who directly stimulates sexuality in this sense may be fully aware of and may even slyly foster the child's participation in his sexually teasing behavior.

The simplest unwitting seductions may occur from parental efforts to be "modern" and from misinterpretations of Freud's theory of the sexual origin of the neuroses. Thus, these parents may overdo their belief that "an open approach to sexuality provides an emotionally healthful climate." They may ignore conventional modesty, may go about the house nude and respect no bathroom privacy.

Certain situations lead naturally to excessive sexual stimulation. Seductive and sexually stimulating bathing with the parents of the opposite sex, with playful washing becoming increasingly sexual as the child grows older, often occurs. The mother's washing and examination of the genitals may become seductive maneuvers.

Nearly all parents initially and innocently take their children into bed with them. However, most parents forbid it by the time the child has reached school age. But this may be prolonged, even after it is clear that it is ex-

271

cessively stimulating. Often one parent must insist that the child be forbidden to enter the bed to prevent this teasing and tempting excessive stimulation.

Prolongation of this habit into the teen-age period generally provokes extreme stimulation. Fathers may sleep with daughters and engage in all degrees of caressing and sexual stimulation. One recent study of delinquent girls found that 15 percent of them had had such sexual relations with their fathers. These were mostly verified cases and the true incidence is believed to be much higher.* Similarly, mothers may continue to lie with sons although well aware of the child's sexual excitement. Such mothers experience, according to Drs. Johnson and Robinson, "a gratification admixed with hostility and anxiety." The teasing, provocative mother in lingerie or half-opened kimono who wants her son to powder her back or comb her hair is not unusual.

What happens to the child as a result of this excessive stimulation? Initially the child may be puzzled but compliant. Eventually mounting frustration and anger force him to follow one of two courses:

1. Regression to the relative safety of dependent, infantile attitudes and behavior. This ends the immediate problem for the child. He remains a dependent child and puts himself entirely in the hands of his parents. But this makes impossible the normal growth and development of the child and his ultimate emergence as an adult.

2. The other course results, in men, in physical aggression and rage against women. In women, it is often the cause of promiscuity of various degrees. Drs. Johnson and Robinson and other authorities point out that actual incest, particularly of the father-daughter variety, occurs far more commonly than any official records indicate.

These investigators point out that generally these seductive maneuvers are carried out by one parent—and condoned by the other. They cite the following case:

We recently studied an eleven-year-old girl of a middle-class family whose mother had known for years that serious genital seduction was being carried out by the father. The mother, frigid and very disturbed, for a time had been glad to be relieved of sexual marital "obligations," but eventually her mo-

* S. L. Halleck, *Journal of the American Medical Association, 180:* 273, April 28, 1962.

bilized anger and jealousy demanded that something be done to correct the situation. The father, himself the product of a distorted background, openly confessed his behavior with the daughter and agreed to a program of long intensive treatment for the child and both parents . . . A complication in this case, magnifying the therapeutic difficulty, was the almost complete absence of shame or guilt on the part of the child because of the apparent approval of the mother.

However, children often imagine or fantasy incestuous relationships. In fact, this is a common type of childhood fantasy. It develops out of the affection and loving attachment of the child for the parent of the opposite sex. While these relationships may be reported as fact, their imaginary character can usually be established. When accompanied by excessive sexual stimulation, which may not necessarily reach the point of being physical, such fantasies limit and hurt the child's development.

In fact, one thing that appears to be required of a parent is a willingness to give the child as much love and affection as one can—and then be willing to be progressively and constantly jilted as the growing child searches for love and affection from others. Some parents, not recognizing this, create such a close emotional bond with the child, often as a result of dissatisfactions in their marital lives, that they prevent the child's development. Such overly stimulating attention from a parent can easily make persons the child's own age seem inadequate and insignificant.

If you were subjected to excessive direct sexual stimulation by your parents or other adults as a child, you probably still retain some of your deep feelings of rage and hostility against members of the opposite sex. While the "inner child of the past" cannot escape bearing an emotional scar from such a betrayal of affection, such an experience does not make it impossible for you to develop a loving sexual relationship—but it will require patience and understanding. In many cases men and women have needed psychiatric help in order to develop sufficient trust within themselves to feel love. Understanding and trying to forgive the parent whose transgression was cloaked in affection may remain impossible. But if the past can be steadfastly relegated to the past, and not applied to those who had no part in that past, your hurt "child of the past" may be helped to recognize his innocence and that he is worth loving. If you have suffered from this kind of hurt, you can help yourself by recognizing that the harm is not necessarily permanent and that men and women can love one another in wholesome ways. If you feel you need help, for this can be a severe problem, do not hesitate to seek it. While psychiatrists are especially trained in dealing with complex emotional problems, they are not numerous and your own physician can help you both directly and in finding a psychiatrist if this becomes necessary.

Cultural Approval of Mass Sexual Stimulation

Our culture does not ostensibly endorse excessive stimulation of the sexual feelings of children. It merely makes it inescapable.

This is true not only for children but for all of us. We are all exposed to it, and all of us are affected by it in one way or another. Today we live in a visible aura of unrestrained sexual stimulation; the seductive, alluring and provocatively posed girl is everywhere, successful and desirable, for the men to respond to and the women to emulate. Our children get the same exposure as adults via our mass media, for this is the character of mass media. While in other cultures attitudes toward sex may be either more restrictive or more casual than ours, nowhere else are they so confused and contradictory. This in itself is a frequent and profound cause of anxiety in every stratum of our society.

The continual and unlimited visual sexual stimulation characteristic of our society represents the end efforts of the revolt against the old puritanical viewpoint which considered the sight of a girl's ankle shocking. Despite all this undiscriminating mass stimulation, our attitude toward seeking sexual satisfaction remains remarkably prudish and puritanical. This contradictory—and again inescapable—cultural attitude is in itself pathogenic.

While this prolonged mass stimulation has broken down the old attitudes regarding display of the innocent body, it has not altered the puritanical behavioral code. Instead sexual fantasies have very nearly become mass-produced, public ones; the mere mention of Brigitte Bardot on a television show results in laughter that essentially recognizes the fantasies about this naked actress. Constantly stimulating sexual fantasies while insisting on puritanical behavior can only result in more tension, anxiety, sexual difficulties and conflicts—and the breakdown of the behavioral code. This is not "new freedom" or "modern living," but a kind of sensual enslavement that is particularly confusing. This helps to explain why each year an increasing number of young girls become unwed mothers; in 1961 these girls numbered an unprecedented 200,000.

The Exploitation of Sex

We long ago passed the line that marks acceptance of the human body as something natural and beautiful, and turned to its commercial exploitation. This is one of the great factors in the current mass sexual stimulation. The sexy girl is selling everything from golf clubs to whiskey, cars, movies and careers, promising satisfaction for everything. Our fashion and clothing industries seek sexually stimulating designs as the key to sales success in everything from beachwear to work clothes. Our television jokes, while inevitably based on expectations aroused by attractive women and our remaining puritanical code against such satisfactions, imply that loose and casual encounters are not only just around the corner, but are desirable and worthwhile. Our adult attitudes approve of impulsive, flirtatious behavior at parties—and piously disapprove of anything coming of it.

The Effects of Mass Sexual Stimulation

Many people sense there is something wrong in the unrestrained sexual provocativeness of our society. But because of the excesses of the past, they are afraid to explore their own feelings and reactions lest they be called puritanical "bluenoses." However, examination of the effects of this mass sexual stimulation indicates such reactions are not puritanical but realistic.

The preoccupation with sexuality that afflicts our society results in a distorted emphasis on the physical and erotic side of sex—and neglect of the personal interchange side. This emphasis causes great and multifaceted unhappiness. We cannot all have the physical attributes of movie stars. Yet such attractiveness is presented as not merely desirable but a guaranteed solution to all problems. For the girl who is not beautiful, this creates an immediate and hurtful attitude within her toward herself. We see millions of women striving endlessly and unhappily for physical beauty, for slenderness, for renewed attractiveness, and a very great part of this is based on "child of the past" feelings that they are not attractive. Many women never do realize that attractiveness is primarily a matter of inner appeal—which starts with acceptance of oneself. Ironically, the beautiful woman often suffers as much from this emphasis on physical beauty as anyone. Beautiful, she expects to find herself satisfied and happy. Instead she is often very unhappy and miserable—for the feelings of satisfaction can be gained only through emotional participation and have little to do with physical beauty.

Another effect of this mass sexual stimulation is that it tends to make the actual sexual experience impersonal. The partner is a negligible factor. The partner does not particularly stimulate, but merely triggers a precharged relationship between a person and his fantasy. The actual stimulation comes across the air waves or across the page in an impersonal fashion; the response is similarly indiscriminate and impersonal. The separation of the interpersonal and physical aspects of love are thus reinforced. The goal of sexual experience has become physical—the release of sexual tension rather than affectionate emotional interchange in a meaningful relationship.

But what must also be said is that this continual stimulation results in continual dissatisfaction and frustration. A girl, for example, must wear provocative, sexually revealing clothes and behave in a flirting, teasing fashion, according to our culture, if she wants to be popular. However, she must resist any sexual overtures from responding males. She is automatically put in a teasing position. If she does not resist, she's considered "bad," "a fool," "easy," "a pushover," "no good." If she does resist, she is in the position of arousing both herself and men without any point to the arousal. Much confused promiscuity, particularly among teenagers, results from this cultural equating of sexual provocativeness with popularity.

This combination of mass stimulation and restrictions is both unrealistic and cruel. For young people, particularly those embarked on long educational programs, it creates many problems. The teenage marriage and the college marriage are efforts to solve this. At a time when they are both economically and emotionally dependent—and experiencing the most powerful sexual impulses of their lives—our culture expects these young people to ignore or be immune to the mass sexual stimulation approved by our society. Causing acute frustration and confusion in our most intelligent young people, it forces the continuation of immature sexual fantasies into adulthood.

The Effect on Children

There is rapidly growing evidence that idealization of the physical and erotic aspects of sex by our mass media is causing significant difficulties for children. In many cases children are being pushed, particularly by mothers who are confusing popularity with sex, into sexual and emotional situations which they are not yet equipped to handle. Because our sexual stimulation is on a mass basis, the ensuing problems will also be on a mass basis.

Yet except for some physicians and psychiatrists particularly concerned with children, and some social workers and perceptive observers of cultural trends, this situation is largely ignored. But let me quote from a *Time** article on children in the "pre-teen" group to demonstrate some of the ramifications of our mass sexual stimulation that are obviously making future trouble. It also demonstrates that this is no mere isolated incident.

In Massapequa, N.Y., Kathy came home from school and announced she would need nylons and a garter belt to wear at her girl friend's birthday party because "all the other girls" would be wearing them. Kathy is eight years old.

In Los Angeles, Bill's parents gave him his first "sit-down" dinner and dance (live music) for his tenth birthday. Tuxedoed boys escorted dates who wore corsages. One boy showered too much attention on another's date. "I had to talk with him and remind him he brought his own little date," explained Bill's mother.

* *Time*, April 20, 1962.

In Chicago's suburban Evergreen Park, a dozen girls from age six upward, whooshed into the local beauty shop for their regular Saturday appointments, emerged topheavy with "beehive" and "lioness" hairdos. Sighed Manager Warren Miller: "They've got more hair than they've got face. I'd call it a mop."

In San Francisco, Beverly, daughter of a Berkeley professor, asked her parents for a "training bra." She needed to feel a little glamorous, since she was planning to go to a drive-in movie on the back of her boy friend's bicycle. Beverly is nine, her boy friend eleven.

In short, dating, dancing, kissing games and all the rest of the natural delights that once were the preserve of adolescents, are becoming part of the everyday life of an increasing number of eight- to twelve-year-old grade-schoolers all over the U.S. The latest social discovery of the pre-teeners, particularly popular in the nation's suburb-nests, is "making out," a tentative version of adolescent necking: the boys and girls get together at somebody's home, and the parents discreetly disappear, leaving the room darkened and the boys at liberty to "make out." Preteeners in Los Angeles have developed a modern version of the post-office and spin-the-bottle kissing games. They call it "Seven Minutes of Heaven (or Hell)." The boy takes the girl who is "it" into a closet or some other room and, depending on his inclination kisses her (Heaven) or hits her (Hell) for seven minutes.

All of this excessive sexual stimulation and emphasis on the physical is basically coming from parents who are the "carriers" of the current cultural attitude. Professor Carlfred B. Broderick,* of Pennsylvania State University, has commented on this situation as follows: "Many parents appear to operate under the mistaken theory that sex starts at puberty. They assume that early kissing is meaningless. But pre-teen dating starts the youngster earlier on the road to progressive intimacy. By the time these children have reached their teens, they have pretty well covered the field, and are ready for nothing less than marriage."

Marriage for such children is hardly a solution; it is more likely to be a promise of unhappiness. The divorce

---

* Carlfred B. Broderick, *Time,* April 20, 1962; see also *PTA Magazine,* December, 1961; *Marriage and Family Living,* February, 1961.

rate among people who married in their teens is about five times as great as for those who married in their mid-twenties.

Today's children, stimulated by the flow of sultry romance from television, movies and cheap magazines—which is often supplemented by the excessively stimulating emphasis on physical aspects of sex by their parents—can hardly avoid a distorted picture of love and affection, marriage and responsibility. They are being thrust into sexual and emotional situations far beyond their capacities. Dr. Benjamin Spock, whose concern for children has made him the best known baby authority in the nation, has also concerned himself with this problem. He says: "The trouble is that Nature is working for a marriage at about fifteen or sixteen years. Early dating and going steady for months will encourage intimacy even before fifteen. But our society expects everyone to be in school until at least seventeen or eighteen. Some children who aren't at all ready are forcing themselves to compete for partners and to play the roles of people in love."*

There are reports of parents trying to introduce dating as early as the fifth grade. It is common now in many places in the seventh grade. And many parents are frantic with anxiety if their daughter is not dating or going steady by the time she reaches high school. Boys are similarly pushed. Many parents interpret any failure to date as a lack of sex appeal—and as a result of our cultural over-emphasis on sex come to the conclusion that the child is going to be an "old maid."

The price we will ultimately pay for this continuous, generalized stimulation is of course incalculable. But by recognizing it for what it is, and in particular how it appeals to and sustains the immature sexual interest of the "child of the past," we can begin to relieve ourselves of some of the pressures and tensions it creates.

A Realistic Approach to Sex

Recognizing how the mass sexual stimulation of our culture tends to depersonalize sex can help you begin to find your way to genuine sexual satisfaction. In reality, human beings are not long satisfied with physical sexual relations

---

* Benjamin Spock, *Ladies' Home Journal*, April, 1958.

as such. The deeper satisfactions come from the day-to-day interchange and mutual concern which embellish and enrich a loving relationship. Sexual relations are satisfactory only when there is respect, consideration and interest in the person *who happens also to possess sexual glands*.

Our Puritan ancestors made the mistake of trying to negate bodies and suppress sexuality. What resulted were excessive sexual fantasies and disturbing feelings of guilt because one's body could not be denied.

Instead we must recognize that our bodies and their sexual glands exist, and intertwine their functioning with our emotional feelings of love and desire for our partner's welfare. Sex and consideration for the other person, a loving willingness to assume responsibility for the fullest development of the partner as a person, create the deepest sexual satisfaction when they are completely and inextricably intertwined.

This is not an idealistic but a realistic goal. It will prevent you from being carried by the tide of impersonal sexual stimulation intrinsic in our culture into the ultimate loneliness of living wholly in fantasy.

In order to achieve this goal, you must:

1. Set limits on your own sexual fantasies. You can do this respectfully, recognizing that many of these excessive fantasies are stirred up by the emphasis given sex in our mass media. Such fantasies belong to your "child of the past" and as a parent to yourself you can put them aside.

2. Recognize that you, as a human being, have sexual glands and sexual feelings which deserve consideration.

3. Connect your sexuality with your emotional attachment to a human being, and seek your real satisfaction in your day-to-day interchange and not in the exaggerated promises of fantasy.

PART III

Changing Yourself
and Your Life

CHAPTER 19

BECOMING A NEW KIND
OF PARENT TO YOURSELF

If this book were written exclusively for physicians, this chapter would be titled "Therapy" or "Treatment." It is devoted to some practical problems you will encounter in abandoning the pathogenic parental attitudes of your childhood and developing new ways of being a helpful parent to your "inner child of the past."

This book has no "peace of mind" pep-talk to offer. You can have peace of mind by reducing the struggle between your "child of the past" and your adult self. This is an inner satisfaction and contentment that can only be earned. No one can bestow it on you. Life itself is filled with struggle, its satisfactions are achieved in struggle. The unhappiness and discontent of many of us is caused by the fruitless struggles of the "child of the past" which thwart adult fulfillment. To change your life, you must accept and manage your inner "child of the past" in new ways, with understanding, kindness and firmness. In describing the most common pathogenic areas, I have attempted to show specific areas in which you may have to wrestle in order to guide your "child of the past" in new ways. I have also tried to show how a pathogenic attitude is transmitted and how it can be taken apart and altered.

Yet the outcome is always going to depend on what efforts you make in changing the old parental attitudes that you use on yourself. Reading this book is not wrestling with these old attitudes, although it may give you some much needed leverage in the form of understanding your difficulties. And a psychiatrist or physician cannot change your attitudes. You must do it yourself. Similarly, no ex-.

planation—or exploration—of your childhood will end your problems. Finding the sources of your difficulties can tell you where the struggle must take place. But for your life to change in any significant fashion, you must make the effort.

Identifying Feelings of the "Inner Child of the Past"

Your first concern, in becoming a new kind of parent to yourself, is to learn to identify the feelings of your particular "child of the past." Because each child is different, and each family is different, each person is unique. Your "child of the past" differs from that of your brother or sister, even if you are twins. Your particular "child of the past" has had specific experiences that differ from everyone else's in some respects. So do his feelings. You must learn to recognize these feelings and childhood longings as important, deserving of respect, and separate them from your adult feelings. This distinction is important because it will help distinguish your adult goals. It will clearly indicate whether the "child of the past" is interfering or adding to your satisfactions. By recognizing and accepting the feelings of your "child of the past" in a respectful way, you can begin to function as a kind and helpful parent with full awareness of this role toward yourself. This will help you move toward achievement of your adult goals.

As a practical matter, your first recognition of the feelings of your "inner child of the past" may be made more easily at a time of stress. Your "child of the past" is not dominating or controlling your actions all—or even most —of the time. But at times when you are tired, ill or under great strain, your "inner child of the past" is more likely to assert himself—and thus emerge clearly. Or when the external situation you face is reminiscent of those of your childhood, the feelings of the "child of the past" are often sharply delineated.

You do not need to wait for a stressful situation in order to see clearly the role of your "inner child of the past." Your memories of your reactions to past stresses will provide an accurate guide. Take a notebook and itemize the stresses—and your reactions. This will begin to clarify the role your "child of the past" has played in your life. You can begin to anticipate both your parental attitude toward yourself—and the reaction of your "child of the past." This anticipation will help you manage your "child of the past," just as a mother taking away a dangerous item from her child must anticipate that the child will be angry with her—and not be upset by it or give in to this rage and let the child continue to play with it.

Secondly, by carefully and methodically checking the common pathogenic attitudes described earlier, you will find some which apply to you. This will help you identify more of the feelings of your "inner child of the past." List the pathogenic attitudes which seem to have been particularly involved in the formation of the reactions of your "child of the past." Take note of how these attitudes now interfere in your adult life. Or if they provide for deep satisfactions, as they well may, especially in recreation, make note of that too. However, the attitudes which you need to change are those which interfere with your adult capacities and efforts. Make notes on what seems to trigger these attitudes—and the emergence of the "child of the past."

Sorting Out Pathogenic Attitudes

In doing this certain aspects of these attitudes should be borne in mind:

1. *Any parental attitude that is pathogenic or trouble-making is excessive.* The attitudes described in this book are the most common pathogenic parental attitudes, but they are by no means the only ones. You may have been subjected to excessive parental attitudes which are not described. We have all felt, at some point in childhood, neglected, overindulged, harshly punished, overcoerced, pushed toward perfection, made fearful of germs, permitted to be impulsive and rejected in some degree. What matters, however, is whether this reaction was the result of a persistent and excessive attitude pattern. It is the excessive and continuing character of an attitude which makes it pathogenic. We all need to learn, for example, that germs cause disease, but when a fearful attitude toward germs is excessive, it becomes incapacitating.

2. In the preceding pages common pathogenic attitudes have been described as though they existed in a "pure culture" form. In reality these attitudes are invariably mixed

with other attitudes, often interwoven and interlocked in such a way that one pathogenic attitude forces creation of another. For example, the perfectionistic parent may feel guilty about his excessive demands and turn to overindulgence, alternating a shower of gifts with new demands for perfection. It is in this fashion that pathogenic attitudes are often linked in a kind of push-pull connection. Generally speaking, one excessive attitude often creates others which serve to help maintain the imbalance caused by the primary pathogenic attitude.

3. It may help you to identify the feelings of your "inner child of the past" by recalling the different attitudes held by your mother and father, both in general and in specific areas. It is not at all unusual for one parent to be overcoercive while the other is overindulgent and overly submissive. In such a situation, the child may adopt both attitudes toward himself. What attitudes characterized your father? Your mother? Perhaps clues as to what their childhoods were like will help you clarify their attitudes —which are now part of your "heritage."

In listing in your notebook parental attitudes that seem to be significant in your life, you may find that some contradict one another. However, these attitudes are all a part of your specific individuality. How they fit into one another and the effect they have on one another may require some time to puzzle out.

The best procedure for you to follow is to take your time and try to clarify both:

(1) the parental attitudes and
(2) your reaction to them.

When You Became a Parent to Yourself

As a child you naturally reacted to your parents' attitudes—and you still do, using these attitudes on yourself. Long before your adolescence you began a process of "internalizing" these attitudes, absorbing and integrating them into your way of considering, treating and guiding yourself. During adolescence, when you gradually separated yourself from your parents' control, you began to be a parent to yourself.

This is a process which you can alter in a significant fashion. Knowing that you have "borrowed" the attitudes you are now using on yourself will help you. These are not your creations and you do not have to use them, but can develop your own parental attitudes toward yourself. You do not have to change everything in your life, but only those parental attitudes which are limiting your satisfactions and achievements.

Sometimes you may feel that you have to change everything in your life. This indicates that you have a low appreciation of what you have accomplished and little satisfaction in your present efforts. When you begin to find satisfaction in your efforts in some areas, you will be less downcast and depressed—and see that not everything needs to be changed. You have, even if you are not aware of them, elements on which you can build new attitudes and new satisfactions. The attitudes which must change are those parental attitudes which limit your satisfactions and achievements.

Mutual Respect

To change an old parental attitude which you are now using on yourself, it is important to recognize the feelings this attitude engenders in your "child of the past" and respect these feelings. You need to understand how a specific attitude destroys mutual respect between the adult you and your "child of the past." Most parental attitudes, as I have emphasized, are based on consideration of the parent, his feelings, rights, needs, demands, convenience. The feelings of the child are often belittled, overlooked or ridden over roughshod. Even in overindulgence, which takes on the appearance of concern for the child, the child's real developmental needs and deeper feelings of satisfaction with himself and his efforts are ignored. Ultimately bored with this endless, unsought shower of gifts, he is made nearly incapable of actively seeking his own satisfactions.

Thus, you must begin by respecting the feelings and needs of your "inner child of the past." You should consciously and patiently recognize how these feelings have come about—and your own innocence in their creation.

Acting as a kinder and more helpful parent than your own parents were able to do, you must then set limits on your response to these feelings and to their expression. You must set firm limits even on feelings that continue to arise from genuine harshness, deprivations and inadequacies in your childhood home. You will not help yourself by feeling sorry for yourself—and you may be pursuing the outdated and unrealistic goals of childhood. You can set such limits on the expression of the feelings of your "child of the past" and still maintain a respectful attitude toward this part of yourself.

Start with respect for the feelings of your "child of the past" and you have made a big step toward reducing your difficulties. Without it, you can make no progress but will only thrash around, fighting and blaming yourself.

Setting Limits

There are very practical ways of knowing when your "inner child of the past" is interfering in your adult life —and these are important in limiting his expression. For example, when you are responding to a situation with more emotion and feeling than is warranted by the situation and it leaves you "steaming," annoyed, vexed, disappointed with yourself, you should look for the "child of the past" and his role in this emotional upheaval. Ask yourself why he is reacting so strongly—and limit his expression of feelings respectfully.

If you are in conflict with others more often than is actually warranted, it is probably due to your "child of the past," who is reacting to both your parental attitude and the external situation. Many people could reduce their difficulties considerably if they would set limits on their expressions of anger. In childhood they did not develop any tolerance of frustration—and their parents gave in, perhaps even indulged them, when they raged over frustrations, demanding their "way." As adults, they constantly aggravate their relations with others by giving vent to what are the feelings of the "child of the past." The situation seldom calls for the degree of rage which they express.

If problems of control are major difficulties in your life, such as drinking too much or emotional blowups of rage, or you are loafing and "goofing" much of the time, you should seek to determine the role played by the parental attitude and your "child of the past" response to it in order to break up the cyclic action involved.

If a definite lack of balance between work, rest and play exists in your life, you should seek to determine what part the "inner child of the past" is playing in the creation of this imbalance. You need to rest and to vacation away from your work. Excessive work, rest or play is usually the result of demands of the "child of the past."

The pursuit of the past goals of childhood must be limited because they are unrealistic and wasteful. We already know this to some extent. The little boy who dreams of being a cowboy gives up the idea when he finds out something of the cowboy's real existence, and his growing interests become absorbed in other endeavors which seem more attractive and more reasonable. However, some goals are not easily put aside—often because they are not recognized as goals. The "child of the past" is often filled with longings and wishes which constitute goals and which he seeks to satisfy. For example, if you have been deprived of adequate love and attention from your mother in childhood, your "child of the past" will continue to seek this tenderness and prefer it rather than the more robust mutual interchange of living adults. Setting firm limits against the pursuit of childhood goals, which cannot be fulfilled because they belong to the past, is a necessary parental activity.

Basic Directions

If you can identify the main primary pathogenic attitudes to which you were subjected as a child, the following table will give some general directions in which you can move in becoming a new kind of parent to yourself:

If in Childhood You Experienced	You Can Today
Perfectionism Overcoercion	*Take off pressure and demands which you put on yourself*
Rejection Perfectionism Punitiveness	*Put your emphasis on kindliness, respect and gentleness in the way you treat yourself and limit your self-criticism*
Overindulgence	*Make demands on yourself to accomplish things; limit your dependence on others*
Oversubmission	*Enforce firm limits on your impulsiveness, work to overcome your tendency not to respect feelings and rights of others*

Neglect Rejection	*Consciously do little kindnesses for yourself, indulge yourself when you can and reduce your self-criticism*
Hypochondriacism	*Refuse to give in to your aches and pains*

This guide, while oversimplified, will give you a sense of what direction to take. As you clarify the old parental attitudes—and your reactions to them—you can consciously and effectively begin to treat yourself differently, with more respect and firmness.

Sometimes people think that simple awareness of these pathogenic attitudes and how they have been continued will be sufficient to cause them to disappear or lose their strength. Actually, awareness is not enough. It must be coupled with conscious, continued efforts and practice in treating your "inner child of the past" in a new way. Only in this manner can you alter the old troublemaking attitudes and their patterns.

What to Expect as You Change

Changing these old parental attitudes requires patience and hard work. It is much easier to slide along in the old patterns. Indeed, because these old attitudes have the security of the familiar, they will "feel right" for some time—and your new respectful approach will "feel wrong." You must prepare yourself to face some feeling of inner strangeness, of not feeling "at home" within yourself, even of definite anxiety. Learn to view this anxiety as a sign of progress. In time this feeling of strangeness and anxiety will fade as you become accustomed to your new attitudes —and begin to feel the benefits of them.

You should also expect a constant "pull" toward the old attitudes. Success in treating yourself differently on a few occasions does not mean the struggle is over. You must prepare yourself for a continuing struggle—and recognize that you are trying to establish a pattern. Gradually the relief from former miseries and the new satisfactions you will enjoy will make this worthwhile. However, the shadow of the past will always remain and seem more comfortable any time you are under pressure, fatigued or ill.

I am sometimes asked whether a person can make these changes without the help of a physician or psychiatrist.

Basically, and in most instances, I believe a person can significantly alter his parental attitudes toward himself without any more help than he can get from this book. However, the struggle may be prolonged and more difficult than if he had the help of a physician, particularly one trained in emotional illnesses and problems. To be realistic, a physician cannot do the wrestling with the old parental attitudes—you have to do that. But he can help explain the strange, "not at home" feelings which you may develop as you abandon the old parental attitudes and develop new respectful ones. A book such as this one, while it may adequately serve as a guide, is not a human relationship and cannot provide the warmth and appreciation of your efforts which an interested physician can.

In order to make steady and persistent progress, I suggest that every two months you review your progress. Keep your review date marked on your calendar. Keep notes on parental attitudes—and the reactions of your "child of the past." Give yourself a regular daily time to consider some aspect of your effort to alter these old troublemaking attitudes. In this fashion you will keep yourself oriented toward the persistent effort needed until you feel "at home" with your new way of being a parent to yourself.

Your Satisfactions in Prevention

Most pathogenic attitudes are passed from generation to generation. One of the most satisfying aspects of being able to alter these troublemaking parental attitudes is knowing that you can, as a present or future parent in real life, prevent a pathogenic attitude from afflicting the next generation of your family. As a psychiatrist who has worked with hundreds of parents and children, I consider this preventive aspect a primary consideration. It is one of my chief motives for writing this book.

Prevention requires the creation, in place of the emotional atmosphere which fosters pathogenic parental attitudes, of an atmosphere of mutual respect between parents and children. Each person must be respected in his right to the activities, the frustrations and satisfactions of his particular age level—and be limited only when this pursuit infringes on the rights of other family members.

291

Limits must be set firmly enough to insure that the rights of others are respected on a continuing basis.

This has three implications:

1. That each family member—from father to baby—is respected; the respect does not depend on the person's age or production or position in the family.

2. That there are continuing, firm limits against the infringement of the rights of others.

3. These limits must be reinforced with a willingness for conflict at the point of infringement. Life is filled with conflict and the romantic, "sweetie-pie" idea that married and parental life should be devoid of it has hurt all of us. Conflict does not, in itself, mean a lack of respect.

After many years of working with parents and children attempting to maintain a mutual respect balance, I am convinced that each family must have:

1. *Limits for children* whenever the adult feels that his rights or dignity are intruded upon. The child may be isolated, sent to his room, until he is ready to come around without infringing on other people's rights. Respectful limits are not punitive. The child must make at least partial restitution for anything stolen, broken carelessly or lost. In the preschool years firm limits must be placed to protect the child from the common dangers, i.e., streets, medicine cabinets, light sockets, stoves, knives, needles, scissors, open stairways, cleaning fluids.

2. *Chores*, beginning at school years, increasing as the child gets older, in order to develop work habits, self-respect and satisfaction in accomplishments. Children have a right to grumble about them, parents have the right to insist.

3. *Study hours for children*, particularly older ones, with TV and radio turned off and an interested adult available as a consultant but not to do the work.

4. *Freedom for all* to pursue individual interests from mudpies to serious hobbies without *anxious admonitions, pressure, lectures* or *criticism* from others as long as these efforts do not infringe on the rights of others.

5. *When children quarrel*—and they do quarrel—isolation for both in separate rooms until they can agree to come together peaceably again.

6. *Adult recreation* is necessary. Adults can be more capable of maintaining a mutual respect balance if they can get away from the children for an evening with a fair degree of regularity. And children need to experience the

fact that parents have a vigorous life of their own to pursue—that adults weren't put on earth solely to administer to the needs of children.

Each family can work out its problems and conflicting interests along lines of mutual respect. Such respect makes pathogenic attitudes unable to flourish. Having seen this work successfully in hundreds of families, I know that it is possible and practical—if each parent will recognize the need to treat the child he once was with respect, rather than with the belittling parental attitudes of the past. If the parent is respectful toward his own past feelings, he will be able to respect his real child's feelings.

Illumination—and Solution

Yet your present satisfactions and happiness, as well as preventing pathogenic parental attitudes from afflicting your children, depend on your ability to be a new kind of parent to yourself. In the opening chapter, it was pointed out that while this book might illuminate your emotional difficulties, it could not solve them. The application of whatever knowledge and insight you may have gained depends on you.

If you can accept your role as parent to your "inner child of the past," with respectful understanding and kindness born of your own intimate knowledge of how his intense, troublesome feelings were created and are now expressed, you can gradually free your adult life from the distortions of the past. You will have more freedom and energy to act in an appropriate and satisfying adult way, to participate in and enjoy life's activities without interference from the past.

What this requires is not easily achieved. You will have to think when you are not used to thinking. You may have to push yourself when you are not used to pushing. You may have to silence complaints when you are used to whining. You may have to endure some new anxiety and strange feelings.

By becoming a conscious, active parent to your "inner child of the past," kindly but firmly limiting when necessary, you can do something no one can do for you: create a new and satisfying life for yourself—and a new way of thinking about yourself and those close to you.

About the Author

Dr. W. Hugh Missildine is assistant professor of psychiatry at the Ohio State University College of Medicine, and a diplomate of the American Board of Neurology and Psychiatry. He received his psychiatric training at the Johns Hopkins Hospital, Phipps Clinic and Children's Psychiatric Service, Baltimore, Maryland. For nine years he was director of the Children's Mental Health Center in Columbus, Ohio, and it was there that he conceived his new approach to adult emotional problems. Dr. Missildine is editor of Feelings and Their Medical Significance, a publication which goes to thousands of physicians in the United States every month, and in which the concepts in this book are often expressed.

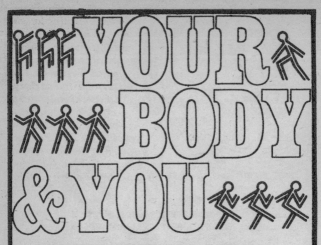